I0467622

Financial Terms Dictionary

Real Estate Terminology Explained

Published June 30, 2017

Revision 1.1

Financial Terms Dictionary

Limits of Liability and Disclaimer of Warranties

The materials in this book are provided "as is" and without warranties of any kind either express or implied. The Author disclaims all warranties, express or implied, including, but not limited to, implied warranties of merchantability and fitness for a particular purpose.

The Author does not warrant that defects will be corrected, or that that the site or the server that makes this eBook available are free of viruses or other harmful components. The Author does not warrant or make any representations regarding the use or the results of the use of the materials in this book in terms of their correctness, accuracy, reliability, or otherwise. Applicable law may not allow the exclusion of implied warranties, so the above exclusion may not apply to you.

Under no circumstances, including, but not limited to, negligence, shall the Author be liable for any special or consequential damages that result from the use of, or the inability to use this eBook, even if the Author or his authorised representative has been advised of the possibility of such damages.

Applicable law may not allow the limitation or exclusion of liability or incidental or consequential damages, so the above limitation or exclusion may not apply to you. In no event shall the Author's total liability to you for all damages, losses, and causes of action (whether in contract, tort, including but not limited to, negligence or otherwise) exceed the amount paid by you, if any, for this eBook.

Facts and information are believed to be accurate at the time they were placed in this book. All data provided in this book is to be used for information purposes only. The information contained within is not intended to provide specific legal, financial or tax advice, or any other advice whatsoever, for any individual or company and should not be relied upon in that regard. The services described are only offered in jurisdictions where they may be legally offered. Information provided is not all-inclusive, and is limited to information that is made available and such information should not be relied upon as all-inclusive or accurate.

You are advised to do your own due diligence when it comes to making business decisions and should use caution and seek the advice of qualified professionals. You should check with your accountant, lawyer, or professional advisor, before acting on this or any information. You may not consider any examples, documents, or other content in this eBook or otherwise provided by the Author to be the equivalent of professional advice.

The Author assumes no responsibility for any losses or damages resulting from your use of any link, information, or opportunity contained in this book or within any other information disclosed by the author in any form whatsoever.

About the Author

Thomas Herold is a successful entrepreneur and personal development coach. After a career with one of the largest electronic companies in the world, he realised that a regular job would never fully satisfy his need for connection on a deep level. The only way to live his full potential was to start building his own business and find new ways to be in service to others.

For over 25 years he has helped many people - including himself - build their dream businesses. Toward that goal, he focuses on education, simplified and enhanced by modern technology. He is the author of 15 books with over 200,000 copies distributed worldwide.

Other than his passion for creating businesses, Thomas has spent over 20 years in the self-development field. Placing emphasis on the exploration of consciousness and building practical applications that allow people to express their purpose and passion in life, Thomas's work in this area has provided ample and happy proof that this approach works.

He believes that every person has at least one gift and that, when this gift is developed and nourished, it will serve as a fountainhead of personal happiness and help contribute to a better, more sustainable world.

For the past twelve years Thomas has studied the monetary system and has experienced some profound insights on how money and wealth are related. He has recently committed to sharing this financial knowledge in a new venture - the Financial Terms Dictionary, a hub of financial term descriptions designed to help people get started on their own money makeover and get a financial education in the process.

Thomas's ultimate vision for the Financial Terms Dictionary is to empower people to adopt a wealthy mindset and to create abundance for themselves and others. His ability to explain complex information in simple terms makes him an outstanding teacher and coach.

For more information please visit: Financial Terms Dictionary

Financial Dictionary Series

There are 12 books in this financial dictionaries series available. Click the links below to see an overview and available formats. There is also a premium edition available, which covers over 900 financial terms!

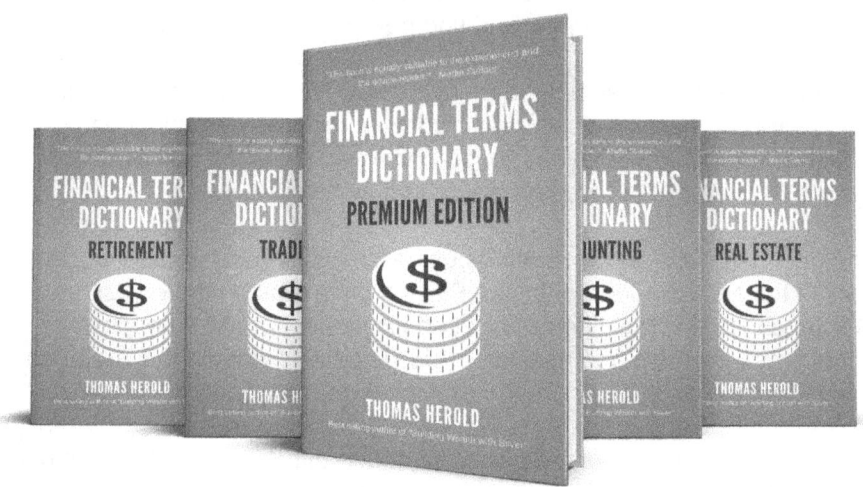

Standard Editions
Financial Terms Dictionary - Accounting Edition
Financial Terms Dictionary - Banking Edition
Financial Terms Dictionary - Corporate Finance Edition
Financial Terms Dictionary - Economics Edition
Financial Terms Dictionary - Investment Edition
Financial Terms Dictionary - Laws & Regulations Edition
Financial Terms Dictionary - Real Estate Edition
Financial Terms Dictionary - Retirement Edition
Financial Terms Dictionary - Trading Edition
Financial Terms Dictionary - Acronyms Edition

Basic & Premium Editions
Financial Terms Dictionary - Basic Edition
Financial Terms Dictionary - Premium Edition

Table Of Contents

Absorption Rate

Absorption rate is a term used in real estate. It represents the speed with which homes available in a real estate market are sold in a certain amount of time. Real estate professionals figure out this absorption rate by taking the number of houses that are available and dividing this by the average number of sales in a month. The result provides a useful number. It is the total number of months it will require before all of the homes on the market are sold.

It is important to note that this absorption rate does not consider any supplies of other houses that enter the real estate market. As such it is a snapshot of a fixed moment in time. Higher absorption rates will usually signify that the numbers of available houses will decrease quickly. This means that a homeowner would likely sell his or her house in a shorter time frame.

In historical context, when the rates of absorption rose over 20%, this has meant that the market was ideal for sellers. Homes would sell fast. When the absorption rate proved to be lower than 15%, this means that a buyer's market is in effect. Buyers are being pickier. This slows down the rate at which homes are being sold.

The absorption rate is easier to understand by looking at an example. In this scenario, a given city has 2,000 houses that are up for sale. If buyers came into the market and bought up 200 homes each month, then the home supply would be depleted in 10 months. This is simply figured by dividing the 2,000 houses by 200 homes bought each month.

When buyers purchase the 200 houses from the 2,000 houses total, it means the rate of absorption equals 10%. This number is derived by taking the 200 houses buyers purchase every month and dividing it by the total 2,000 houses for sale. It would mean that the market is optimal for buyers. Any homeowner who was hoping to sell a house would be aware that the market should half sell out over a period of five months.

There are a number of different individuals who work with this important figure. Real estate industry professionals are most interested in the number. Real estate brokers would put this number to use when they price houses. If a market showed signs of lower rates of absorption, the agents might have no choice but to lower the listing price in order to attract a buyer. In the opposite case, the market might exhibit a higher rate. This would allow the realtor to raise the home price without eliminating demand on the property.

Home builders also look at these absorption rates when they are thinking about building new properties. A higher rate is often interpreted by the construction industry as an optimal time to begin building new houses. When the conditions on the market show higher absorption, it means demand can likely support them developing additional properties. The opposite is true if there is less absorption. This tells them that demand is lower. Construction may pause in efforts to build new houses.

A last group that carefully studies the rates of absorption are the property appraisers. They think about these rates when they are considering the total value of a given property. In 2009, new appraisal rules came into effect. These mandated that every home value appraisal connected with a home loan had to take into account the active rate of absorption. The reasoning behind this was that home values should be less in times where lower absorption resulted in fewer and more drawn out sales at lower prices.

Adjustable Rate Mortgage (ARM)

Adjustable Rate Mortgages, also known by their acronym ARM's, are those mortgages whose interest rates change from time to time. These changes commonly occur based on an index. As a result of changing interest rates, payments will rise and fall along with them.

Adjustable Rate Mortgages involve a number of different elements. These include margins, indexes, discounts, negative amortization, caps on payments and rates, recalculating of your loan, and payment options. When considering an adjustable rate mortgage, you should always understand both the most that your monthly payments might go up, as well as your ability to make these higher payments in the future.

Initial payments and rates are important to understand with these ARM's. They stay in effect for only certain time frames that run from merely a month to as long as five years or longer. With some of these ARM's, these initial payments and rates will vary tremendously from those that are in effect later in the life of the loan. Your payments and rates can change significantly even when interest rates remain level. A way to determine how much this will vary on a particular ARM loan is to compare the annual percentage rate and the initial rate. Should this APR prove to be much greater than the initial rate, then likely the payments and rates will similarly turn out to be significantly greater when the loan adjusts.

It is important to understand that the majority of Adjustable Rate Mortgages' monthly payments and interest rates will vary by the month, the quarter, the year, the three year period, and the five year time frame. The time between these changes in rate is referred to as the adjustment period. Loans that feature one year periods are called one year ARM's, as an example.

These Adjustable Rate Mortgages' interest rates are comprised of two portions of index and margin. The index actually follows interest rates themselves. Your payments are impacted by limits on how far the rate can rise or fall. As the index rises, so will your interest rates and payments generally. As the index declines, your monthly payments could similarly fall, assuming that your ARM is one that adjusts down. ARM rates can be based on a number of different indexes, including LIBOR the London Interbank

Offered rate, COFI the Cost of Funds Index, and a CMT one year constant maturity Treasury security. Other lenders use their own proprietary model.

Margin proves to be the premium to the rate that a lender itself adds. This is commonly a couple of percentage points that are added directly to the index rate amount. These amounts vary from one lender to the next, and are commonly fixed during the loan term. The fully indexed rate is comprised of index plus margin. When the loan's initial rate turns out to be lower than the fully indexed rate, this is referred to as a discounted index rate. So an index that sat at five percent and had a three percent margin tacked on would be a fully indexed rate of eight percent.

Affidavit

An Affidavit is a declaration in writing which includes a sworn oath or positive confirmation that written contents are factual and true. These declarations and statements could be made related to court cases. They also could be made to support an important document as with mortgage applications or tax returns.

Though many people may not be aware of it, a great number of forms prove to be affidavits. This is because they have a line that states the individuals have filled in the form to the best of their knowledge. The line must also mention that deliberately entering information that is incorrect will lead to perjury charges. If a person is found guilty of perjury charges, it can lead to significant time spent in jail.

The word affidavit is originally taken from the Latin. The Latin roots signifies that individuals have pledged their faith with complete knowledge of the law. It is interesting that affidavits are always voluntarily undertaken documents. This means that no parties in a court case are able to make a person give such statement under oath. Courts can force individuals to give deposition accounts. Depositions differ from an affidavit. They may both be statements that are written, but depositions will be cross examined in a court.

Affidavits must involve knowledge that is personally known by the individual who declares them. This means that persons who do not include information of which they were unaware will not be punished or deemed to be in perjury. Personal knowledge can cover a person's opinion too. In such cases, the statement must be unequivocally stated to be opinion instead of a known fact. Any individual is allowed to provide an affidavit if he or she maintains the necessary mental ability to comprehend how serious the oath given actually is. This is why guardians of mentally ill patients are able to provide such an affidavit on their behalf.

These documents are generally formally witnessed by a qualified official such as a notary public or an account clerk. Notaries are agents who receive a small fee in exchange for witnessing the signing of legal documents for individuals, as with mortgage forms or real estate transactions. This witness signing the document means that the person pledges that the information is accurate and realizes how important this oath is. Documents like these can be utilized in court as evidence. They can also be submitted alongside supporting materials with various kinds of transactions, including for social services.

Individuals who sign affidavits should be extremely careful that they read the documents several times, especially if another individual is recording them. This is because the documents are oaths which are legally binding. The statements contained within must be correctly and clearly related. When the signor recognizes errors in the document, as with facts on a mortgage application, these need to be corrected in advance of signing. This is more important than the inconvenience it will cause the officials who have written down the information and who are witnessing the signing and oath that accompanies it.

Appraisal

Appraisals are professionally done estimates of a property's real value. These are conducted by appraisers. Many things can have an appraisal done on them, including smaller items like artwork or jewelry, as well as larger things like businesses, commercial buildings, or homes.

Appraisals are commonly required before many different transactions can be performed. In advance of getting a house, piece of jewelry, or an artwork insured, appraisals must be performed. Homes and offices have to be appraised for insurance, loans, and tax purposes. Appraisals ensure that these loans and insurance policies are comparable to the property's tangible market value.

Several different types of appraisals can be performed. Real property appraisal involves properly estimating Real Estate value. Personal property appraisal involves determining the worth of valuable individual objects like expensive china, jewelry, pottery, artwork, heirlooms, and antiques. Mass appraisals merge real property and personal property appraisals into a single appraisal. Business value appraisals consider all of the valuable tangible and intangible assets that a business owns, including logos, services, equipment, property, inventory, other assets and goodwill.

Perhaps the most commonly used type of appraisal is a home appraisal. Home appraisals prove to be professionally done surveys of a house to come up with an opinion or estimate of the home's value on the market. These kinds of appraisals are usually performed for banks that are considering the approval of a loan for a person purchasing a home. Such home appraisals turn out to be detailed reports. These cover many things including the home's neighborhood, the house's condition, how rapidly area houses sell, and what comparable houses actually sell for at the time.

Such a home appraisal could similarly be done for a replacement value for insurance purposes or as a sales comparison in marketing a home, as well. Cost and replacement appraisals determine what the actual cost to completely replace your home would be if something destroyed the house. This type of appraisal is most often employed for new houses. Sales comparison appraisals more often examine various additional properties within your house's neighborhood to determine at what price they are presently selling. The appraiser will then determine how such houses compare and contrast against your particular home.

Home appraisals commonly cost in the range of from $300 to $500 when people decide to order one done themselves. Such appraisals are not often accepted by banks. They will want to have their own contracted appraiser make the estimate in order to get a more independent number that they trust.

Home appraisers are always licensed by the state in which they operate. The highest of ethical standards are demanded of them. Their sole purpose is to act as an independent third party who will give their truthful opinion of a home's market value. Appraisers are not supposed to be associated with any party that is involved in the selling of a home.

Appraised Value

Appraised Value refers to the property value evaluation from a certain frozen moment in time. Professional appraisers perform these appraisals when the origination process of the mortgage is underway. Lenders themselves typically select specific property appraisers to do them. It is the borrowers who are expected to pay for getting the appraisal.

Home appraised value proves to be a critical factor in getting through the process of loan underwriting. It enjoys a special place in deciding the amount of money that buyers can borrow and according to what terms. As a key example, the LTV Loan to Value ratio is determined utilizing the appraised value. When the LTV proves to be higher than 80 percent, the lender will insist that the borrowers purchase PMI private mortgage insurance. Once the LTV declines to 78 percent or lower with an appraisal, the need for expensive PMI payments can be excused.

This appraised value should not be confused with market value. The two are both important in residential home transactions, for retail buildings, commercial property, land, and farms. Yet real distinctions between the appraised value and market value of real estate exist. The market values will be driven by consumers and their demand versus available home supply in a given city, county, or even region. The experts make the appraised values.

Appraised values of given properties relay the information in the form of a precise number on the value of the home or other property in question. These appraised values come from both the professional opinion of the appraiser as well as the data they gather from similar home sales on the same street, in the neighborhood, and in that section of the city. Market values on the other hand vary more dramatically. Buyers have great influence on the property's market value. This is because any home is ultimately truly worth as much as a buyer will actually pay for it.

Sometimes people also confuse the idea of assessed value and appraised value. Assessed values are those which the city or town assessor's office will put on a given property. They do this so that they can decide what amount of taxes should be levied and collected for the property tax. Whole towns and cities become assessed in a particular (from four months to twelve months) period. Qualified assistants will actually determine the final values once they interview the owners and examine the properties in question. Municipalities then combine all of the assessed values for all properties within their jurisdiction to determine how much the tax rate should be for the year in question. It is possible for the town or city to revalue its tax rate every year in order to gather the revenues they require to run the municipality. This means that while assessments do not typically change on a yearly basis, tax rates could.

It is only in cases where the city or town's assessed values are deemed to be outdated that they will reassess the properties in the jurisdiction. This happens as dramatic inequities arise between one property and the next. It would require a sufficient reason to spend the money on conducting a new assessment of all properties within the municipality. There are states which have standard regulations that each home must be reassessed on an individual basis whenever it becomes sold or transferred. It is also true that rarely will the assessed values versus the appraised values for a given property be precisely the same dollar amount. This is because while assessed values are not impacted by market activity in a certain time period, the appraised values will inevitably be influenced by them due to actual market activity of homes selling in the area.

Assessed Value

Assessed Value refers to the specific dollar value amount which a municipality assigns to a certain property. They do this for the purpose of determining the relevant taxes for the property and owner. These assessed valuations actually create a given residence's tax purpose value. They do this through considering inspections and any comparable home sales in the area. Once this is all completed, the municipal government will set a value on the home and then assess the due property taxes. The owner then receives the final bill for municipal taxes on the property. The assessment value is also called the ad valorem tax.

Most of the time, such Assessed Value proves to be less than the associated fair market value or appraisal value for the property in question. This assessment value is a number with very limited uses. It only applies to the relevant property tax in question.

The person who has the role for determining the Assessed Value turns out to be a government assessor. These individuals are typically assigned by particular taxing districts. It is true that every taxing jurisdiction maintains its own rules and procedures for determining the actual assessment value. Despite this, the general standards which they rely on are nearly identical.

The assessors are expected to make these valuations on a yearly basis. This is where the property tax bill comes from every year. Most years, the assessment value will not change. The Assessed Value is derived from the fair market value, of which they set a certain percentage. They consider a number of different elements in determining this. Chief among these are comparable property values, condition of the property, features of the house, total square footage and air conditioned square footage, and conditions in the market. A great number of such calculations prove to be derived from the computer models. These come from official real estate databases on regions and neighborhoods.

Besides such computer-based real estate data, the government assessors will do physical assessments onsite when necessary. Some states have exacting and specific requirements for the ways in which their government assessors have to visit the various properties which are being assessed in person. There are also rules regarding property owner objections to a set value. They can dispute the value on their given house and can ask for a reassessment visit. This is carried out in practice as a property second evaluation.

In the majority of states, the final numbers which the jurisdictions come up with represent a certain percentage of the fair market value for a given property. This assessed value ratio can range significantly from one state to another. It could in theory be as wide a variance as from 10 percent to 100 percent of the fair market value of the property in question. At only ten percent assessed value ratio, Mississippi boasts among the lowest ones in the United States. Coming in at a staggering 100 percent assessed value ratio is Massachusetts in the typically tax-heavy Northeast and New England regions.

Most states utilize a set property tax formula when determining their so-called millage rate. Millage rate refers to the actual tax rate compiled for the assessed value. This is the value times millage rate times assessment ratio equals the effective property tax. They are commonly described per $1,000. A single mill equates to $1 of tax for each $1,000.

The majority of the states also require a personal property tax to be levied. This comes from the assessed value of other forms of property. Personal property that has tax assessed on it includes cars, mobile homes, boats, and motorcycles.

Asset Protection

Asset Protection and planning refers to strategies and practices for protecting personal wealth. It happens through deliberate and involved planning processes that safeguard individuals' assets from the potential claims of any creditors. Both businesses and individuals alike can employ these specific techniques to reduce the ability of creditors to seize personal or business property within the legal boundaries of creditor debtor law.

What makes Asset Protection so powerful is that it is able to insulate a variety of assets and all legally. It does not require any of the shady or illegal activities inherent in concealing assets, illegal money transferring, bankruptcy fraud, or tax evasion. The asset experts will warn their clients that efficient protection of assets starts in advance of a liability, incident, or claim occurring. The reason is that it is generally over late to begin arranging such protection afterward. There are a wide variety of normal means for protecting such personal or business assets. Among the most popular are family limited partnerships, accounts receivable financing, and asset protection trusts.

In the heavily litigious society of the United States, Asset Protection involves protecting property from those who might win a judgment in court. There are a variety of lawsuits that could threaten a person's or business' assets. Among these are car accident claims, unintentional negligent acts, and even foreclosure on property lawsuits where the mortgage is no longer paid. The ultimate goal in Asset Protection is to take any nonexempt from creditors assets and move them to a position where they become exempt assets beyond the reach of any claims of the various creditors.

Asset Protection which an individual or business does when a lawsuit is already underway or even imminent to be filed will likely be reversed by the courts. This way they can seize the hidden assets that were deliberately transferred to protect them from an imminent court case judgment. This is the ultimate reason why effective protection of assets has to start well in advance of the first hints of litigious activity or creditor claims.

Two principal goals must be combined in order to effectively construct an efficient and ironclad Asset Protection plan. These include achieving both long term and short term goals and reaching estate planning goals. The financial goals component involves clearly understanding present and future income sources, the amount of resources needed for retirement, and any resources which will remain to leave to any heirs via estate planning. This helps people to come up with highly detailed financial plans.

After this has been done, individuals will want to examine carefully any present assets to decide if they are effectively exempted from any and all sundry creditors. The ones that are not should be clearly repositioned so that they are exempt. This also involves planning to position future assets so that they are similarly effectively protected.

The next step is to come up with a complete and all inclusive estate plan. It should encompass all forms of asset protection and relevant planning via advanced techniques of estate planning. Among these are irrevocable trusts for the individuals, their children, spouses, and beneficiaries as well as family limited liability companies.

The most common mistake that people or businesses make with this Asset Protection planning is waiting until it is too late to safeguard the assets. The other mistake is assuming that such planning can be done rapidly or as a short term fix for a longer term problem. Protecting assets is ultimately longer term planning that must be done carefully and ahead of potential creditor claims on assets or pending lawsuits.

Assumable Loan

An assumable loan is one that permits a home buyer to take over, or assume, a home seller's contract on their mortgage. This is not permitted by every mortgage lender in the place of a typical home purchase. Loans that do not have Due On Sale clauses, such as the majority of VA and FHA types of mortgages, can usually be assumed and are considered to be assumable loans.

Assumable home loans work in the following manner. A current home owner will simply transfer over his or her mortgage contract and obligations to a purchaser who is qualified to take over. In the past decades of the 1970's and 1980's, these types of mortgage note assumptions proved to be quite popular. Back then, they could be done without even having to obtain the mortgage lender's authorization. These days, the only types of mortgages that may be assumable loans without needing a lender's actual permission are those that are made by the FHA or VA.

Assumable loans provide opportunities for both buyers and sellers. It is often the case that a home buyer will not be able to secure a better rate for a new mortgage than that provided by an already existing mortgage. This could result from the negative credit history of the buyer in question or the conditions existing in the market place at the time. As existing interest rates rise, the appeal of non-existent lower rates on mortgages commonly pushes prospective home buyers to look out for assumable loans. Such a home buyer who secures an assumable loan then has the responsibility for the mortgage that the home seller previously carried.

The existing rates of the mortgage carry over for the buyer as if the person had made the original contract themselves. This assumable loan process also saves the buyer a number of the settlement costs that are incurred in making a new mortgage. This can be a substantial cost savings benefit.

Sellers similarly benefit from assumable loans. It is not uncommon for sellers to wish to be involved in the savings that buyers realize in the process of transferring over an assumable loan. Because of this, the two parties commonly share in the savings.

As an example, when the sale price of the home in question is greater than the amount owed on the mortgage itself, then the buyer will often have to put down a significant down payment, which goes straight to the home seller in this case. Otherwise, the buyer might have to get another mortgage to come up with the difference in amounts. A seller's principal benefit in participating in such an assumable loan transfer lies in having a good chance of getting a better price for the home.

Automated Underwriting

Automated underwriting proves to be one of the biggest changes that has come to the mortgage lending business in the last several years. The process uses computers to handle the process of underwriting mortgage loans. There are numerous benefits to the concept. Among them are lower closing costs, quicker loan approvals, fewer requirements for documentation, and approval for applications which human underwriters denied in the past.

Underwriting itself is the means whereby the underwriters approve or deny mortgage loans. They do this by considering the property, the ability to pay back the loan, and the credit worthiness of the individuals applying. For most of mortgage loan history, people exclusively handled these activities. In recent years, programs have demonstrated that computers are able to perform these jobs quicker, with greater accuracy, and generally better.

There are now automated underwriting systems that handle much of this work load. Both Freddie Mac and Fannie Mae have created their own such systems to evaluate mortgage loans. They are the two biggest investors in mortgages within the United States. Freddie Mac has a system called Loan Prospector. Fannie Mae developed Desktop Underwriter to perform these same functions. Both computer systems display their abilities via a predictive model. They take the specific mortgage applications and compute a quantitative risk factor for them.

Automated underwriting systems are easy to apply through. The lender or mortgage broker queries the applicant for information. He or she enters this data into the underwriting system. The system pulls a credit report to accompany it. The system next creates a Findings Report using the credit report and application information. The Findings Report reveals the determination on the loan application approval. It provides the list of documents that will be required in order to verify the data of the application.

Consumers benefit from these systems. The approvals they issue represent binding commitments from either Freddie Mac or Fannie Mae. If the information put in is correct and can be documented, then the consumers can enjoy the confidence of knowing that their loan will be issued.

Borrowers no longer have to come up with voluminous amounts of application documents and complete major paperwork thanks to these systems. The new automated underwriting systems commonly only require a single pay stub instead of the two months that human underwriters typically wanted.

Approval time spans are significantly shorter now with these computers. The Findings Report appears in only minutes after the lender enters the information into the system. Less documentation also means that the time frames are reduced.

Consumers receive the benefit of the savings from these systems. Appraisal fees are typically $100 less. Credit report costs come down by $50 or more. Loan origination fees may be less as well.

The greatest single benefit of the new systems is that with automated underwriting, consumers who used to be refused loans are many times approved now. Consumers with excellent credit but fewer down payment resources especially benefit from this system. In the past they would not have been approved, but the system model assigns less importance to the full down payment amount that human underwriters did.

One helpful characteristic of these automated underwriting systems revolves around property identification. Human underwriters often required the property for which they were applying for a mortgage to be stated on the application. The new systems do not have such a requirement. This benefits consumers who are still shopping for a house. Once they are approved by the system, they gain a powerful tool for negotiating deals with the sellers of properties.

Blanket Loans

Blanket loans are those which cover multiple properties or parcels of land. They handle the costs for or can be secured by more than a single piece of real estate. These are most typically employed by commercial land developers or investors. For individual consumers, they can be utilized as a type of bridge between new and old properties and mortgages. For these consumers, such a blanket loan will make it possible to pay for both mortgages until the owner reaches the point of selling the old property.

The feature that makes these mortgages most useful for developers is their release clause. These permit the borrowers to sell a single or even several pieces of real estate without the need of being forced to refinance the mortgage. This makes them significantly different from traditional mortgages. Normal mortgages make borrowers completely pay down their loan balance before they can sell the property which secures them.

For developers of residential properties, they find these blanket loans particularly helpful. They employ them to pay for large tracts of land on which they will build. When it is time for the loan to fund, it becomes secured by the full piece of property. The developer is allowed to subdivide his property and sell it in individual lots. For part of the security to be released, the developer must utilize some of the sale proceeds to pay down part of the loan.

This is helpful when builders are constructing subdivisions. Such a developer could put the blanket loan to use to buy the consecutive pieces of land while they are available. The developer would then be able to subdivide the total land into specific lots for building houses. With each home that he finishes and sells, the property becomes detached from the blanket loan without the financing having to be disrupted on the remainder of the development project.

Consumers also find these types of blanket loans helpful in making it possible to transition from the sale of their current home to the building or buying of the new house. This makes much more sense than having two concurrent mortgages or obtaining a more costly short term bridge loan. It can also help them so that they do not have to sell the property early and move into a rental while they look for a property to purchase.

These kinds of blanket loans are often governed by a contingency clause. These clauses detail that the newly purchased house and its mortgage will not close until the person is able to sell the existing home. The problem with such a contingency clause is that they have limited time frames on them. They may force a borrower into selling the home in a panic in order to meet the clause expiration date. This can lead to a lower selling price or disadvantageous terms on the sale.

Blanket loans get around such a dilemma by providing the borrowers with an extended period of time in the clause to sell their old house. Sometimes they are arranged as interest payment only loans for a full 12 months before amortizing starts. This gives the seller a sufficient time period to sell the house for a good price and reduces the overall burden of the mortgage at the same time.

The main downside to blanket loans for individuals is that they are significantly harder to find since the real estate crash and Great Recession of 2009. Their advantages include both flexibility and efficiency in financing. For an individual consumer, this means a single mortgage payment rather than two. Developers do not have to worry about constantly refinancing their property debt as they sell off parts of the property. Should a developer default on his loan, the bank simply assumes control of all remaining property which secures the loan.

Bridge Loan

A bridge loan is a temporary short term loan whose purpose is to help a home owner to afford to buy a new house before they are able to sell their present house. They might do this to avoid having to move into a rental in between houses. The home buyer's existing house secure these loans. The money that comes from these loans is utilized to purchase the house into which the buyers are moving.

A bridge loan can be more popular in real estate markets which favor the buyer, or a buyer's market. The home owner may find it easier to buy a new house than to sell his or her existing one in these cases. This means that the buyers will have to come up with the down payment through either these types of loans or by using a home equity loan. Home equity loans can be less costly than bridge loans are.

A bridge loan will offer some borrowers greater advantages. Besides this, a great number of lenders will refuse to make a home equity loan on a house that is already up for sale. The best thing is to compare the advantages of the two different kinds of loan in order to decide which works best for a given buyer's unique scenario before he or she puts in an offer on another house.

Bridge loans do not always involve credit score minimums and set debt to income ratios. It depends on the lender and the underwriting process that is involved. Instead approvals are more often granted based on whether such underwriting makes sense to the loan officer and lender. There would be stricter guidelines on the part of the loan that pertains to the new house and its long term mortgage.

There are lenders who will make conforming loans and not consider the bridge loans' payments when qualifying the borrower for the new mortgage. In other cases the borrowers become qualified to purchase the new house by combining the present loan payment with the additional mortgage payment on the new house.

A great number of lenders will qualify the borrowers on two payments for a variety of reasons. They understand that the majority of buyers already have a current first mortgage on the home which they own. Banks also know that buyers would probably close on the new house they are buying before they sell their present home. Most importantly, banks are aware that home buyers in this scenario will own two different houses, even if for a short time frame. Qualifying on a bridge loan based on two payments requires a greater income or a lower payment on one of the houses.

With conforming loans, banks and lenders can find more room to work with a greater debt to income ratio. They can do this by using one of the automated mortgage underwriting programs with Freddie Mae or Fannie Mac. In general with jumbo loans, the restrictions are greater. The majority of lenders will limit the borrower to a maximum of 50% debt to income ratio.

Bubble

In economic terms, a bubble is high volume levels of trade at prices that are significantly out of line with actual intrinsic values. A simpler definition is the trading of assets that have over inflated values. Bubbles are also called market bubbles, speculative bubbles, balloons, financial bubbles, and speculation mania. Prices within bubbles can vary wildly. At times, they are no longer predictable using the traditional market determining forces of only supply and demand.

There are countless explanations offered for the reasons that bubbles occur even when there is no speculation, uncertainty, or limited rationality in the market. Some have theorized that bubbles could be caused in the end by prices coordinating against each other and by changing social scenarios. Bubbles are generally identified with certainty after they have burst, in the light of drastic drops in prices. This results from the difficulty of ascertaining real intrinsic values in actual trading markets. Bubbles burst, sometimes violently, in what is known as a crash or a bursting bubble.

Mainstream economics holds that you can not predict or call bubbles before they happen or while they are forming. It argues that you can not stop bubbles from developing, and that attempting to gently prick the bubbles leads to financial crises. This school of economic thought favors authorities waiting vigilantly for bubbles to burst by themselves, so that they can handle the aftermath of the bursting bubble with fiscal and monetary policy tools.

The Austrian school of economics argues that such economic bubbles are most always negative in their impacts on economies. This is because bubbles lead to misappropriation of economic resources to inefficient and wasteful uses. The Austrian business cycle theory is based on this argument concerning bubbles.

Examples of economic bubbles abound within the U.S. economy. In the 1970's, as the United States departed from the gold standard, American monetary expansion led to enormous bubbles in commodities. Such bubbles finally ended after the Federal Reserve tightened up massively on the excess money supply by increasing the interest rates to in excess of 14%. This led to the bursting of the commodities bubble that caused gold and oil to fall down to more historically normal levels.

Another example of price bubbles proved to be the rising housing and stock market bubbles created by the extended period of low interest rates that the Federal Reserve enacted from 2001 to 2004. These bubbles burst once the interest rates returned to more normal levels.

An enormous amount of dislocation occurred in the following years as this bubble burst rippled over to the financial system and the entire economy in 2007 and 2008. The Great Recession and financial collapse were created in the wake of this bursting bubble. This example demonstrates how the larger bubbles grow before they finally pop, the more dangerous and damaging they become when they finally do burst.

Capital Appreciation

Capital appreciation refers to the increase in an asset's value. This gain is based on the increase in the market price of the asset. It primarily happens as the asset which an investor backed goes for a greater market price than the investor first paid for the asset in question. The part of the asset which is considered to be capital appreciating covers the entire market value which exceeds the cost basis, or original amount invested.

There are two principle sources of returns on investment. The largest of these is typically the capital appreciating component of the return. The other return source is from dividends or interest income. The total return of an investment results from the inclusion of both the appreciation of capital and the dividend return or interest income.

There are a wide variety of reasons why capital appreciation can occur in the first place. These differ from one asset class or market to the next, but the idea is the same. With financial assets like stocks or hard assets such as real estate, this can occur similarly.

Examples of this appreciation of capital abound. If a stock investor buys shares for $20 a piece while the stock provides a yearly dividend of $2, then the dividend yield is ten percent. A year after this, if the stock is trading at $30 and the investor obtained the $2 dividend, then the investor has enjoyed a return of $10 in capital appreciating since the stock increased from $20 to $30. The percent return of the stock price increase amounts to a capital appreciating level of 50 percent. With the $2 dividend return, the dividend yield is another ten percent. That makes the combined capital appreciation between the stock price increase and the dividend payout $12, or 60 percent. This stunning total return would please most any investor in the world.

A variety of different causes can lead to this appreciation of capital for a given asset. A generally rising trend can support the prices of the investment. These can come from such macroeconomic factors as impressive GDP growth or accommodative policies of the Federal Reserve in lowering their benchmark interest rates. It might also be something more basic having to do with the company that issued the stock itself. Stock prices could rise when the firm is outperforming the prior expectations of analysts. The real estate value of a house or other property could increase because it has good proximity to upcoming new developments like major roads, shopping centers, or good schools.

Mutual funds are another investment example which seeks out capital appreciation. The funds hunt for investments which will likely increase in value because of their undervalued but solid fundamentals or because they have earnings which outperform analysts' expectations. It is true that such investments often entail larger risks than those alternatives picked for income generation or preservation of capital, as with municipal bonds, government bonds, or high dividend paying stocks.

This is why those funds which focus on capital appreciation are deemed to be more appropriate for those investors who have a higher tolerance for risk. Growth funds are usually called capital appreciation investments since they pour their funds into company stocks which are rapidly expanding and boosting their shareholder values at the same time. They do employ capital appreciation as their primary investment strategy to meet the expectations of lifestyle and retirement investors.

Case Shiller Index

The Case Shiller Index represents the collection of United States' Home Price Indices. These were developed by economists Karl Case and noted Yale Professor Robert Shiller. The two men's company Case Shiller Weiss, Inc. produced the statistics from 1991-2002. Allan Weiss their partner oversaw the production and release of the index on a regular basis.

This index is a collection of house price indicators for where the market has come and currently is. Among the many versions of the Case Shiller Index is the 20 city composite, the 10 city composite, and also twenty metro individual regions. The commercial versions of the Case Shiller Indices data points start in January of 1987 and run to date.

CoreLogic has since taken over the production of the index where David Stiff and Linda Ladner assumed direction. There is now a wide variety in this Case Shiller Index because Standard & Poor's 500 produces and owns a number of them. For example, Standard & Poor's publishes the Case Shiller twenty cities, condominium indices, high, medium, and low tier home price indices, and the national U.S. index. Anyone who is interested in following them can do so on the S&P company website. Eleven of the various S&P produced indices can be traded as futures on the Chicago Mercantile Exchange. Standard and Poor's set their value to a level of 100 for the prices based in January 2000.

Robert Shiller and Karl Case calculated the original Case Shiller Index on a different basis. Their index gathered home price data back to 1890. In their calculations, the 100 value was based on the house prices for the index in 1890. Robert Shiller's version of the index on his website comes out quarterly. His calculations are probably different than the ones Standard and Poor's uses as is his reference point. This is why in 2013 for the fourth quarter, the S&P 20 city index showed in the 160s, while the same point for Robert Shiller's data was in the 130s.

Professor Shiller wrote and published a book in 2000 about the housing market called Irrational Exuberance. In this book, he made the statement that no other country in the world seems to have published this type of housing data going back to the 1890s.

There are some important economic inferences that the Case Shiller Index shows. Shiller also detailed these in his book. He insists the idea that housing prices have been in a continuing uptrend over time in the United States is false. Instead, the prices of houses have a powerful tendency to go back towards their levels in 1890 as adjusted for inflation. He also notes that there is no correlation between changing home price patterns and the changes in population levels, interest rates, or even construction costs.

The Case Shiller Index also gives Shiller enough information to explain why there is no constant uptrend in the inflation adjusted home prices. Part of this is mobility. He has stated that if the prices of houses rise enough then people can simply move to another area of the country. This is because urban land makes up less than 3% of the U.S. total land area.

Improvements in technology are another reason Shiller has discussed for this phenomenon. As technology of home construction has consistently improved, it has become quicker and less expensive to build houses. This keeps a lid on the inflation adjusted cost of homes.

Between these reasons, Shiller argues that there is no trend in home prices either up or down. He has observed this not only in the United States, but also in other countries. The real house price indices of Norway and the Netherlands show the same truth.

Certificate of Title

A certificate of title represents a document which states who the owners or owner of real estate or personal property actually are. It is issued by a municipal or state government. This certificate gives evidence of any ownership rights.

In general a title insurance company will issue a certificate of title opinion on a house or piece of property. This is their statement of opinion regarding the status of a title. They draft this opinion after carefully looking through public records pertaining to the property.

Such a certificate of title opinion will not necessarily assure the buyer of a clean title. It will list out any encumbrance on the property. Encumbrances are often items that keep the property from being freely sold. These could include easements or liens. The title companies will issue such certificates to financial institutions which are making the loan. Many of these lenders must have such documents in hand before they will approve a mortgage loan for a house or piece of property.

Certificates of title are extremely important with real estate. This is why a title company will issue their opinion that the person selling the property actually owns it. Personal property is easier to give to another person than is land. Where land is concerned, a person might be living on a given property and yet not own it. This makes the certificate opinion from the title company critical. It promises that the company has performed the complete background check regarding who owns the land and so has the right to sell it.

This certificate of title is a statement of fact when a state or municipal government actually issues it. These documents contain a good deal of useful information on them. All of them will have the name and address of the owner of the property. They also have information that identifies the property itself in some specific way.

If the certificate pertains to a real estate property, then it will have the location of or address for the land in question. If it is instead for a car or other vehicle, it will have the license plate number and possibly the vehicle identification number. These certificates will also state what the encumbrance is on the property if there is any. If there is a lien on a vehicle or mortgage on the house or land, this will be noted.

State agencies will also issue certificates of title on a variety of vehicles. This covers such things as buses, trucks, motorcycles, trailers, motor homes, boats and watercraft, and airplanes. When a lender makes a loan on such a vehicle, it is able to keep the title in its possession until the debt has been paid in full. They then release the lien at this point and send back the title certificate to the actual owner.

Certificates of title should not be confused with deeds though they share certain common characteristics. Each of these two documents offers a proof of ownership for the property in question. The certificate of title has sufficient information to specifically identify the property itself and any relevant encumbrances. Deeds have additional information on the real property. This includes any conditions for the ownership as well as more detailed information on and about the property. Deeds are critical elements in any transfer of real estate.

Cession Deed

A cession deed is used to give up property rights to a government authority. It is possible for individuals, companies, or organizations to sign a cession deed with a state or the federal government in the U.S. Cession deeds have generally been utilized between great imperial powers like the United States or Great Britain and smaller independent entities such as islands or Indian tribes ruled by chieftains. Both American Samoa and the British colony of Fiji were created by a cession deed in the 1800's.

American Samoa arose because of the Deed of Cession of Tutuila. The local chiefs from the island of Tutuila signed this treaty with the United States on April 17, 1900. As part of the cession deed, the chiefs ceded their island to the U.S. and swore allegiance to the country. Four years later in 1904, the chiefs of neighboring island Manu'a also agreed to cede their territory to the U.S.

In exchange for this, the chiefs received guarantees that they could continue to exercise control over their individual villages. Their rule had to be maintained according to the American laws that pertained to Samoa. The control also could not obstruct any advances of civilization or the peace of the people over which they ruled. The U.S. promised to protect and respect the rights of the inhabitants, particularly their property and land rights.

Congress did not ratify this cession deed until the Ratification Act of 1929. The navy administered this new American Samoa during the years of 1900 to 1951. At that point the President of the U.S. issued executive order 10264 and transferred control of the American Samoa territory to the Secretary of the Interior. American Samoa has been a territory of the U.S. with a locally elected governor, lieutenant governor, and legislative assembly since the 1960s. The territory is self governing under its constitution that took effect in 1967.

The British Empire also signed a cession deed when in gained control of the Kingdom of Fiji. This process began in 1871 when the British honorary consul John Bates Thurston persuaded the other chiefs of Fiji to accept the great war chieftain Cakobau as constitutional monarch. Actual power resided in the legislature and cabinet that the Australian cotton settlers dominated. The assembly had its first meeting in November 1871 in Levuka.

This constitutional monarchy arrangement did not work out well for Fiji. The government spent more money than it had and built up an unmanageable debt in only a matter of months. Two years of economic and social unrest followed in the islands kingdom. At this point, Cakobau asked the British consul Thurston to talk with the British government about ceding control of the islands to the empire. This was the second time Cakobau had attempted to cede his control to Great Britain.

Two British commissioners came to Fiji to consider the practicalities of annexing Fiji. Cakobau presented a final offer on March 21, 1874. The British accepted this deal. Sir Hercules Robinson who was eventually to be appointed governor arrived in September on British naval ship Dido. Cakobau enjoyed a royal 21 gun salute as Robinson received him.

King Cakobau, rival chief Ma'afu, and other senior Fijian Chiefs signed two separate copies of the Deed of Cession on October 10, 1874. One copy remained in Fiji while the other copy went back to Great Britain. The British ruled Fiji for the next ninety-six years under a series of appointed governors before granting the island nation its independence.

Chain of Title

A chain of title refers to the consecutive historical transfers in a title on a particular piece of real estate property. These chains start with the current owner of the property and trace their way back to the property's first owner. Reconstructing such a chain can be extremely important when a lender needs complete ownership documentation. Such title documents are generally kept by registry offices with local and municipal governments.

The field of real estate places tremendous importance on such a chain of title. Because it can be difficult to construct them, companies have come up with systems to track ownership and registration of real estate property. One of these is the Torrens Title system.

Insurance companies in the United States will provide title insurance on a property. They do this using the chain of title on real estate that the owners are transferring. These chains are so important that many title insurance companies will keep their own private title operations to track such titles so they do not have to rely on only official government records. In cases where it is difficult to come up with a complete chain, abstracts of title can be utilized. Attorneys will sometimes certify these.

Lack of a clear chain of title has caused significant problems during the Great Recession of 2008. These problems began when many lending companies made the choice in 1995 to use an electronic registry to hold the title. The best known company in this arena was MERS Mortgage Electronic Registration Systems. The banks tried to use this system so they could sell and purchase mortgages without needing to register ownership changes with the appropriate local governments. Without clear title chains, the banks were often not able to come up with the original titles needed to force foreclosures and evictions as individuals defaulted on their mortgages. A number of states throughout the U.S. sued the banks over these actions.

The chain of title is also utilized in intellectual property areas. With the film industry, they refer to documentation that demonstrates the ownership rights of a particular movie. These chains can be used in other creative endeavors in the movie business. If many individuals contributed to the creative work, authorship is owned by a large number of the writers. Film distributors and buyers must carefully examine these chains of title to know the proprietary rights or rights under license of the owner. This is also important with books and encyclopedias.

Documents on chains of title for films can include a number of other intellectual properties. Trademarks can be included. Musical copyrights often form part of these chains as well. Talent agreements are an important part of these. They provide the talent's legal release to utilize their images, works, appearance, and personal rights in movies. This covers everyone from directors to actors to choreographers and cinematographers. There are even insurance policies that cover omissions and errors of movie producers who do not obtain sufficient chains of title.

Specific organizations compile these reports for copyright property on behalf of the movie studios. To do so, they consult with the U.S. Copyright Office regarding author claimants, screening searches, and registration renewal searches. This detailed work requires that records from the Copyright Office dating back to 1870 and extending to the present be consulted. There are also other databases and trade publications which have to be reviewed for possible ownership claims.

Closing Costs

Closing costs are the fees that are charged when you buy a house. Many other costs are associated with buying a house than only the down payment. These closing costs are fees like recording fees, title policies, courier charges, inspections, lender fees, and start up reserve fees to create an impound account.

The most expensive component of these closing costs is the lender charged fees. Such closing costs are charged beyond the home's purchase price. Most closing costs are set and predetermined, meaning that they are not open to negotiation.

The total price of closing costs is fairly standard. Typically, a good guideline for closing costs is that they will run you somewhere between two and four percent of a house's purchase price. The range is as large as this spread because the origination fees and points for making the loan vary significantly from one lender to the next. These points and origination fees that are charged by the lender are always revealed to a buyer in the Good Faith Estimates that are provided to the buyers. For example, a home that is $400,000 will have closing costs that run from around $4,000 to $16,000. They could be even higher than this amount, on some occasions.

Some closing costs are of the non-recurring kind. Such fees are charged to a buyer of a house on only a single time. They include escrow or closing, title policies, courier fees, wire fees, notary charges, endorsements, attorney costs, city or county or state transfer taxes, recording, natural hazard disclosures, home protection plans, lender fees for the HUD-1 800 line, and home inspections.

Other closing costs are called prepaid closing costs, or recurring closing costs. Although these are paid for in a single lump sump up front, they cover those costs that continue to recur throughout the life of the home loan. There are comprised of property taxes, flood insurance when required, fire insurance premiums, prepaid interest, and private or mutual mortgage insurance premiums.

Closing costs are also impacted by the month of the year in which you close on the house in question. This is because future insurance and tax payments will be collected on a pro rated basis for the number of months of premiums for the year. Not all loans come with an escrow or impound account either. Yet loans that are for in excess of eighty percent of the purchase price of your house will mandate such an escrow account and impound be established.

Closing costs are some of the unfortunately high expenses associated with buying a house. They are only avoidable when a person takes over an assumable mortgage. In these cases, most closing costs, such as lender points and origination fees, are side stepped by a buyer.

CMG Plans

CMG Plans are special mortgage plans. In these types of plans, the mortgage of the borrower is set up to work like a checking account does. Instead of depositing the employee's payroll to a traditional checking account at a bank, the individual's company deposits paychecks directly into the mortgage account. Once a check deposits, the mortgage balance owed by the individual becomes reduced by this deposit total.

The CMG Plans accounts also work like a checking account as the individual writes checks against the account. When the checks clear or the owner withdraws money from an ATM machine, the balance increases by the amount taken out or cleared. Money that remains in the account that has not been taken out by the end of the month becomes permanently applied to the mortgage balance. This acts as principle repayment.

There are significant benefits to such CMG Plans. As paychecks become deposited to the account, the average outstanding principle amount for the month on the mortgage is reduced. This average outstanding monthly principle turns out to be the amount on which banks charge interest. Interest accrues on a daily basis with these plans. This means that interest totals on the mortgage are reduced even if the principle amount at the conclusion of the month remained the same as it was on the first day of the month.

The balance actually would not be the same at the month's end. These CMG Plans require that minimally 10% of the mortgage holder's paycheck stays with the account by the end of the month. This is how the principle balance becomes permanently reduced over time. Such a 10% of payroll savings towards the mortgage means that principle reduces quicker than typical 30 year amortizing mortgages require. The final result is that the amount of time on the mortgage is significantly less. Greater interest charges will be saved by the mortgage holder this way.

With interest rates at historic lows, these CMG Plans make greater sense than simply keeping the money in a non interest paying checking or negligible interest bearing savings account. The borrower literally begins to earn the same interest rate of the mortgage on the literal day that his or her company affects the payroll deposit. It does not hurt the borrower or cause any negative consequences in the account as bill pays, cash withdrawals, or check writing activities are performed. Regardless of how much of the money is taken back in expenses, the average monthly balance of the mortgage and associated interest rate charges come out lower.

There are two downsides to such CMG Plans. It is possible that these types of mortgages will come with a higher interest rate than a more typical mortgage would. Paying a higher rate for this service turns out to be mostly unnecessary, since borrowers can get the same results of early principle retirement simply by paying additional principle repayments on their normally amortizing mortgages.

The other downside concerns eligibility requirements. Only consumers with strong and consistent income streams are able to utilize these types of CMG Plans. The average person would not qualify for them.

Collateral

Collateral refers to an asset or piece of Real Estate which borrowers provide as security to lenders in exchange for a loan. This property actually secures the mortgage or other form of loan. In the event that the borrowers do not continue to make the agreed upon payments on the loan according to the laid out schedule, the financial institution has the right to seize this property in order to recover the principal losses.

Because such collateral provides at least nominal security to the lending institution in the scenarios where the borrower refuses to or is unable repay the loan, these forms of loans are commonly provided with lower interest rates as compared to those loans which are unsecured entirely. When such a lender has interest in the underlying property provided by the borrower then this is referred to as a lien.

In the end there are several arrangements with such collateral. The type of loan often determines which form will be required within the contract. With car loans or mortgages, the loans are secured by the property upon which the financial institution issues the loan. Other forms of loans have more flexible security, as with collateralized personal loans. In order for any loan to be called secured, the backing security has to be at least equal to or greater than the balance that remains on the loan in question.

Such secured loans entail far less risk for lenders because the underlying property serves as an incentive for the borrower to keep paying back the loan. Borrowers know all too well that if they do not complete the required payments then the financial institution which holds the loan may legally possess (or repossess) this collateral in order to recoup the money it is owed on the rest of the loan.

With mortgages, the collateral in question will always be the home that the borrower buys using the loan in the first place. If and when they fail to pay the debts, then the lender may seize possession of the property by utilizing a procedure called foreclosure. After the lender completes the necessary court process and has the property back in its possession, it is allowed to sell off the home to someone else. This will permit the bank to cover the principal which remains on the original loan along with their costs for the foreclosure.

Houses also can also be utilized for second mortgage collateral, or against HELOC's (Home Equity Lines of Credit). In such scenarios, the credit delivered by the financial institution may not be greater than the equity which exists within the home itself. As a tangible example, a home could have a market value of $300,000. At the same time, it might be that $175,000 of the original mortgage balance remains to pay. This would mean that the majority of HELOC's or even second mortgages would not exceed the available equity of $125,000.

Collateral is also utilized in margin accounts' trading of stocks, commodities, and futures. In this case, it is the securities themselves that become the property which secures the brokerage loan. In the event that a margin call has to be issued and the account holder will not or can not pay it on demand, then the securities' value ultimately makes certain that the brokerage will get back its loaned money.

Sometimes financial institutions will require additional collateral be put up for a given existing loan, if the contract allows such a scenario. This will reduce increasing risks for the lending institution. A creditor could give notice that without such additional security, they will be forced to raise the interest rate on the loan. Additionally accepted security could be certificates of deposit, cash, equipment, letters of credit, or even shares of stock.

Collateralized Debt Obligations (CDO)

Collateralized Debt Obligations are one of the financial weapons of mass destruction that helped to derail the global financial system in the financial crisis of 2007-2010. They are literally securities that are supposed to be of investment grade. The backing of collateralized debt obligations proves to be pools of loans, bonds, and similar assets. These investments are rated by the main ratings agencies of Moody's, Standard and Poors, and Fitch rating companies.

The actual value of collateralized debt obligations comes from their asset backing. These asset backed securities' payments and values both derive from their portfolios of associated assets that are fixed income types of instruments. CDO's securities are divided into different classes of risk that are called tranches.

The senior most tranches are deemed to be the most secure forms of securities. Since principal and interest payments are given out according to the most senior securities first, the junior level tranches pay the higher coupon payments and interest rates to help reward investors who are willing to take on the greater levels of default risk that they assume.

The original CDO was only offered in 1987 by bankers for Imperial Savings Association that failed and became folded in to the Resolution Trust Corporation in 1990. This should have been a warning about collateralized debt obligations, but their popularity only grew apace during the following ten years. CDO's rapidly became the fastest expanding part of the synthetic asset backed securities market. There are several reasons for why this proved to be the case. The main one revolved around the returns of two to three percentage points greater than corporate bonds that possessed identical credit ratings.

CDO's also appealed to a larger number of investors and asset managers from investment trusts, unit trusts, and mutual funds, to insurance companies, investment banks, and private banks. Structured investment vehicles also made use of them to defray risk. CDO's popularity also had to do with the high profit margins that they made for their creators and sellers.

A number of different investors and economists have raised their voices against collateralized debt obligations, derivatives in general, and other asset backed securities. This includes both former IMF Head Economist Raghuram Rajan and legendary billionaire investor Warren Buffet. They have claimed that such instruments only increase and spread around the uncertainty and risk that surrounds these underlying assets' values to a larger and wider pool of owners instead of lessening the risk via diversification.

Though the majority of the investment world remained skeptical of their criticism, the credit crisis in 2007 and 2008 proved that these dissenters had merit to their views. It is now understood that the major credit rating agencies did not sufficiently take into account the massive risks that were associated with the CDO's and ABS's, such as a nationwide housing value collapse.

Because the value of collateralized debt obligations are forced to be valued according to mark to market accounting, where their values are immediately updated to the market value, they have declined dramatically in value on the banks' and others owners' balance sheets as their actual value on the market has plummeted.

Collateralized Mortgage Obligation (CMO)

Collateralized mortgage obligations are investments that contain home mortgages. These mortgages underlie the securities themselves. These CMO yields and results derive from the home mortgage loans' performance on which they are based. This is true with other mortgage backed securities as well.

Lenders sell these loans to an intermediary firm. Such an intermediary pools these loans together and issues certificates based on them. Investors are able to buy these certificates to earn the principal and interest payments from the mortgages. The payments these homeowners make go through the intermediary firm before finally reaching the investors who bought them.

The performance of collateralized mortgage obligations depends on the track record of the mortgage payers. What makes them different from other types of mortgage backed securities is that it is not only a single loan on which they are based. Rather they are categorized by groups of loans according to the payment period for the mortgages within the pool itself.

Issuers set up CMOs this way to try to reduce the effects of a mortgage being prepaid. This can often be a problem for investments based on only a single mortgage as owners refinance their loans and pay off the initial one on which the investment was based. With the CMOs, the risk of home owners defaulting is spread across a number of different mortgages and shared by many investors.

Tranches are the different categories within the mortgage pools on which the collateralized mortgage obligations are based. The tranches are often divided according to the mortgage repayment schedules of the loans. For each tranche, the issuer creates bonds with different interest rates and maturity dates. These CMO bonds can come with maturity dates of twenty, ten, five, and two years. The bondholders of each individual tranche receive the coupon or interest payments out of the mortgage pool. Principal payments accrue initially to those bonds in the first tranche which mature soonest.

The bonds on collateralized mortgage obligations turn out to be highly rated. This is especially the case when they are backed by GSE government mortgages and similar types of high grade loans. This means that the risk of default is low compared with other mortgage backed securities.

There are three types of groups who issue these CMOs. The FHLMC Federal Home Loan Mortgage Corporation issues many of them. Other GSE Government Sponsored Enterprises like Ginnie Mae provide them as well. There are also private companies which issue these CMOs. Many investors consider the ones issued by the government agencies to be less risky, but this is not necessarily the case. The government is not required to bail out the GSEs and their CMOs.

There are investors who choose to hold their CMO bonds until they mature. Others will re-sell or buy them using the secondary market. The prices for these investments on this market go up and down based on any changes in the interest rates.

The other most common type of mortgage backed securities besides these CMOs are pass through securities. Pass throughs are usually based on a single or few mortgages set up like a trust that collects and passes through the interest and principal repayments.

Common Securitization Platform (CSP)

During the financial crisis that started back in 2008, the federal government took control of both Fannie Mae and Freddie Mac the government sponsored enterprises because they became insolvent. One of the ideas that the since-then managing agency the FHFA Federal Housing Finance Agency came up with is the Common Securitization Platform. This strategic goal resulted from the FHFAs *2014 Strategic Plan for the Conservatorships of Fannie Mae and Freddie Mac* report.

The hope with this Common Securitization Platform is to create a new and greatly improved securitization infrastructure for both Freddie Mac and Fannie Mae. These two groups are collectively known as the Enterprises. Their new platform is to be for American mortgage loans which are backed up by single family kinds of properties.

In order to put this vision into reality, the two GSEs have established a joint venture called CSS Common Securitization Solutions. It is actually designing the Common Securitization Platform under the leadership and direction of the FHFA. The CSS fills the role of agent for both enterprises to help with issuing the single family mortgage securities. It also is handling disclosures when the securities are issued and in the future. Besides this, CSS is administering such securities after they are issued.

Among the more important tasks the Common Securitization Solutions is carrying out with regards to the program surrounds the operational capabilities of the Common Securitization Platform. CSS is responsible for creating these so that the CSP will run. The CSP will eventually support the securitizing activities of the GSEs and their single family mortgage program. This will culminate in the two Enterprises issuing one Single Security, which will actually be a single mortgage backed security.

Issuing this Single Security is important for several reasons. The FHFA along with Fannie Mae and Freddie Mac all want to see their securities' all around liquidity improve. This will also aid in the mission of the two GSEs to ensure the country's housing finance markets remain liquid too.

Common Securitization Platform is both a technology and operating platform then. In the future, it will handle a great number of the critical back office functions and operations of the Single Security. It will also take over the majority of the two GSEs present securitization operations in the single family mortgages for them. Without the CSP, it would be practically impossible to actually launch and integrate the Single Security.

Single Security is the future of Freddie Mac and Fannie Mae. It will help to ensure that adequate financing for fixed rate mortgages and loans continues for the one unit to four unit single family properties. The way that it will actually do this is by taking elements from both of the GSEs and combining the best of each.

There are three areas where these different procedures have to be aligned for the Single Security to function properly. The key features of the Fannie Mae mortgage backed securities and the Freddie Mac participation certificates will be taken mostly from Fannie's mortgage backed securities model. Investor disclosures will be modeled after Freddie's participation certificates. A final area to be aligned concerns the practices and policies that will be utilized to take loans out of securities.

The Single Security endeavor also promises to allow for some exchanges of old for new securities. This pertains particularly to the 45 day Participation Certificates of Freddie Mac. These will be exchangeable for 55 day time frame Single Securities that Freddie Mac will issue.

Constructive Eviction

Constructive eviction is a backdoor way of evicting a tenant. It is not done through legal means because of a tenant failing to pay rent or seriously breaking the property rules. It is instead the process of a landlord making a rental uninhabitable for the tenant. Though the term sounds positive, it is quite the opposite. Landlords who engage in this type of eviction are failing to carry out their legal obligations.

For constructive eviction to take place, a residential rental property must deteriorate into enough disrepair that it becomes very difficult or near impossible to live in the property. It could also be that the landlord allows a condition to exist that makes inhabiting the home or apartment intolerable. As the condition becomes so severe that the property is no longer fit to live in, the tenant is forced to leave. An uninhabitable property exists in a state that compels the renter to move away, or to be constructively evicted. Because the renter is incapable of completely utilizing and possessing the property, he or she has been evicted technically.

There are a number of way in which a tenant could be a victim of constructive eviction. The landlord might turn off the electricity, gas, or water utilities. The owner might disregard an environmental problem such as toxic mold or flaking off lead paint and not properly clean it. He or she could also not fix leaking roofs. This causes water damage to walls and eventually leads to mold. The owners could block the unit entrance or change the locks. They might do something extreme such as take out sinks or toilets from the property as well. When the conditions deteriorate to the point that tenants abandon the rental then constructive eviction has occurred.

A landlord might engage in this type of unethical behavior because of rental controls. Many cities limit the amount by which rent can be increased. They may also allow the tenant to remain in the rental with an automatically renewing lease so long as they fulfill the contract obligations.

Tenants have the ability to fight back against this type of eviction. This starts with providing the owner a notice in writing of the constructive eviction. The landlord must be given a fair amount of time to address the issue. This may not translate to an instant repair that happens in 24 hours.

Many repairs require more time to have completed. Water and gas leaks are examples of these. Still the repairs have to be done in a time frame that is reasonable.

Renters who find themselves in living conditions that are poor should take pictures. They also should invite independent inspectors to examine the property. These types of inspectors come from the permit or building department, as well as from the area health department.

When landlords are unwilling to address the uninhabitable living conditions in a reasonable time frame after having been given fair written notice, renters have rights. They are usually allowed to leave the property without having to pay rent that would still be owed according to the rental or lease agreement. In general, tenants have to move away from the property while they begin the legal process of terminating the lease and suing the owner for damages.

It is often better to compel the owner to make the necessary repairs or to address the issues that are creating the uninhabitable living conditions on the property in the first place. This is easier in cities and states that have strong legal enforcement of the landlord obligations. New York City and state are an example of places in the United States that make it difficult for owners to practice constructive eviction by requiring that they fulfill their maintenance duties.

Cost Segregation

Cost segregation proves to be a procedure of identifying assets of personal property that commonly become lost or bunched together in the real property asset. Cost segregation involves reclassifying costs of assets to a depreciable life that is the shortest one possible.

This allows owners of real estate to optimize their tax deductions in the depreciation category, which lessens the amount of present income tax due. Any investor who is buying a building, renovating a building, or getting into a construction project can qualify for significant Federal and state tax advantages using cost segregation.

Particular assets that pertain to these types of projects may be eligible for such accelerated depreciation. This translates to you being capable of realizing bigger tax deductions now in a shorter time frame. Advantages in bigger tax deductions now include a less expensive capital cost and greater positive cash flow over the principal several years after a purchase has been made or a project completed. Cost segregation studies help you to find such chances to claim more accelerated tax purpose depreciation. These cost segregation studies show always be performed by well qualified Certified Public Accountants.

Cost segregation is able to reduce the time frame for depreciation significantly via s simple strategy. These studies go through all of the costs involved in a property that are currently being tax depreciated over the usual thirty-nine year time frame. Many of these might be reclassified to far shorter time periods of depreciation, including fifteen years, ten years, seven years, or even only five years. The shorter the time frame of depreciation, the greater the tax deductions will be in this far shorter period of time. Greater amounts of depreciation are realized immediately when this is done properly. In this way, not only are tax savings in the present and coming years maximized, but cash flow is similarly increased.

Cost segregation studies make sense for anyone who is purchasing an already existing building. They are efficient for investors who are putting up a new facility. They similarly help those who are engaging in leasehold improvements to a present building. Finally, they give tremendous advantages to businesses or individuals who are renovating, improving, or expanding a building that already exists. Even older buildings can be cost segregated for better tax deprecation purposes.

Cost segregation should not be confused with simple deprecation analysis. A great deal more is involved than simply taking line items off of construction invoices to classify them. The procedure actually involves a team of professionals who are familiar with tax laws and accounting rules, along with construction and engineering concepts. A CPA will be the center of such a team, since he or she will have to make various building components tangible to quantify them in a way that they can be estimated as costs that work with IRS rules. This team would also feature an engineer, contractor, and possibly architect much of the time.

Between them, these professionals will examine in depth electrical and mechanical plans, working drawings, and even blueprints to break segregate out the electrical, mechanical, and structural parts of the building from other components that are associated with the personal property. Even engineering and architect fees as they pertain to various parts of the project are included as soft costs.

Counter Offer

Counter offers are those made by home sellers after buyers have turned in an official offer to buy the house. Usually, such counter offers spell out the terms with which the seller will accept the buyer's official initial offer. Many different specifics can be addressed with a counter offer.

Some of these things include the consideration of a higher offering price, presenting a larger earnest money deposit, and modifying time frames for contingencies. Others counter offer elements might revolve around altering service providers, excluding any personal property from the home selling contract, or changing the possession date or closing date. A seller might also refuse to cover the costs of certain fees or reports.

Not only can sellers counter a buyer's original offer, but buyers can similarly submit counter offers back to the seller on their counter offer. This is labeled a counter-counter offer. No limit to the actual numbers of counter offers which can be handed back and forth exists.

Counter offers are easily rejected. A number of purchase contracts for houses have places at the bottom of the contract for a seller to put his or her initials if the offer is being rejected. Many offers have time frames, or expiration dates, when the offer will be rejected if the seller has not responded. Sellers can simply write the word rejected over a contract's face, then date and initial it to reject a counter offer.

In some states, sellers are allowed to come back with various counter offers at once. For example, in California, sellers are allowed to counter more than one offer at a time and every counter offer is permitted to be different. Should one of these buyers choose to affirm the counter offer of the seller in this scenario, the seller is not required to agree to the acceptance of the buyer. This can become confusing, so talking with real estate attorneys can be a good idea in these complicated cases.

Counter offers can similarly be accepted without difficulty by the buyer. All that a buyer needs to do to take the counter is to accept the offer and send it back to the entity to which it goes. Like with anything, timing is critical. Counter offers expire much as purchase offers do. This means that a seller could always elect to take an alternative offer while a buyer contemplates whether or not to sign off on the counter offer.

Even though many agents become discouraged at the mention of a counter offer being on the table, this should not be the case. Houses can be secured with new offers submitted even while a counter offer is out. In such a scenario, sellers commonly go ahead and take the second buyer offer. They then withdraw their counter offer from the first buyer. This is permissible and proper in every state.

Credit Bureaus

Credit bureaus are agencies that collect financial information. They go by different names in various countries around the world. In the United Kingdom they are known as credit reference agencies. In Australia, the bureaus are called credit reporting bodies. India knows their credit agencies as credit information companies.

Within the United States, these organizations are called consumer reporting agencies. Whatever name they go by, they all serve the same function. The bureaus gather information from banks and other financial sources to deliver consumer credit information about individual consumers.

The U.S. consumer reporting agencies are governed by the Fair Credit Reporting Act. Other laws that regulate the activities of the bureaus are the Fair and Accurate Credit Transactions Act, the Fair Credit Billing Act, the Fair Credit Reporting Act, and Regulation B. These acts attempt to safeguard consumers against unfair practices and mistakes made by the data providers and the credit reporting agencies themselves.

The U.S. has two separate government organizations who oversee the credit bureaus and their data suppliers. These are the FTC and the OCC. Primary oversight of the credit reporting agencies as they deal with consumers belongs to the Federal Trade Commission. The banks are monitored for all of the information that they provide the reporting agencies by the Office of the Controller of the Currency. This government agency supervises, regulates, and charters all of the national banks and any information they turn over to the consumer credit reporting agencies.

Three main credit reporting bureaus dominate nearly all credit reporting in the U.S. These are Experian, Equifax, and TransUnion. None of these three agencies are owned by government entities. All of them exist as companies seeking to make a profit and are traded publically. They are carefully monitored for fairness by the government provided oversight organizations.

The consumer reporting agencies operate through a vast network with the credit card issuing companies, banks, and other financial entities with which individuals have accounts. All of these ties ensure that credit account information and histories show up on the credit reports of one, two, or even all of the bureaus.

The credit bureaus compile all of this information into a consumer credit report. They each then utilize proprietary trade secret formulas to determine every individual's FICO credit score. Each of the three bureaus formulates its own score that is different from that of its competitors. They also come up with educational credit score numbers which are often vastly different from the official scores.

Consumers do not have to settle for educational credit scores. They have the rights to see what is on their credit reports. Each and every year, individuals are able to obtain an official credit report from each of the three credit bureaus. This can be done by going to the government mandated website AnnualCreditReport.com.

Besides this, consumers are allowed to go to the websites of the three main consumer reporting agencies and order credit reports and scores from them directly. The only way to get the official credit score is to pay for and order it from the credit bureaus themselves. These are not provided in the annual free reports. Experian and Equifax offer all three credit reports in a single convenient to view document.

Sometimes the credit bureaus will make mistakes with individuals' credit reports. When this happens, it is important to get in touch with the credit bureau itself in order to dispute any information that is inaccurate. These organizations also should be contacted directly if there is concern about fraud so that they can place a security alert or fraud alert on the person's credit report.

Credit History

Credit history is an official record that shows the company or personal history of borrowing and paying back loans. This history provides business or personal identifying information, a record of credit that the individual or company has, and negative elements such as bankruptcies and late payments.

It describes how individuals use their money and finances. It lists out the number of credit cards, loans and other obligations, and bills that a consumer has. It keeps records of whether they pay these bills in a timely fashion. The credit history information is compiled as companies send in data on credit cards and loans to one of the three main credit bureaus. These are Experian, Equifax, and TransUnion. They act as the gatekeepers of credit history.

These companies compile all of this information on credit and bills into a file called a credit report. This credit report is the repository of all an individual's credit history. It contains a great deal of personal information that starts with the owner's name, social security number, and address. All credit cards and loans are itemized out and detailed. It states the total money a person owes. Finally, credit reports put together a profile on the individuals as to whether they pay their bills late or on time.

Credit history and credit reports are important for individuals. Businesses will not loan out money to people until they know all about them and their spending and borrowing habits and past. Businesses find all of this information on personal credit history in these credit reports and then make decisions as to whether they will extend credit in the form of a credit card or make a loan to the applicant.

Some employers choose to examine a candidate's credit report along with a job application. Insurance companies also consider it when they are determining rates of their customers. Even cell phone and utility companies often look it up when they are deciding how much a person will need to pay in deposits to start service.

Credit history is also used to create a credit score. Credit scores are numbers that the three credit reporting bureaus maintain for individuals using their credit history. If the credit history is good, then the credit score will be as well. Individuals can see their credit history and obtain their credit reports for free every year. Credit scores are not available unless people pay for them.

High credit scores convey a good credit history. Lower credit scores refer to a poor credit history for an individual. Each of the three credit bureau companies will have a slightly different score for a person. High credit scores range from 700-850. Low credit scores start from 300 to 600.

Credit history as shown in a personal credit report is very important to know. Each of the three companies is required to send individuals their credit report every year showing personal credit history on demand. Individuals are able to request this at no charge by going to AnnualCreditReport.com.

There are other companies that advertise offers to provide credit scores for free along with free credit reports. These are usually promotional offers that require individuals to sign up for a monthly service of some type in order to qualify for them. Such offers are often monthly credit monitoring services for a fee. As a rule, a person will generally have to pay something to obtain his or her credit scores.

Credit Report

A credit report is an individual or business' credit history. This includes their record of borrowing and repaying money in the past. It similarly covers data pertaining to any late payments made or bankruptcies that have been declared. In some countries, credit reports are also referred to as credit reputations.

When an American like you completes a credit application for a bank, a credit card company, or a retail store, this information is directly sent on to one of the three main credit bureaus. These are Experian, Trans Union, and Equifax. These credit bureaus then match up your name, identification, address, and phone number on the application for such credit with the data that they keep in their bureau's files. Because of this match up process, it is essential that lenders, creditors, and other parties always provide exactly correct information to the credit bureaus.

Such information in these files at the three major credit bureaus is then utilized by lenders like credit card companies in order to decide if you are deserving of having credit issued to you by the creditor. Another way of putting this is that they decide how likely that you will be to pay back these debts. Such willingness to pay back a debt is usually indicated by the timeliness of prior payments to other lenders. Such lenders will prefer to see the debt obligations of individual consumers, such as yourself, paid on time every month.

The second element considered in a lender offering loans or credit to individuals like you is based on your actual income. Higher incomes generally lead to greater amounts of credit being accessible. Still, lenders look at both willingness, as shown in the credit report and prior payment history, along with ability, as shown by income, in deciding whether or not to extend you credit.

Credit reports have become even more significant in light of risk based pricing. Practically all lenders of the financial services industry rely on credit reports to determine what the annual percentage rate and grace period of repayment of a loan or offer of credit will be. Other obligations of the contract are similarly based on this credit report.

In the past, a great deal of discussion has gone on considering the information contained in the credit reports. Scientific studies done on the issue have determined that for the most part, this credit report information is extremely accurate. Such credit bureaus also have their own authorized studies of fifty-two million credit reports that show that the information contained therein is right a vast majority of the time.

Congress has heard testimony from the Consumer Data Industry Association that in fewer than two percent of credit report issue cases have there been data which had to be erased because it was wrong. In the few cases where these did exist, more than seventy percent of such disputes are handled in fourteen days or less. More than ninety-five percent of consumers with disputes report being satisfied with the resolution.

Credit Union

A credit union represents a financial cooperative. Members own these financial institutions. It is these members who both start and run them so that they can reduce costs for financial services and share profits with each other.

There are a variety of sizes of these institutions. A credit union might be a small operation that volunteers run. It could also be a substantial outfit with thousands of members or more. The idea is the same in either case. The business model has members pooling their savings within the credit union so that they can make loans to other members and receive financial benefits. Such benefits include lower interest rates on loans and higher savings rates.

Credit unions are similar to building societies in Britain, Australia, and other countries. Many of the building societies that allow members to invest their money to help members buy or build houses were started in the 1800's. Halifax in the United Kingdom is the largest in the world with 18 million members.

It is easy to become a member of a credit union, especially when individuals are invited. Once they deposit initial funds into the account at the institution, they become part owners of the organization. This allows them to share in the profits that it makes. They also gain the rights to vote for the board of directors of the credit union and in other important decisions.

Many credit unions get started because a large corporation or other organization wants to offer these benefits to their employers or their members. In cases like these, profits can be invested in community services, membership interests, or projects that benefit the members. Credit unions are considered not for profit. This is because they are helping the community or their members out rather than making a profit for the organization itself.

When credit unions began in America, the membership had limitations to those who held a common bond with others in the group. They might have to live in the same town or work in the industry of the other members. Credit unions have since loosened up the rules for becoming a member. Banks have been frustrated by this development that permits many people to participate in a rival organization which does not have to pay taxes.

There are some risks to belonging to this type of organization. If the union is unable to cover its expenses beyond the services, they could possibly fail. Should the organization not possess enough cash flow, it will be unable to run the operations smoothly enough to take care of the members. At this point, it would be closed.

The benefits of belonging to such an organization are significant. The friendliness and feeling of community is greater than from an average bank. The unions also give benefits that a bank will not, like less expensive loans, better rates for credit, and other financial services without fees or with lower costs. Other unions provide the membership with significant advantages like free insurance coverage or reduced cost and free education.

The building societies of Europe predated credit unions in America. The first ones in the U.S. appeared in the 1900s. St. Mary's Bank Credit Union of Manchester, New Hampshire became the first such organization in America. They are now found all over the globe. Some of them in the U.S. now run under the regulations of the Federal government instead of state regulations.

Creditor

Creditors are those financial institutions or individuals who extend credit to a business or other individual. They carry this out by providing financing which they expect will be paid back at a set time in the future. There is another type of creditor as well. This is a company which delivers services or supplies to a person or other business yet does not insist on immediate payment. Since the customer actually does owe the company money for the goods or services provided in advance of payment, that company becomes their creditor de facto.

Within the universe of a creditor there are real and personal categories of them. Finance companies and banks represent real creditor situations. This is because they possess official and legally binding contracts which they sign with the borrower. In this action, they bind assets of the borrower as collateral against the loan in many cases. Typical collateral would be the underlying asset for which the borrower is obtaining credit in the first place. This is often a car, a house, or some other piece of Real Estate. A personal creditor is a family member of friend choosing to loan out money to their loved one or friend.

Real creditors do not loan out money out of the goodness of their hearts. Instead, they intend to earn profits by charging the borrowers interest for these loans. Looking at an example helps to clarify the concept. A creditor might loan out $10,000 to a borrower at a six percent rate of interest. The lending institution will realize earnings in the form of loan interest.

For this accommodation, the creditor is taking on some amount of risk that the borrowing business or individual might potentially default on the loan. This is why the majority of those extending credit will price the interest rate which they charge the borrower based on the business or persons' prior credit history and creditworthiness. It becomes important to borrowers of especially large amounts of money to have high credit quality so that they are able to obtain a more advantageous interest rate and save money on the interest payments.

The rates of interest on mortgages depend heavily on a host of different variables. Some of these are the nature of the lender, the credit history of the borrower, and the amount of the upfront down payment. Still, it is usually the creditworthiness that overwhelmingly determines the final interest rate which becomes applied to a loan such as a mortgage. This is because those borrowers who boast fantastic credit histories and scores come across as low risk for the creditor in question. It is why they enjoy the lowest of interest rates. As lower credit score-carrying borrowers prove to be considerably riskier for the creditors, they manage their risk by requiring a greater rate of interest in compensation.

There are cases where a creditor will not obtain repayment. In such cases, they do have several options. Banks and official real credit issuing entities are allowed to repossess the underlying collateral. This would mean they have the ability to seize either the car or home which secured the loan. Where unsecured debts are concerned, it is more difficult to collect. They might sue the borrower for the unpaid debts in these cases. Courts could choose to issue orders attempting to force the borrower to pay them back. They might do this by seizing assets in their bank accounts or by garnishing their wages with their employers.

Sometimes the borrowers will choose to file for bankruptcy. In these cases, the courts will be the ones to alert the creditor to the situation. There are cases where any non- necessary assets can be liquidated so that debts can be paid back. The order of priority will make unsecured creditors last in the receiving line.

Deed in Lieu of Foreclosure

A deed in lieu of foreclosure represents an alternative option to a standard foreclosure on a house. In this deed in lieu arrangement, the owner of the property decides to hand over the property in question to the lender on a completely voluntary basis. In exchange for agreeing to this, the lender cancels out the mortgage loan. The deed to the house becomes transferred from the owner to the lender. As part of this conciliatory arrangement, the mortgage lender guarantees that it will not start the foreclosure process on the owner. If there are any foreclosure actions that have already begun, the lender will also terminate these. It is up to the lender to decide if they will forgive any extra balance that the sale of the home does not cover.

There are some tax issues that can arise with a deed in lieu of foreclosure deal. One potential downside to this type of debt forgiveness involves the consequences of it with the IRS. Federal law in the United States requires creditors to file 1099C forms for tax purposes when they choose to forgive any loan balance that amounts to more than $600. This debt forgiveness is then considered to be income and it becomes a tax liability for the home owner.

Fortunately for many home owners during the financial crisis, Congress passed the Mortgage Forgiveness Debt Relief Act of 2007. This delivered tax relief on a number of loans that banks forgave in the years starting from 2007 till the end of 2013.

The main issue and advantage that a deed in lieu of foreclosure offers centers around this excess balance debt forgiveness. Anyone who enters into such a voluntary agreement should carefully review the contract to learn how the deficiency balance topic will be addressed. Sometimes the documents are not clear on this point.

In this case, the homeowner should take the deed in lieu document to a lawyer who specializes in property law. It is not inexpensive to have a lawyer review such a contract document. The money it can save the home owner in the future for signing a contract he or she does not understand and may suffer significantly from will make the fees seem reasonable by comparison.

There are a number of requirements in order for a deed in lieu of foreclosure to be accepted. First the house would have to be on the seller market for a minimum number of days. Ninety days is usual. There also may not be any liens on the house. The property typically could not be in the process of foreclosure already. Finally, the deed in lieu offer has to be voluntary on the part of the home owner.

Another option that can be pursued in place of this deed in lieu of foreclosure is a short sale. Short sales have the same requirements as do the deed in lieu arrangements with several additional stipulations. The home seller must be suffering from financial hardship. The home itself has to be offered at a reasonable price.

In an alternative short sale, the mortgage lender will consent to receiving a lesser amount from the sale than the remaining mortgage balance that the owner still owes. It is up to the bank and the contract if any additional balance which exists will be forgiven or not. The same tax issues apply if the lender agrees to forgive more than $600.

Delinquent Rent

Delinquent Rent refers to rent that tenants pay their landlords late. This is called one of the two greatest frustrations for landlords in the renting process. The other one is handling tenants who vandalize a place. Making good on late or unpaid rent is a hassle for landlords that is almost always an expensive and time consuming process. There are various processes available to landlords for them to obtain their unpaid or late rents. These vary widely based on the state where the property lies, as each state has its own laws pertaining to rentals. The rental agreement also plays its part based on the provisions it contains.

Rental relationships were once arranged with mere handshakes, but that simpler time is now long gone forever. In today's complicated and litigious world, such business arrangements become specified by the law and in contracts instead of on a trust basis. In today's rental arrangements, the rental agreement governs the means of obtaining Delinquent Rent or unpaid balances. This is why it is so important to obtain a solid rent contract template before individuals become landlords and execute rental agreements for the first time.

Oral arrangements are never a good idea in these scenarios. This is because courts frown on enforcing them and they may even doubt their existence or validity. Well-defined lease contracts spell out each provision of the rental arrangements. This includes the amount of rent that has to be furnished and at what point said rent must be paid. Landlords who are unable to specify the precise date on which the rent must be paid will find they are often stymied in their subsequent late and unpaid rent collection endeavors.

It is similarly important for landlords to never agree to verbal alterations to a written out and executed contract. Verbal changes become hotly contested and debatable in law courts. They often will diminish the ability to collect on late rents which the written contract adequately specified. This is why instead the landlords must focus on writing in the maximum number of self help (for rental collection) avenues as the laws in a given state will permit.

In the majority of cases, the state laws provide for two different forms of dealing with unpaid and Delinquent Rent. The ones mentioned above are called self help remedies. These involve any methods a landlord may enforce without needing to make court appearances, file lawsuits, and involve judges. They can only include the relevant property code and state rental law provision allowances. Some of these so-called self help remedies include the ability to enforce liens on the personal property of the renter, to post a notice of eviction, and to physically engage in a lockout of the tenant by changing the locks on the property.

There are states that restrict the kinds of personal property that landlords may seize against Delinquent Rent or back rent. State contract law usually has provisions governing lockouts and eviction notices too. Landlords have to obey the contractual and state law requirements for both methods carefully. For example, shutting off electricity, water, and gas is typically not permitted by most states among the procedures for collecting late rent.

Eviction notices are often the most effective means of dealing with back rent. This is because the majority of tenants do not actually wish to be evicted forcefully by the sheriff from the property. The will generally respond to such a notice by paying any and all rent which they owe at this point.

When self help remedies do not resolve the situation, the small claims court is the place that handles the majority of landlord-tenant disputes. The landlord will have to pay filing fees in order to lodge a rent collection lawsuit. Tenants must be notified of the opening of such a rental dispute lawsuit. Every jurisdiction has its own regulations for the format of the notice which the landlord must provide to the tenant. Among these are in person notification, by fax, by mail, or other means of notification. Once a hearing is held before the judge, a judgment will typically be awarded for the rent that remains unpaid or delinquent.

Discount Fee

Discount fee refers to an upfront closing cost on a mortgage. This one time arrangement provides a mortgage borrower with the ability to enjoy lower mortgage rates than the general market offers. These discount points are often tax deductible. This is because the IRS counts these points as mortgage interest that is prepaid. The discount fee varies from one bank to another in how much it lowers the interest rate on the mortgage. Typically, a single discount point that a buyer pays in the closing will reduce the interest rate on the mortgage by 25 basis points, or .25%.

Mortgage lenders commonly quote their own current mortgage rates as two parts. In the first part, they provide the official mortgage rate which they are offering. In the second part they reveal the amount of discount fee that the borrower will need to pay to reach that rate. Generally speaking, the more points the home buyer pays, the lower the quote on the mortgage rate will become.

Ultimately the discount fee is a means of buying down the interest rate. This lowers the monthly payments. It is separate from origination points. These are costs that banks levy in order to prepare the mortgage loan.

Settlement statements may label this discount fee under another name. They can be termed mortgage rate buy down or discount points. These points carry a cost of 1% of the total size of the loan. With a $300,000 loan, a single point would cost $3,000. Half a point would amount to $1,500. A quarter point would equal $750.

The tax advantage of these discount points pertains to taxes a home buyer pays now. They are completely deductible in the year the borrower buys them. Individuals are not allowed to claim the full deduction on loans for home refinance. These must be spread out for the entire life of the refinance loan. This means that for a home owner who buys points for a 30 year refinance mortgage, he or she is able to claim 1/30 of the fees every year in tax deduction. For any borrower who decides to buy these points on a mortgage, it makes sense to discuss it with the tax advisor so that the deductions on federal income tax can be maximized.

The other reason that a home buyer would be interested in buying points is because it can lower the monthly payments and the total amount of money paid during the life of the mortgage loan. On a $100,000 loan a standard discount point would reduce payments by $14 each month for every $1,000 spent. This leads to a breakeven time frame of 71 months.

In order for buying points to make sense, the mortgage borrower has to decide how long he or she will likely hold the house or the mortgage. If the owner plans to sell the house in less than this amount of time, or he or she will refinance the loan sooner, then paying for points becomes a waste of money. If an owner will hold a mortgage for more than the six years in this example, then the savings over the remaining 24 years of the mortgage can be substantial.

Freddie Mac keeps statistics on average mortgage loans and points. In the year 2015, the average fixed rate loan came with .6 discount points. With the average ARM adjustable rate mortgage, .5 discount points came in the contract. The exact amount of an interest rate break that a point carries depends on the bank in question. Some banks also do not give multiples of .25% interest rate breaks on each point the borrower purchases.

Discount Mortgage Broker

A discount mortgage broker is one who claims that the lender is paying his or her fees. These mortgage brokers shop for competitive loan deals on the behalf of consumers looking for mortgages. Upfront mortgage brokers by contrast are ones that spell out exactly the fees they will receive from the borrower. Their charges are part of the closing costs of the loan.

The phrase discount mortgage broker gives the connotation that the individual is offering services for a reduced price. This is usually the opposite of what they do. Discount brokers usually charge higher fees. The borrower is not able to recognize this much of the time because the fees are buried in the higher interest rate which he or she will pay over the life of the loan. When the borrower pays in the rate, the payment becomes extended over years instead of a single upfront fee.

Lenders do not ever truly pay the fees of mortgage brokers. Borrowers always front them in one of two ways. With upfront brokers, the borrower pays the costs upfront in cash when it is time for the mortgage loan to close. This makes the fee for the broker a part of the closing costs.

The other way is for the borrower to pay a higher rate of interest to the lender. The lender then covers the broker cost during the closing in exchange for the higher interest rate. This means that the fee would not be a closing cost for the borrower. The borrower is still paying the fee. He or she is paying it instead each month of the loan in the form of a higher mortgage payment.

A discount mortgage broker prefers to have the fee paid by the lender in the closing. The reason for this is that resistance from the borrower to the fees is considerably less when the borrower does not understand the way it works. Consumers are usually extremely focused on the cash which they must come up with at closing than they are on payments they will make in the future.

The disclosure forms which are required do not clearly spell out rebates that the broker receives. The home buyers know all too well how much these fees are when they pay it personally at closing. They often have little idea of how much the broker is charging and receiving when they pay it from the interest rate.

This is why a discount mortgage broker is always looking to receive its compensation completely in the form of rebates from the lender. There is nothing illegal or unethical when borrowers pay their brokers via a higher interest rate in lieu of a cash payment. Transparency would argue that a home buyer should at least be able to make the choice intentionally.

Some borrowers can actually benefit from paying the discount mortgage broker through the rate and rebate. In the cases where the home buyers will not pay this greater rate for too long, then it can save them money over the upfront out of pocket mortgage broker fees. For individuals who will keep their mortgage a greater amount of time, it saves them money to pay the broker directly at closing. This is provided they have the cash available.

Discount Points

Discount points are also sometimes known as simply points. They represent a type of interest that is paid in advance. A single discount point is equivalent to one percent of the total loan amount. Through charging borrowers points, lenders boost their loan's yield to a total that is higher than the expressed interest rate.

Borrowers are able to give a bank or lender payment as a way of lowering the loan's interest rates. The up front sum of money gives them a lower monthly payment. With every point that a borrower buys, their loan's rate commonly falls by .125 percent. A buyer paying for points is not without risk. At some time within the life of the loan, the cost of the money given to lower the rate of interest will equal out to the money that you saved in being able to make lower amount loan payments because of the loan's better interest rate.

Should you refinance the loan or sell the house in advance of attaining this break even point, then you will actually take a loss on the transaction. On the other hand, if you hold on to the property and accompanying mortgage for a greater amount of time than the break even, then you will actually save money on the purchase.

It goes without saying that the longer amount of time that you hold the property mortgage and financing with the bought discount points, the better this money used for the points actually rewards you. At the same time, a person who plans on purchasing the property and then selling it or refinancing it quickly will only lose money by not simply paying the higher rate of interest on the loan in lieu of buying points.

Discount points can also be bought to help you qualify for loans. If the loan qualification basis is grounded in your monthly loan payment against your monthly income, then you may only be capable of getting approval by buying the discount points to lower the rate of interest which will result in the lower monthly payment that your approval requires.

Discount points should not be confused with broker fees or origination fees. Discount points only serve to lower the interest rates. Origination fees are those that the lender charges for creating and closing the loan. They could sometimes be a different name for lowering the interest rate as well.

Borrowers who will stay in the house for a longer period of time should definitely consider buying points. Lower interest rates will pay off in savings over time. Any changes in the fees and costs for the loan will be shown to you in the last good faith estimate that the lender provides.

Sometimes when you buy points, you may be able to get a no closing cost loan. This usually happens when the bank is getting a premium interest rate. As their fee is made off of a higher starting interest rate on the note, it can be utilized to cover the closing costs.

Discount Rate

The term discount rate actually has several meanings. Where interest rates and banks are concerned, the discount rate proves to be the actual interest rate that central banks charge their member depositing institutions. When these banks choose to borrow funds from the central bank or the Federal Reserve as their lender of last resort, then this is the rate that they will be required to pay them as interest.

Besides this, the discount rate can refer to the annual effective discount rate in investments. This rate turns out to be the yearly interest divided up by the capital that includes the interest. The rate provides a lower value than does the interest rate. The value following a year delay would be the nominal value in this case. The upfront value is this nominal value less a discount. This annual effective discount rate is commonly utilized for financial instruments that are like Treasury Bills.

For businesses, the discount rate is important as they are making critical decisions regarding their profits and what to do with them. When it is time to contemplate whether to purchase new equipment pieces or to instead return the profits to the share holders, this discount rate is helpful. If all else is equal, then the company will only elect to purchase the equipment if it returns a greater profit to the share holders at a future point.

The share holder discount rate would then be the dollar total that share holders expect to receive in the future so that they would rather have the company purchase the equipment now instead of return the profits to them now. Share price data is utilized to figure up the discount rate for estimating share holders' preferences. This is called the capital asset pricing model. Businesses commonly use this discount rate when they make choices regarding buying equipment by using the net present value in the decision making process.

This discount rate proves to be the weighted average cost of capital. It shows the cash flow risk. The discount rate can also be used by companies to show two different things. It demonstrates the time value that money has, or the risk free rate. Investors generally prefer cash now than cash that they must wait for, meaning that businesses have to compensate them by making them wait for it. The discount rate also establishes a risk premium.

This proves to be the additional return that investors want as payment for the possibility that they might not ever see this money if the cash flow is not there in the future.

Down Payment

A down payment is an upfront amount that is given as a portion of the price on a purchase of large ticket items such as houses or cars. These are given in cash or by check when the contract is signed. The balance of the sum due is then given as a loan.

Down payments are principally intended to make sure that the bank or other type of lending institution is capable of recovering the remaining balance that is owed on a loan should the borrower choose to default. In transactions of real estate, the underlying asset becomes collateral that secures the associated loan against potential default.

Should the borrower not repay the loan as agreed, then the bank or institutional lender is allowed to sell this collateral asset and keep enough of the money received to pay off the rest of the loan along with the interest and fees included. In these cases, down payments decrease the exposure risk of the lender to an amount that is smaller than the collateral's value. This increases the chance of the bank getting the entire principal loaned out back should the borrower default.

The amount of such a down payment therefore impacts the lender's exposure to the loan and protects against anything that might lessen the collateral's value. This includes profits that are lost from the point of the final payment to the final collateral sale. The making of this down payment assures a lender that the borrower has capital available for long term investments, further proof that the finances of the borrower are able to afford the item in the first place. Should a borrower not successfully pay down the full loan amount, then he or she will lose the entire down payment.

Down payments on houses bought in the United States typically range anywhere from 3.5% to 20% of the full purchase amount. The Federal Housing Administration helps first time borrowers to pay merely 3.5% as a down payment. In the excesses of the years leading up to the financial collapse of 2007, many banks were making loans with no down payments. On car purchases, these amounts of down payments might be in the range of from 3% to 13%.

Dual Index Mortgage

Dual Index Mortgages are products of Latin American countries. They are especially popular in places like Mexico that have experienced significant inflation levels historically. These kinds of mortgages permit borrowers to buy houses even when a substantial amount of inflation risk exists. They are not and have never been offered in the United States, though they have been compared to ARM Adjustable Rate Mortgages.

Dual Index Mortgages do show some similarities to the American Adjustable Rate Mortgages. Such ARMs have always been in demand in places in the U.S. that are more expensive to buy houses. As with these types of loans, the dual index ones provide the borrower with lower early monthly payments that will cause negative amortization to occur. This means that the loan balances will rise for many months before they gradually begin to decline.

With Dual Index Mortgages, the rate that the lender earns is indexed. This means that the rate becomes adjusted at periodically set time intervals. The banks are able to adjust the rate on the loan according to the market rate changes.

The borrowers suffer from other aspects of the Dual Index Mortgages. On the positive side, the first payments are designed to be affordable for the borrowers to be able to make. The payments and the interest rates are not the same with these loans. This is where they are significantly different from American ARMs. The payment could be figured at 5% for example while the interest rate due to the lender is 25% or even higher. The substantial difference between these two rates becomes an add on to the loan balance in the form of negative amortization. This means that it may be a great number of years before the balance on this kind of loan starts to go down.

The actual payment amount is determined based on a salaries and wages index. This amount will change each month. The reason the Dual Index Mortgages are dual is because the payments adjust with the income index at the same time as the interest rate adjust to the interest rate index. The hope with these mortgages is that the payment made by the borrower will one day reach the level where it more than covers the interest rate so that the loan balance can decline finally.

The problem with this is that salaries and wages may not match inflation increases in Mexico and other Latin American countries. This would cause the borrower payments to not increase quickly enough for the loan principal to be paid down. In this case, there are remaining unpaid principal balances at the end of the loan terms. Some lenders in Mexico have been willing to underwrite Dual Index Mortgages where they take on this significant risk. The majority of them receive insurance from the government of Mexico. If there are unpaid remaining balances, the government will absorb the losses.

Besides these Dual Index Mortgages, Mexico has also experimented with some other kinds of home loans. One of these is known as the PLAM, or Price Level Adjusted Mortgage. These are less common than the dual index types.

Economic Occupancy

Economic Occupancy refers to the rate of paying tenants for an apartment building or some other rented out space like an office building. The managers and owners of apartment buildings and complexes commonly measure their success with both physical and economic occupancy rates. While these two concepts are related, they are not exactly the same. With physical occupancy, this pertains to the percentage of the total apartments (or commercial office suites) that the owners successfully rent. The rate of economic occupancy describes how many of these tenants are actually paying rent. The economic assessment speaks volumes more than the physical occupancy rate, since ultimately the economic one explains the apartment complex of office building's financial performance.

Another way to think of economic occupancy pertains to the percentage of rents which the owners and managers successfully collect from their tenants as measured against the total sum of money which could physically be collected. This ultimately describes how successfully or unsuccessfully management is optimizing potential revenues.

A number of reasons present themselves for why a building's unit might not be paying rent. The simplest explanation is that the units could be vacant. There are also gaps which exist from when one tenant leaves a unit until another finishes moving into the unit. Some buildings or complexes will find they need to offer discounts to lure in tenants. This might be half off the first rental month costs. Other tenants could depart while still owing the management company rents or fees. Many times, the manager of the apartments, maintenance head, or security guards will live rent-free on the property as part of their benefits as well. The downside is that while it is useful to have such key personnel living on site, it lowers the revenue stream on the property every month.

Figuring up the true economic occupancy is simple. This requires the property manager to divide the actually collected rent by the potential maximum collectable rent if every tenant paid the full price. It helps to consider a real world example of the concept. For any complex that possess 20 occupied apartments which rent for $1,000 per month, perhaps 16 actually pay the rent for one reason or another. This would amount to $16,000 divided by $20,000 for an 80 percent rate. Yet the physical occupancy would amount to a full 100 percent in any case. The best case scenario is to have as close as possible an economic occupancy as physical occupancy rate.

The measure for economic occupancy has various helpful applications. It demonstrates any complexes or office buildings which are suffering from serious issues. If the rate is low, then problems exist with either rent collection, tenant turnover, or both. It may mean that the complex or office building management is inadequate or the base of tenants is unable or unwilling to pay their rent because of property problems. Low rates of occupancy eat into the ability to pay operating costs of the property. Ultimately they mean that profits will be lower or outright losses will be present instead.

Realtors often use the economic assessment over the physical occupancy rates when they are attempting to value an apartment complex or commercial office building. Those properties which are losing money display an inability to retain their tenants. It is also important to compare apples to apples with this measurement. Calculating the economic occupancy on a week by week basis will show a bias of high economic results the final week of the month and a low result the first week of the month. This is why realtors will prefer to have the occupancy calculated economically on a month by month basis, as it filters out the discrepancies of weekly fluctuations.

Equity

Equity represents the homeowner's total dollar amount of ownership in their property. Determining equity is a simple calculation. It is found by taking the home's assumed fair market value and subtracting out the balances of liens and debts secured by the property along with the mortgage balance that is still unpaid. As a home owner pays down the mortgage, reducing the outstanding principal balance, the equity of a home owner goes up. It similarly increases as the property gains in value. To obtain one hundred percent equity in their property, home owners have to pay down both any outstanding debts that are secured by the property and the full mortgage.

Associated with the equity value of a home is the LTV, or loan to value ratio. This loan to value ratio proves to be a means of stating the property's value as against the total dollar amount of your actual loan. The loan to value ratio is simply figured up by taking the amount of your loan and dividing it by your property value. Alternatively, you could divide the amount of your loan by the purchase price or selling price, whichever of the two is the lower amount.

An example helps to illustrate the concept. If you were to purchase a $300,000 house, you might put down a $60,000 down payment using your money. The remaining $240,000 would be covered by taking out a mortgage. Dividing the $60,000 amount by the $300,000 home value yields equity of twenty percent. If you divide the $240,000 by the $300,000 home value, then you will get the loan to value ratio that amounts to eighty percent.

Should you determine later that you will sell this house, then the equity that you have will be concretely and accurately figured up for you. This will simply prove to be the fair market value of your house minus the loan that you still owe the bank on the house. Using the example from the paragraph above, consider what would happen if you lived in and made payments on your house for five years following the purchase.

In this time frame, your monthly mortgage payments lower the balance that remains on the loan to the tune of $10,000, diminishing it from $240,000 to $230,000. Besides this, over those five years, your home value goes up.

This allows you to realize a selling price of $330,000. Since the balance that you owed is still $230,000, then your equity is simply figured by taking the $330,000 selling price and subtracting the $230,000 from it. This leaves you with a final equity value of $100,000. Once all selling costs and realty commissions are figured up and taken out, you would be able to utilize the $100,000 equity in order to invest or to put down the down payment on the next house that you purchase.

Naturally, this home value can cut both ways. Should the value on the home drop from $300,00 to $250,000 in the time that you own it, then your remaining equity would be only $50,000, less than the original $60,000 that you put into it upfront.

Equity of Redemption

Equity of redemption refers to a property owner's legal rights. This term represents the right of a home owner to reclaim his or her property which a mortgage loan secures. Such a right pertains to the period before the bank or lender has foreclosed on the home when the home owner is in default on the mortgage payments that include principle and interest.

As a home owner gets behind on his or her monthly mortgage payments, the lender has the right to accelerate the loan. They will generally not do this until they have attempted to work with the owner to help them get caught up on the mortgage. It is everyone's best interest for the home owner to remain in the home. Banks often lose money on houses which they sell through foreclosure.

Accelerating the loan means that the bank demands payment in full. It is still possible that the lender may be willing to let the behind home owner catch up on the mortgage payments which are in arrears at this point. Otherwise, if the owner does not meet this demand or make full payment, then foreclosure on the property begins in earnest.

In order to meet this order for full payment, home owners are permitted to find an alternative source of funds to pay off the original mortgage principle, interest, and late fees. If they are able to secure such a funding source, then the equity of redemption gives them the rights to keep the house. The problem for most home owners is that if they are in financial trouble and can not pay their mortgage, then they probably will be unable to secure another loan with which to pay off the first one.

This equity of redemption right only lasts until the home has been foreclosed upon and sold. The equity of redemption is also considered to be a valuable interest in the property and a legal estate in and of itself. This means that the home owner can sell or even transfer away this right to another individual or a company.

Equity of redemption should never be mixed up with the statutory right of redemption. The right of redemption is a separate legal right that is not universal throughout the United States. Some of the states allow for this separate right of redemption which gives home owners significantly greater maneuvering room and legal avenues.

In fact a right of redemption means that for an amount of time determined by state law, the owner is able to redeem his or her house and property simply by paying all principle, interest, costs, and fees. This right is for the period after foreclosure or seizure for unpaid taxes has already occurred. By paying the amounts demanded, the right of redemption means that the owner is able to reclaim his or her home, even if it has already been sold.

How long the statutory right of redemption period lasts depends on the state in question. This amount of time could be for several months. In other states and scenarios, it could stretch on for several years after the foreclosure has been completed. Investors who buy houses in states with this legal right must be aware of the repercussions.

Those who buy seized or foreclosed upon houses could run into a situation where the original owner comes up with the money to pay off the entire original obligation on the house. In this case, the original owner would receive back his or her home. The investor would be left to work out compensation for the lost property with the lender from whom they had purchased it.

Escrow

Escrow is a concept that relates to a sum of money that is kept by an uninvolved third party for the two parties involved in a given transaction. In the U.S., this escrow is most commonly involved where real estate mortgages are concerned. Here is it utilized for the payment of insurance and property tax during the mortgage's life.

When you place your money into such an escrow account, an escrow agent who is a neutral third party holds it. This agent works on behalf of both the borrower and home lender. The escrow agent's job in the transaction is to act as the principal parties instruct him or her. As all transaction terms are fulfilled, the money is then released. These escrow accounts may be a part of transactions ranging from small purchases affected on online auction sites to building projects that total in the multiple millions of dollars.

Escrow is utilized in these property transactions when it is time for your mortgage to close. At this point, the borrower's lender will commonly insist that you establish an escrow account for paying for both home owner's insurance and property taxes. You are required to make a first deposit to the account. After this, you make payments into the account each month. Typically, these are simply a part of your monthly mortgage payments. When it is time for your insurance premiums and taxes to be paid, your escrow agent then releases the funds.

The concept behind this escrow is to give your lender peace of mind and protection that your insurance and taxes are both paid in a timely manner. Should you not pay your property taxes, the city might place a lien on this house, making it hard for the bank to sell it if they needed to. Similarly, if a fire burned down the house and the insurance premiums had not been paid, the bank would not have any underlying collateral for the mortgage anymore.

You the borrower also benefit from this escrow account. It allows you to stretch out your taxes and insurance costs over the course of the entire year's twelve payments. As an example, your annual property taxes might prove to be $3,000, with a yearly insurance cost of $600. This would mean that when spread out over twelve even payments, the escrow costs would amount to only $300 each month.

The nice thing about escrow accounts and payments is that they come with an included safeguard built in. Should you miss a single payment, then the responsible lender is still capable of paying the accounts in a timely manner. The U.S. Federal law actually stops these lenders from storing up in excess of two months' worth of payments in escrow. As insurance and tax amounts will vary a little from one year to the next, the lender will have to examine and make adjustments to your annual escrow payments.

Eviction

Eviction involves the forced removal of a rental tenant from a landlord's rental property. Other terms that convey the same or a similar meaning include repossession, summary possession, and ejection. Eviction proves to be the term most commonly utilized in landlord and tenant communications. Evictions can not simply happen without going through a legal process that could include an eviction lawsuit.

A notice must first be given to the tenant by the landlord. This is most often referred to as the notice to vacate or notice to quit. It has to be delivered to a tenant in advance of beginning official legal eviction procedures. In most cases, the tenant will then receive somewhere from three to ten days to address the issue causing eviction. These offenses likely are caused by either a failure to pay the rent in a timely manner or contractual breach of the lease for something like have a pet.

Should the tenant refuse to leave the property in question after the expiration of the notice to quit, then the landlord next provides the tenant with a complaint. These complaints mandate that the tenant in question will have to go to court. If the tenant refuses to appear at the court date or does not provide an answer to the complaint, then the landlord is able to seek a default judgment, in which he or she automatically wins the case. A tenant response should include his or her side of the story as well as defense that could include the tenant not being provided with repairs that the lease stipulates.

Following an appropriate answer, trial dates are determined. With the issues being dependent on time, these cases are commonly hurried through the system. Should a judge back up a tenant, then the tenant is allowed to stay, although he or she would have to pay back due rent. Should the landlord be victorious, then the tenant receives a little window to move out of the property before being forcefully evicted. This is commonly only a week, though with a stay of execution, the tenant could be given more time.

Some jurisdictions permit a tenant to have a right to redemption in the eviction process. This would allow a tenant to cancel a pending eviction and to stay in the rented property by catching up immediately on the back rent along with other appropriate fees. These rights become waived should the tenant constantly be late in paying the rent.

Finally, after a tenant has lost his or her eviction lawsuit, the tenant is commonly given a particular number of days in which to abandon the property. This has to be done before other repercussions occur. Sometimes the tenant will be told to leave immediately.

Landlords are given writs of possession by the court after the tenant has lost the lawsuit and still refused to leave. These writs of possession are then turned over to a law enforcement officer. Such an officer would then put up an official notice for a tenant to depart the property before the date on which the officer will return to forcibly remove the tenant. If the tenant is not gone when the officer returns, he is permitted to take the tenant and anyone else on the property and remove them. They will be allowed to take away their possessions or place them in storage before the property is given back to the landlord.

Experian

Experian is one of the three main credit reporting bureaus in the United States. As such it maintains a credit report, history, and FICO score on all adult Americans. The company does so much more than this most commonly understood function.

The company is also an international leader for global business and consumer credit reporting as well as marketing services. Experian is headquartered in Dublin, Ireland and is based on the London Stock Exchange where it is a member of Britain's FTSE 100 stock index. The company has customers in over 80 countries of the world and maintains offices and employees in 37 countries. Besides its Dublin base, Experian has operations headquarters found in Nottingham in the United Kingdom, California in the United States, and Sao Paulo in Brazil.

Experian serves as the corporate leader in global information services. The company received the 2015 honor of "World's Most Innovative Companies" from Forbes magazine for being among the leaders in driving improvements and change.

They deliver analytical tools and data to their clients found all over the world. The company helps businesses to prevent fraud, to manage their credit risk, to automate functions of decision making, and to specifically target marketing offers.

Experian also assists individuals with information and security needs. They aid individuals in checking out their credit reports and credit scores through copies that they can purchase and download directly over the Internet. They help people to safeguard themselves against the very real dangers of identity theft with credit report monitoring services. The company also provides a great source of information for education that is both hands on and interactive. This education helps both marketing personnel and credit professionals along with individual consumers.

Experian prides itself on its analytic and data services. They are in the business of assisting businesses and individuals with managing, protecting, and optimally using their data. They offer a number of different services to help people to do this effectively.

Their Experian Credit Tracker product gives consumers their FICO score, Experian credit report, and a credit monitoring service that comes with fraud alerts. They also staff a dedicated support team for fraud resolution when individuals become victims of identity theft. Help with identity theft or credit fraud is an area that is critical to consumers when they become victims.

Consumers can also choose from their higher level Experian Protect My ID service. This gives individuals an Experian credit report, 3 bureau credit monitoring services and alerts, daily checking of ID via Internet scanning, and access to their dedicated support for fraud resolution.

Experian provides a higher level view of individuals' credit reports and scores also. Their 3 Bureau Credit Report and FICO Scores service delivers copies of the person's credit report and FICO score for Experian, TransUnion, and Equifax. They also sell just their own credit report and FICO score for a lower price.

Experian offers even more services to its big business customers. Among their business product offerings are customer acquisition, customer management, fraud management, risk management, debt recovery, consulting services, regulatory compliance, and thought leadership. In customer acquisition, the company offers direct mail tools and big data analytics.

For risk management they verify applicants' identities and backgrounds. Experian can manage data breaches and prevent money laundering as part of their fraud management offerings. Debt recovery services include locating debtors and managing collection efforts. Among their consulting services are strategy, product, and fraud consulting areas.

Small business customers also have a variety of services offered to them by Experian. These include help with business and consumer credit, marketing and managing the business, and collecting debt.

Fair Housing Act

The Fair Housing Act of 1968 is officially known as Title VIII from the Civil Rights Act of 1968. It makes it illegal to discriminate with regards to renting, selling, or financing homes or apartments. No one may consider color, race, sex, religion, or national origin in these activities.

Congress amended the Fair Housing Act of 1968 with the Fair Housing Amendments Act in 1988. These amendments expanded the rulings of the original act in a number of important ways. No one was permitted to discriminate with housing because of an individual's disability or based on their family status. This meant that home sellers or renters could not disallow families with pregnant women or who had children less than 18 years of age living with them.

To prevent disability discrimination, the act included construction and design accessibility rules for some multifamily homes. Those that were to be occupied initially after March 13, 1991 had to comply with the accessibility provisions for disabled people.

The amendments also created new means of enforcing and administering the rules. HUD Housing and Urban Development attorneys were now able to take cases to administrative law judges for victims of such housing discrimination. The jurisdiction of the Justice Department became expanded and revised in such a way that it could file suits in Federal district courts for discrimination victims.

HUD has been tasked with the principal responsible to administer the Fair Housing Act of 1968 since the government adopted it. Thanks to the amendments in 1988, the department has become substantially more involved in enforcing the provisions. This is because the newly protected families and disabled brought many new complaints. The department also had to move beyond investigating and conciliating. They were tasked with mandatory enforcing the rules.

Any complaint regarding the Fair Housing Act of 1968 that individuals file with HUD becomes investigated. The FHEO Fair Housing and Equal Opportunity office handles this responsibility. When complaints can not be resolved voluntarily, the FHEO decides if there is sufficient evidence for a reasonable case of discrimination in housing practices. If they find reasonable cause, then HUD issues a Determination and Charge of Discrimination to the complaint parties. Hearings are next scheduled in front of a law judge for the HUD administration. Either the complaining party or the accused can terminate this procedure to instead have the matter resolved in Federal courts.

At this point, the Department of Justice assumes HUD's responsibility for the aggrieved party's complaints. They act as counsel that seeks to resolve the charges. The matter then becomes a civil case. In either the case of the HUD law judge hearing or the civil action held in the courts, the U.S. Court of Appeals can review the outcome.

The Fair Housing Act of 1968 proved to be historic as the final major act in the civil rights movement legislation. Despite this, housing remained segregated throughout much of the United States for decades. During the thirty years from 1950 through 1980, America's urban centers' black population grew from 6.1 million up to 15.3 million people.

At the same time, white Americans continuously abandoned the cities in favor of the suburbs. With them went a great number of the jobs that the black population needed to communities where they did not find welcome. The result of this ongoing trend caused urban America to be filled with ghettos. These are the communities inside the American inner cities where many minority populations live. They have been dogged by consistently high crime, unemployment, drug use, and other social problems.

Fannie Mae

Fannie Mae is the acronym for the FNMA Federal National Mortgage Association. This entity is a GSE Government Sponsored Enterprise along with brother organization Freddie Mac. It became a publicly traded company in 1968. This home lending giant proves to be the largest mortgage financing provider anywhere in the United States. As such, it funds significantly more mortgages than any competing company or entity. It ensures that homebuyers, homeowners, and renters around the U.S. all can obtain financing options which they can afford.

As the GSE became established in 1938, it has provided funding for the housing market of the country for over 75 years. Franklin D. Roosevelt's New Deal established the company in the midst of the Great Depression. This is why the mission of the company is to aid individuals in purchasing, renting, or refinancing a home whether economic times in the country are good or bad.

The company's explicit purpose is to boost the size of the secondary mortgage market. They do this when they securitize mortgages and package them into MBS mortgage backed securities. This process returns the mortgage loaned money to lenders who are then able to reinvest this money into additional lending. It also acts to grow the numbers of lending institutions who are issuing mortgages. This ensures that there are more than just savings and loan associations making local loans for housing.

The model worked well until between 2003 and 2004. At this point the subprime mortgages crisis started. It began when the mortgage market turned away from the GSEs like Freddie Mac and Fannie Mae and began to migrate rapidly to unregulated MBS Mortgage Backed Securities that major investment banks put together. This shift to private MBSs caused the GSEs to lose their control over and ability to monitor mortgages in the country.

Increased competition between the investment banks and the GSEs reduced the power and market share of the government mortgage backers further and boosted the mortgage lenders at their expense. This radical change in the way mortgages were overseen and made caused the underwriting standards for mortgages to dangerously decline. It turned out to be one of the major reasons for the ensuing mortgage and financial crises.

The situation became so severe at Fannie Mae by 2008 that the FHFA Federal Housing Finance Agency had to get directly involved. FHFA Director James Lockhart on September 7, 2008 placed both this organization and Freddie Mac under FHFA conservatorship. This proved to be among the most dramatic and far reaching government involvements in free enterprise financial markets for literally decades.

Among Lockhart's first actions, he fired both companies' boards of directors and CEOs. He then made the companies issue a new class of common stock warrants and senior preferred stock to Treasury for 79.9% of both GSEs. Those who had been holding either preferred or common stock in either entity before the conservatorship began saw the value of their shares massively decrease. All prior shares' dividends became suspended to try to hold up the mortgage backed securities' and company debt values. FHFA pledged that it had no intentions of liquidating the GSEs.

Since 2009, Fannie Mae has made great strides in its business of helping make housing work better for individuals and families. They have injected trillions of dollars into the mortgage markets in lending liquidity. This has gone a long way to helping the housing markets and overall economy to recover.

The company has also gone back to high quality eligibility and underwriting standards. In the first quarter of 2016, they have extended $115 billion in mortgage credit that has allowed for 210,000 homes to be purchased and 256,000 mortgages to be refinanced. They also financed the construction of 161,000 multifamily rental units.

Federal Housing Finance Agency (FHFA)

The Federal Housing Finance Agency is a government regulating agency. They are independent and responsible for overseeing several agencies within the secondary mortgage market. These include Freddie Mac, Fannie Mae, and the Federal Home Loan Banks. They work to keep these critical government sponsored organizations, along with the entire American housing financial system, in good health.

As such, the FHFA labors constantly to build up and safeguard the secondary mortgage markets in the United States. They do this through their leadership in and delivering excellent research, dependable data, strong supervision, and pertinent policies. The three government sponsored entities of Freddie Mac, Fannie Mae, and the Federal Home Loan Bank system together deliver over $5.5 trillion in financial institutions and mortgage markets funding throughout the United States.

The FHFA helps to keep this all possible by providing their independent regulation and careful oversight of these vital mortgage markets. Besides this, they are also the conservator of both Freddie Mac and Fannie Mae since the financial crisis and Great Recession that began in 2007-2008 wreaked havoc on the two giant government sponsored agencies along with the housing market they guaranteed.

The Federal Housing Finance Agency is concerned with creating a better market of secondary mortgages for the country's future. To this effect, they are working on a sequence of strategies and initiatives to boost the housing financial system in the future. Among these new ideas is the construction of a new and improved database called the Common Securitization Platform. This will have dual roles. It will take the presently outdated infrastructures and modernize them. It will also allow for the possibilities of other players in the market choosing to utilize this same infrastructure.

The FHFA considers itself to be in a partnership. They strive alongside the entities they regulate to keep home ownership alive and affordable through a variety of programs. These include the HARP Home Affordable Refinance Program and the HAMP Home Affordable Modification Program. The two programs deliver significant and tangible aid to both communities and their homeowners. So far such programs have assisted literally millions of home owning Americans to keep or stay in their houses.

The FHFA does not have a long history. It is a new organization that grew out of the housing market collapse and Great Recession. President Obama signed the Housing and Economic Recovery Act of 2008 to create the Federal Housing Finance Agency back on July 30, 2008.

The ongoing mission of the FHFA is to make certain that the government sponsored enterprises for housing function in a manner that is both economically viable and safe. This is so that they can continue to provide a dependable source of both funds and liquidity for investment in communities and the financing of home purchases. As part of this, they envision a housing financial system that is stable, dependable, and liquid for both the present and the future.

The FHFA values four virtues. They prize excellence in all areas of their work. The organization appreciates respect for their team members, resources, and the information they collect. They value integrity and commit themselves to the greatest possible professional and moral standards. The group also encourages diversity in all of their business dealings and employment arrangements, as well as in the entities which they regulate and for whom they are the conservator.

FHFA is also an important member group of the Financial Stability Oversight Council. Chief among their tasks is to identify financial stability risks in the U.S., to respond to rising threats to the American financial system, and to encourage discipline in the market. They serve on this council with fellow members that include The Federal Reserve governors, CFTC, FDIC, Comptroller of the Currency, SEC, and Treasury Department.

Financial Crisis

A financial crisis refers to a period where the value of assets and/or financial institutions declines quickly. Such a crisis is commonly connected with runs on the banks or at the least fear and panic. In these difficult and dangerous economic periods, investors will fire sell any assets they can to pull back their cash out of investment and savings accounts. They do this hoping to repatriate their funds home before they decline or vanish altogether at the financial institution.

Such a financial crisis happens because of assets and banks becoming overly valued. They are typically made far worse because of the inexplicable behavior of mass groups of investors. Often times, a rapid-fire domino effect of selling leads to still lower prices of the associated assets in the crisis and even more bank account withdrawals. If the crisis does not become resolved relatively quickly, it can lead an economy and nation into a deep and painful recession or even a lasting and devastating depression.

The sad part of finance is that it is not only prone to numerous incidents like these, but it is also shaped by financial crisis. There have been many such significant financial crises over the past three hundred years. These included the 1720 South Sea Bubble crisis, the Panic of 1792, the Latin American Crisis of 1825, the Cotton Crisis of 1837, the Railroad Crisis of 1857, the Long Depression of 1873, the Knickerbockers Crisis of 1907, Black Monday and the Wall Street Crash of 1929, the 1973-1974 Arab Oil Crisis, 1987 Black Monday, the Asian Crisis of 1997, and the Dotcom Crash of 2001.

The most recent financial crisis which rocked the international world was the Global Financial Crisis of 2008. Economists have determined that this proved to be the most devastating economic disaster for the world since the 1929 Great Depression which lasted nearly a decade. It led to what has become known as the Great Recession. Strangely enough, while the other financial crises which preceded it could be pinpointed to a main reason or singular event, the Global Financial Crisis could not be.

Instead this economic disaster resulted from a chain of events. Each of these had their own trigger. The crisis was so severe that it nearly caused a complete failure of the American and global banking systems. Economists have made the case that the crisis' roots dated back to the decade of the 1970s. The Community Development Act proved to be responsible for developing the market for the one-day toxic subprime mortgages. It was this act that mandated banks had to relax their credit standards for those minorities who were lower income earners.

It turned out to be these quasi-government agency guaranteed subprime mortgage debts that expanded dangerously through the early years of the 2000s. Both the primary government sponsored entities Fannie Mae and Freddie Mac were guaranteeing the toxic mortgages. As these loans were booming, the Federal Reserve (American Central Bank) was drastically slashing interest rates after the dotcom crash of 2001 to stave off a national recession from the stock market collapse. In the end, these dual scenarios of cheap money fueled by dramatically lower interest rates and loosened credit requirements brought on by the Community Development Act worked together to create a housing bubble. The ensuing speculation and positive feedback only encouraged home prices to rise still further.

At the same time, the wily investment banks were seeking easy money gains after the 2001 recession and dotcom bust. They invented the fanciful CDOs collateralized debt obligations from mortgages they bought up on the secondary market. By bundling both prime and subprime mortgages together into single instrument investments, they deceived unknowing investors into purchasing highly risky CDO products.

As the CDO market really took off, the housing bubble started bursting. Along with falling home prices, the subprime borrowers started defaulting on their loans en masse. They either could not or would not make payments any longer on those loans that then turned out to be higher than the value of the homes. This only exacerbated the home price decline situation.

Investors next realized that the CDOs they had bought in droves were declining to near worthless. This resulted from the toxic mortgage debt that underlay them. Investors attempted to offload the paper, but they found the market had disappeared. This then led to a perilous wave of subprime lending institution failures. It caused a dry up in liquidity and a subsequent contagion which filtered through to the highest echelons of the banking world and system.

Thanks to their huge exposure to the subprime mortgages and CDO debt obligations, the two enormous investment banks Bear Stearns and Lehman Brothers collapsed without warning. Over 450 other banks then subsequently failed throughout the following five years. Had it not been for a government-administered and taxpayer-funded bank bailout, a few of the mega banks would have failed as well alongside those that did, including such national venerable institutions as Washington Mutual, Wachovia, and Merrill Lynch.

Financial Mentor

A financial mentor is a trusted guide or counselor that helps a person in the arena of business, personal finance and investments. Mentors can be many different people, but they typically have several characteristics in common. They are all loyal advisers who have the person's best interests at heart.

Mentoring is most widely used in business. Other settings that use it include medical fields and educational settings. Business experts will tell you that among the most useful, helpful, and valuable career assets that you can have in your business career is a helpful and experienced mentor.

Financial mentors are commonly older individuals who have more wisdom and experience to share with the individual than he or she already possesses. Though they do not have to be older in every single case, they must always have more experience than the person whom they are mentoring. These mentors both guide financial development and assist the person with their overall financial and business goals. They do not engage in this process with the expressed intent of making money or benefiting financially from the arrangement usually.

With financial mentors, you as the person being mentored have some preparation that you can do. You should listen carefully to the mentor and what he or she has to tell you. This is most easily accomplished by coming to the meeting with the financial mentor with some sort of recording means prepared. This might be a voice recorder, PDA, laptop, or even pen and paper. If a mentor made specific recommendations in the prior discussions, then you should have both noted and tried to apply them. Be ready to review any steps that you have taken specifically with the mentor.

You should also allow a mentor to be a part of your big picture goals and plans, and not only the particular details. The overall goals for you who are being mentored should be set together, in conjunction with the mentor. They should talk not only about present challenges and difficulties, but also concentrate on long term and short term goals together.

Good financial mentors will also do more than simply hold official meetings. They will take the time to get to know you. This does not have to be extensive amounts of time, but it should be quality time spent. This might involve a fifteen minute friendly chat over coffee or a quick bite to eat out some night. The key is not to take up too much of the financial mentor's time until you get to know him or her better. Then as the relationship broadens out into a friendship, more opportunities to get together will naturally arise.

Financial mentors can help out with many areas of your life. They can make helpful suggestions for getting out of debt. They can guide you with good concepts for practical and smart investing. They can share personal, actual experience for navigating through difficulties with a business that you own. They might suggest advice to assist you in your career development. Whatever help that you specifically request from a mentor, you should always remember to be appreciative and take the time to write thank you notes.

Financing Terms

There are two different financing terms available for businesses. These are short term financing and long term financing. In today's economic environment following the financial collapse and Great Recession, many businesses require both types. The two types of financing involve more differences than only the time frames.

Short term financing is commonly utilized for the daily business operations' funding and needs. This is also known as working capital. The financing terms for these short term facilities commonly require the short term loans to be paid back in a year or less.

Long term financing is more often utilized for the upkeep or purchase of fixed asset types. This might include a building or machinery that a firm owns. The financing terms for long term loans are for periods of time that are greater than a year.

Among the short term financing means are bank loans, bank overdrafts, trade credit, and leasing. For individuals, bank overdrafts prove to be the most common means of short term finance, since their finance terms permit an individual to draw out a greater amount of money that the person has in the bank, up to a predetermined amount.

Trade credit is useful for small businesses who may require the ability to buy goods and services or supplies before they receive payments and incoming receipts. With such trade credit facilities, the finance terms are commonly from thirty to ninety days to pay the full balance.

Long term financing might also involve bank loans, as well as corporate bonds or mortgages. With corporate bonds, a company is borrowing money from investors and members of the public. The financing terms of these types of instruments commonly require periodic interest payments that are known as coupon payments. The principal is then repaid on the agreed upon day. Many corporate bonds also feature a recall option that allows a company to pay off its long term debts early. This might be of interest to such a firm if they feel that they can borrow the funds for less money elsewhere or with lower interest rates.

Mortgages are extremely long term financing options made available to individuals or consumers for the purchase of a house or commercial property. These financing terms commonly run to thirty years or longer. Mortgages involve complex calculations for figuring out payments that often involve property taxes, mortgage insurance, and loan repayments.

Financing terms can also relate to the specifics of a particular loan, mortgage, or credit facility. They would spell out the interest rate, due dates of payments, and number of payments anticipated. In many cases, they would also specify the amount of interest that would be paid over the course of the loan or credit facility, as well as the penalties for not making the payments on time.

Fixed Rate Mortgage

Fixed Rate Mortgages are products for mortgage loans that the FHA, or Federal Housing Administration, first created. In this type of mortgage, the interest rates in effect on the mortgage note stay at the same level during the entire life of the loan. This stands in stark contrast to loans where the interest rates are adjustable, or floating. There are also hybrid types of loans that involve fixed rates for a portion of the loan's life.

Fixed rate mortgages will have monthly payments that must be made to keep current on the mortgage. Besides the monthly payment there are property taxes and property insurance costs. These are typically set up in escrow accounts. With such escrow amounts, these are likely to change every so often. Still, the main share of the payments, which are associated with interest and principal on the mortgage, will stay the same.

Figuring up the monthly payments with fixed rate mortgages is relatively easy. You will have to acquire three pieces of data to do so. These are the interest rate with compounding of interest period, mortgage term, and amount of loan.

Fixed rate mortgages are also known by their nickname of plain vanilla mortgages. They have this moniker because of how simple they are for borrowers to understand. Such fixed rate mortgages do not entail the many risks and perils associated with adjustable rate mortgages that include pre set teasing rates or Adjustable Rate Mortgages. As such, Fixed rate mortgage default rates and foreclosure rates are commonly far lower than are these more experimental and risky mortgage products.

Several terms are commonly associated with Fixed Rate Mortgages. These include the fully indexed rate and the term. Fully indexed rates are the interest rate index plus the margin charged by the lender. Such a fully indexed rate proves to be the actual interest rate for the loan's entire life.

The term represents the amount of time that the fixed rate loan covers. This is not the same thing as the number of payments. Thirty year terms might have thirty payments if you were on an annual payment plan, or it might alternatively have 360 payments on a more usual monthly payment plan

The most popular and proven form of home loans and mortgage products within the United States are undoubtedly these fixed rate mortgages. Among the various mortgage terms that can be acquired, the most prevalent ones are either thirty year or fifteen year mortgages. Both shorter and longer time frames can be had with fixed rate mortgages.

These days, even forty and fifty year mortgages are presently offered. They are especially utilized in places with housing prices that are exceptionally high, as thirty year mortgage terms do not prove to be affordable for the average income family in such scenarios.

In contrast to fixed rate mortgages are various other types. These include graduated payment mortgages, balloon payment mortgages, and interest only mortgages. These unusual other types of mortgages commonly get borrowers into trouble, which is why they are not nearly so popular as are the fixed rate mortgages.

Fixer-Upper

Fixer-Upper is a term that is commonly associated with real estate property, such as houses, that need some significant repair and renovation work. Although these kinds of houses might be lived in despite their present condition, they usually want redesign, reconstruction, or redecoration of some form. Depending on how much repair or renovation work they require, fixer-upper's can be major projects that require significant investments of time and money.

Fixer-Upper's commonly result from houses that have not been taken care of or properly maintained. Because of this, they tend to possess market values that are lower than comparable houses found in the same locale. Fixer-Upper's can be discovered in the majority of communities, even in neighborhoods whose housing prices are not depressed.

Fixer-Upper's commonly prove to be very popular with buyers who act as investors in houses. They want to acquire the property cheaply so that they can repair it and increase its likely real estate value in order to acquire a nice profit on the investment. These projects as investments have gained greatly in popularity as a result of various do it yourself types of renovation shows that are all about home improvement. Many times in downturns in the real estate market, such as the one that has been ongoing since 2007, the interest in fixer-upper's declines.

There is a danger with Fixer-upper's for many buyers who think to improve and then flip them, or resell the house for profits. This is simply that they do not realize how much time and money will be required of them in repairing the house in question. Making a house salable will require addressing not only relatively simple cosmetic issues, but also potentially structural or service problems. When the plumbing or foundation is in need of major repairs or replacing, the work involved commonly turns out to be very expensive and needs professional contractors.

This is why determining if a Fixer-upper is a viable and worthy investment requires some experience and work. First, you will have to determine for how much the typical house in the neighborhood is selling. It is also wise to know what makes the most desirable houses in the neighborhood so in demand and how much they cost. Real estate agents can be helpful in this respect.

If you decide to pursue buying a Fixer-upper, then you should be watching for the truly cosmetic Fixer-upper's. These only require more basic improvements such as wallpaper, paint, new appliances, some landscape work, and possibly new window and floor coverings. Houses that look run down and require substantial structural repairs can be very dangerous and should be avoided. Houses that are priced too reasonably usually have a reason for this. Intelligent buyers should learn why this is the case before they commit their money.

The best strategy is to find the house that is the least wanted in the best neighborhood possible. The house and estimated repair cost must both be within your budget. Once at full fair market value, such a property should pay you back handsomely.

Foreclosure

Foreclosures represent houses or commercial properties that have been seized by a bank or other mortgage lender. These properties are then sold to recoup mortgage loan losses after an owner and borrower has not made the payments as promised in the mortgage agreement.

Foreclosure is also the legal procedure in which the lender gets a court order for the termination of the mortgagor's right of redemption. This is the case since most lenders have security interests in the house from the borrower. The borrower will secure the mortgage using the house as the collateral.

Borrowers fall into home foreclosure for several reasons, most of which could not be predicted in advance. Owner might have been let go from their job or forced to take a job transfer to another state. They might have suffered from medical problems that prevented them from working. They might have gone through a divorce and split up assets. They could have been overwhelmed by too many bills. Whatever the reason, they are no longer able to make their promised monthly mortgage payments.

Foreclosures represent potential opportunities for investors. They may be purchased directly with a seller in advance of a bank completing foreclosure proceedings. Many investors who concentrate on foreclosures prefer to deal with the owners directly. They have to be aware of many laws pertaining to foreclosures, which are different in every state. For example, while in some states home owners can stay in their properties for a full year after defaulting on payments, while in others, they have fewer than four months in advance of the trustee sale.

Practically all states also allow a redemption period for the delinquent homeowner. This simply means that a seller possesses an irrevocable ability to catch up on back payments and interest in order to retain ownership of the house. The owner will likely be required to pay any foreclosure costs experienced by the bank up to that point.

Another means of purchasing a foreclosure home is to buy it at the Trustee's Sale. When this means is pursued, it is better to bid on a house that allows you to look it over in advance of putting up an offer. This is helpful so that you can determine how many repairs will be needed to make it salable and even possibly habitable. It is also worth knowing if the occupants are still living in the house and will have to be forcefully evicted. The process of going through an eviction can be both expensive and time consuming.

Many Trustee Sales will have certain rules in common that have to be followed for a foreclosure house to be purchased. They may demand sealed bids. They could require you to demonstrate your proof of financial qualifications. They might similarly insist on you putting up a significant earnest money deposit. Many of them will state that the property is being purchased in its present condition, or as is.

Freddie Mac

Freddie Mac is a semi-private company that Congress chartered in 1970. They created the entity to offer stability, liquidity, and affordable prices for the country and its housing markets. They have grown to be responsible for the home purchases of one out of four buyers.

Besides this the company is also among the biggest financing sources for multifamily housing in the nation. From 2009 to 2016, the company has dispersed mortgage market funding that amounts to over $2.5 trillion. This has enabled in excess of 13 million American families to refinance, purchase, or rent a home in that time frame.

In 1970 Congress was seeking to stabilize the mortgage markets of the country. They wanted to grow and improve opportunities for rental housing that was affordable and for home buying. Because of this, Freddie Mac's mission has always been to bring stability, liquidity, and affordability to the national housing market in the United States. They do this in a variety of ways. The company helps the secondary mortgage market. They buy both mortgage securities and mortgage loans outright as investments. They then package and sell these as guaranteed mortgage securities known as PCs. In this secondary market, there are entities which buy and sell mortgages as complete loans or as mortgage securities. Freddie Mac never makes loans to home owners directly themselves.

Because of the collapse of the mortgage backed securities markets in 2007 and 2008 and its impact on their finances, the company is now being run under conservatorship. The FHFA Federal Housing Finance Agency oversees their business to make sure loans are carefully scrutinized and securitized. They want to avoid the mistakes of the financial crisis becoming repeated here.

Freddie Mac operates in three main business areas to ensure that a continuous supply of mortgage funding goes through to the housing markets in the country. They make rental housing and home buying more affordable through their single family credit guarantee business, their multifamily business, and their investment business. They utilize all three of these to promote financing for affordable housing.

The single family line is essentially a recycling operation. They work with securitizing mortgages so that the entity is able to provide funding to millions of different home loans annually. This securitization proves to be the means where they buy up different loans lenders have made and then package these up into various mortgage securities. They then sell these on the worldwide capital markets. The money from the sale of these securities they next funnel back to the lenders. In this way home loan operations have sufficient mortgage money for lending.

The company is also interested in supporting renters as well. This is the role of their multifamily business. In this line, the outfit cooperates with a group of lenders to help finance the construction of various apartment buildings throughout the United States. The lenders make the loans and Freddie Mac buys them to package and resell. This way the lenders receive back the proceeds so they can issue more loans. This is a critical line as multifamily loans prove to be a few million dollars each and require unique underwriting from one property to the next.

Their investment business actually purchases some of their own mortgage backed securities which they and other financial entities like Fannie Mae guarantee. This portfolio further invests into individual loans which they guarantee but choose not to securitize. By bidding on some of their own securities, the investment business and portfolio serves the markets. It gives these mortgage backed securities greater liquidity and offers more funding for mortgages. They do this by issuing their own debt which creates net income for the company after they pay their interest to the bond holders.

Georgist Public Finance Theory

Georgist Public Finance Theory refers to an economic school of thought. Also known as geoism, this relates to the idea that economic value which comes from property including natural opportunities and natural resources ought to belong in kind to every individual in a society. They simultaneously believe the production value each individual produces should be owned by each contributing member according to what they produce.

The philosophy came from the works of Henry George. This Georgist paradigm provides solutions to ecological and social issues. It does this by depending on the concepts of public finance and land rights while striving to combine both social justice and optimal economic efficiency.

As such, this Georgist Public Finance Theory concerns itself with the fair distribution of economic rents created by pollution, monopolies, and the control over commons. This includes privileges and rights such as intellectual property and titles of ownership for natural resources. Those natural resources that have a limit on their available exploitable supply are able to produce economic rents. Georgists claim that placing a tax on economic rents is fair, efficient, and also equitable.

The principle policies of the Georgists maintain that taxes should be assessed based upon the value of the land. They feel that any revenues created by an LVT land value tax will eliminate or reduce those taxes on investment and labor which are both inefficient and unjust. Some of the followers of the Georgist Public Finance Theory argue for the redistribution of extra public revenues to be returned to the inhabitants via a dividend payment to the citizens or a basic income distribution.

Land value tax is called progressive by many economists dating back to Adam Smith and his *Wealth of Nations*. These taxes are mostly paid in by the landowning class of wealthy individuals. They can not pass them on to renters of the land, workers, or tenants. The idea behind land value taxes is that they should ameliorate inequalities in economics, increase wages, lessen the vulnerability which economies suffer from such as property bubbles and credit manias, and take away any motivations to abuse real estate.

The basis philosophically for Georgist Public Finance Theory hails back to a few of its early advocates like Baruch Spinoza, John Locke, and Thomas Paine. Yet the person who made the entire concept of gathering in public revenues from the privileges of natural resource ownership became popularized by the social reformer and economist Henry George via his first work *Progress and Poverty* which was published in 1879.

The ideas of Georgist Public Finance Theory became most influential and widespread in acceptance in the early 20th and late 19th centuries. There were whole communities, political parties, and even institutions which were founded on these ideas at the time. Early followers of George's philosophy on economics were many times called Single Taxers. This was based upon the idea of obtaining public revenues only from privileges on land. Today's Georgists have altered this foundational belief to include a wide range of government funds' sourcing.

There were a few communities founded under the Georgist Public Finance Theory principles back in the late 1800s and early 1900s in the United States. Three of them which still exist and function under these ideals are Fairhope, Alabama which arose under the governance of the Fairhope Single Tax Corporate in 1894; Arden, Delaware that Fran Stephens along with Will Price founded a few years later in 1900; and Altoona, Pennsylvania which still operates under only a single land tax to this day.

Internationally, the German sphere of influence in Jiaozhou Bay or Kiaochow within China fully implemented the Georgist Public Finance Theory policies. The only government revenue source that they relied on came from a six percent land value tax levied throughout the territory. The German Imperial administration hoped that this would eliminate the land speculation problems which had arisen in their southwest African colonies.

This objective was achieved successfully in their China sphere of influence as the hoped. These Georgist ideas became a part of the societal fabric in one form or another in such far flung nations and territories as Hong Kong, Australia, South Africa, Singapore, South Korea, and Taiwan. Such countries still assess one form of land value tax or another today.

Good Debt

Good debt is debt that benefits a person or business to carry. Such good debts demonstrate both the creditworthiness and the responsibility of a borrower. They also create a good base to build on in the future. There are many examples of good debt, which stands in contrast to bad debt.

Good debts are typically those debts that are taken on to acquire an item or investment that only grows in value with time. Examples of this include things like real estate loans, schooling loans, home mortgages, business debt, and passive income investments. Each of these items could provide a significant and real advantage with time. Real estate could increase in value and be resold for profits.

Higher education commonly leads to greater amounts of earnings. Loans on homes are commonly wonderful for building credit and provide properties that serve as excellent collateral. Loans for businesses may result in profits earned from trade and sales. It is important to note that cars and other items are not included in these lists. This is simply because they lose value the moment that they are purchased and driven away.

Bad debts in contrast are those that result in higher interest rates and considerable deprecation of the items purchased with time. Goods that are for short time frame use and bought on credit are commonly considered to be bad debts. Since the item's life span will only decline with time, and the interest rates are typically high, no benefit is derived from purchasing these things with debt. A great number of such purchases rapidly decline in value, even after one use.

A significant benefit to good debts lies in the increase in cash flow that they commonly create. Properly structured good debts lead to tax advantages, to the ability to invest in still more assets that can produce cash, and to higher credit scores as well. Good debts that are paid on time furthermore build up a good financial base for the future. Good debts create cash flow, which stands in contrast to bad debts that do not.

Investments that produce passive income are among the best good debts. For example, purchasing an apartment building using debt will result in both income revenue and substantial tax deductions. This proves to be good debt, since although you are borrowing money, you are receiving passive income and gaining the ability to depreciate assets that can actually appreciate with time. On top of this, you are allowed to live there while you accrue all of these other benefits.

When considering a good debt, you should make certain that the income that the investment will provide is high enough to make the investment and the accompanying debt worth while. A number of experts offer advice on this. They suggest that not tying up in excess of twenty percent of your overall value in debt is a better practice. Higher debt levels than this can sound off warning bells with banks and other lenders.

Government National Mortgage Association (GNMA)

GNMA refers to a United States HUD Department of Housing and Urban Development based government corporation. This agency is different from its cousin Freddie Mac as Ginnie Mae is not a private corporation. Rather it is an actual U.S. government agency.

The roles of GNMA are two-fold. They are to guarantee there is sufficient liquidity for mortgages which are government insured. This comprises all mortgages provided by the FHA Federal Housing Administration, the RHA Rural Housing Administration, and the VA Veterans Administration. The other responsibility of Ginnie Mae is to attract the capital of investors into the marketplace for such loans. This allows for the various issuers to provide still more loans in the future. The majority of those mortgages which Ginnie Mae securitizes and sells are in fact MBS mortgage-backed securities which are guaranteed by the FHA. These are usually mortgages which are offered to lower income borrowers and first time home buyers.

GNMA operates in a fairly straightforward manner. The governmental agency purchases home mortgages off of the financial institutions which make such loans. Then it pools them together into $1 million and higher collections. Ginnie Mae has choices at this point. Some of these pools it holds on to and then directly sells them to investors outright. Others it sells off to financial institutions and mortgage bankers who then sell them on to investors themselves.

After this, either the mortgage banker or GNMA itself will collect mortgage payments off of the pools' mortgage homeowners. For those investors who choose to invest in a GNMA, they typically receive monthly payments which come with at least a portion of the principal (that remains outstanding) as well as an interest payment. The other method has investors just obtaining interest payments. In this case, the principal only comes back to the investors as the mortgage reaches maturity.

Sometimes investors call such bonds from the agency Ginnie Mae pass through securities. This is because the requisite mortgage payments will go through, or pass through, a bank. The bank then collects its fee in advance of passing on what remains of the payment to the appropriate investors. These payments amount to greater returns than comparable U.S. Treasury notes provide investors.

GNMA's also possess other advantages. They are guaranteed not to default and fail by the United States' government and its full faith and credit. They also prove to be extremely liquid. This is partly because they may be easily resold via the active secondary market at any time.

GNMA instruments come with a hefty minimum investment dollar requirement. This amounts to typically $25,000. Once this minimum threshold is met, the size may be increased in only single dollar increments to whatever level is desired. There are opportunities to purchase such Ginnie Mae's which can sell for under the standard $25,000 when they are occasionally offered at face value discounts via the secondary market. This could occur in cases where the applicable interest rates prove to be lower than more current instrument issues' rates or also as the remaining principals have become reduced significantly.

There are also mutual funds which buy into Ginnie Mae's. The cost of shares in such funds are considerably lower than the $25,000 minimum of the instruments themselves. In cases like this, investment trusts or outright Ginnie Mae funds will purchase the bonds directly from the government agency or secondary market. They will then provide their own shares, which represent stakes in such instruments, to the investing public.

It is not only separate investors who purchase the Ginnie Mae's. A great range of different organizations and companies purchase them. Several examples of these other buyers abound. They are credit unions, retirement pension funds, commercial banks, real estate investment trusts, corporations, and insurance companies. There are also a great variety of different institution kinds that actually issue such Ginnie Mae's. Among these are banks, mortgage companies, and credit unions.

Government Sponsored Enterprise (GSE)

A government sponsored enterprise is a financial service operations that the U.S. Congress created by law. Their purpose is to improve the amount of credit that flows into specific areas of the American economy. They were also intended to help those parts of the capital markets become more transparent and efficient as well as to lessen risks for investors and capital suppliers.

The wish of Congress in establishing them was to increase the available finance and lower the cost of obtaining it for certain specific segments of the economy. This was to be accomplished by encouraging investors via lowering the risks of losses to those involved.

The main components of the economy where these were set up were home finance, agriculture, and education. Among these, two of the government sponsored enterprises are best known. These are Fannie Mae, the Federal National Mortgage Association and Freddie Mac, the Federal Home Loan Mortgage Corporation.

The year 1916 saw the first government sponsored enterprise that Congress established. This was the Farm Credit System. Congress moved GSEs into housing finance in 1932 when it established the Federal Home Loan Banks. It focused on education costs and finance when in 1972 Congress chartered Sallie Mae. In 1995, Congress passed a law and permitted this educational GSE to give up its government sponsorship so that it could transform into a fully private company.

The segment of the economy for residential mortgages and borrowing proves to be substantially the largest industry where the government sponsored enterprises function. In mortgages, these GSEs own or pool around $5 trillion in home mortgages.

The way that Congress came up with to boost capital market efficiency and get past the imperfections of the market was to help funds migrate more effortlessly from fund suppliers to fund borrowers in major loan demand areas of the economy. They accomplished this with a type of government guarantee which limited the loss risks for those who offered the funds.

These government sponsored enterprises now mostly serve as intermediaries between agricultural and home borrowers and lenders. Freddie Mac and Fannie Mae remain the two best known and most influential GSEs today. They buy up mortgages and issue them through affiliated companies. Once this is accomplished, they pack them up as MBS mortgage backed securities. These securities come with the important financial backing from Freddie Mac or Fannie Mae. Investors allowed to trade in the TBA to be announced markets find these investments appealing when they carry government sponsored enterprises backing.

These housing GSEs also established a secondary market for loans with their guarantees, securitizing, and bonding. It has helped the main issuers of primary market mortgages to boost their volume of loans at the same time as they reduce the risks of single loans. It also gives investors a wide market of instruments which are securitized and standardized.

The government sponsored enterprise does not actually come with the government's hard guarantee of their credit. Despite this, lenders have always given them better interest rates at the same time that investors in the securities have paid high prices. This stems from the government's implicit guarantee that these critical organizations will not default or fail. It has helped the two main GSEs to save on borrowing costs to the tune of around $2 billion each year.

The subprime mortgage crisis and financial crisis reached a fevered pitch and embroiled Freddie Mac and Fannie Mae in 2007 and 2008. The American government demonstrated the value of the implicit guarantee then by bailing out and putting the two GSEs into conservatorship in September of 2008.

Graduated Payment Mortgage (GPM)

A graduated payment mortgage is a special type of home mortgage where payments are low initially and go up over the term of the loan. These are still considered to be a type of fixed rate mortgages as the interest rates are set and pre-determined even when the payments rise.

The low upfront payment helps financial institutions to qualify the borrowers. Banks only have to take into account the original low rate to approve them. This is why the GPMs assist those who otherwise would not be able to get qualified using the normal FRM fixed rate mortgage. This aids a great number of potential home buyers who might not be able to get qualified to purchase a home. It is best for younger or newer homeowners. Their levels of income should rise with time. This helps them to make the increasing mortgage payments.

The payments rise every year with a graduated payment mortgage until the entire amount has been repaid. The amount that they increase varies from one contract to the next. Typically the payments rises between 7% and 12% each year from the original base amount.

There is a danger with these types of products. If the young home buyers do not see their income rise consistently and significantly enough, the increasing payments on the home will take a greater share of their take home pay every year. Eventually, they may not be able to afford the payments if their salaries do not rise sufficiently.

The original payment for these graduated payment mortgages is not enough to cover the loan's interest. The difference between what is covered and what is not is called negative amortization. This amount adds on to the loan balance with every payment. It takes years for the rising payments to overcome this increase in the loan balance. Lenders do not like the fact that the balance goes up above the initial amount. Because of this they charge greater rates for these types of loans than they do for standard fixed rate mortgages.

The trade-off with a graduated payment mortgage is the larger payment that continues to grow for several years. This generally does not reach its peak level until five years have passed. The higher payment will then stay fixed for the rest of the mortgage term. This is the price to pay for a low upfront payment that a borrower can be approved for and can afford.

There are other kinds of graduated payment mortgages on the market. These alternatives provide varying rates of payment rises for different amounts of time. In one example, homeowners can get a gradually rising rate of 3% per year for ten years rather than pay more than 7% each year for 5 years. These alternative GPMs require a higher upfront payment amount and can also lead to a larger final payment. Because the initial payment is higher, the negative amortization will be less. This will cause the peak loan balance to be smaller.

GPMs are not unique in mortgages that have payments which increase. There are also fixed rate mortgages called temporary buy downs. These come with lower upfront payments during the loan's early years. The advantage to these is that the loan does not incur negative amortization.

Temporary buy downs only work if someone pays for the buy down account. The financial institution takes money from this supplemental account to cover the lower payments in the first two years. This way the lender receives identical payments for the entire life of the loan. Either the home seller or the buyer has to supply the money for the supplemental account.

HARP Program

HARP stands for the Home Affordable Refinance Program. This program that the government sponsored entities Fannie Mae and Freddie Mac created and back is unique. It turns out to be the one refinancing program that works with borrowers who are eligible and who have no or little equity in their houses so that they can receive refinancing benefits and lower interest rates.

The HARP program has changed some over the years. One of the main improvements to the program was to get rid of the underwater limitation amount for home owners. There is now no restriction on how much more the borrowers owe on their mortgage than the property is actually worth.

Thanks to this modification in the HARP program, a great number of home owners who could not qualify before will now be able to do so. The program itself expires on September 30, 2017. This makes it important for buyers who are considering it to take action on it or get more information in the near future.

The HARP program is a good choice for those borrower who have maintained a successful payment history over the last 12 months. It does not require a perfect payment record. Over the last six months there can not be any late payments. From six to twelve months prior there can only be a single payment that is 30 days late. The loan must also be guaranteed by or owned by Freddie Mac or Fannie Mae.

In order to participate, there are several other considerations. The loan only can be modified with this HARP program if it is either the primary residence or a second house or investment property. It makes most sense if the value on the house has declined. It is especially useful for those whose first mortgage amount is greater than the present house market value or if there is little equity in the property. The loan will only qualify if borrowers closed on them before or on May 31, 2009. This information can be obtained with the loan lookup tool and results on the Fannie Mae or Freddie Mac websites.

There are a number of good reasons for borrowers who are not able to take advantage of other refinancing means to utilize the HARP program on their mortgage. It lowers the monthly payment after the process is complete. The refinance procedure also decreases the interest rate. This means that borrowers will save on interest as well as monthly payment amounts.

It can be especially beneficial for those who have adjustable rate mortgages. These HARP interest rates are fixed, which means they will not change with time. Lower interest rates and less interest also help the home owners to build up their equity faster. It is possible to get a refinanced mortgage with a shorter term as well. Because the program does not require any appraisals, this saves the home owners both money and time that it takes to find someone to perform them to most banks' satisfaction.

Participating in the HARP program is not difficult. It requires that borrowers undergo an application process, receive approval, and finalize closing much like with the original mortgage. HARP lenders work with the home owners every step of the way and assist in deciding if the program meets the needs of the borrower. There may be closing costs associated with the refinance. These often can be rolled over into the new loan to reduce out of pocket costs as necessary.

Home Affordable Modification Program (HAMP)

The Home Affordable Modification Program is also known by its acronym HAMP. This stands for a program created by the United States government. They founded it in order to assist those homeowners who were struggling to keep up with their mortgages. For any homeowners who have watched in dismay as their financial conditions deteriorated since they originally purchased their house, they could be able to qualify for loan modifications to make keeping the home possible and affordable.

The program actually helps participants by allowing them to reduce their monthly mortgage payments. This happens as the program approves a lower rate of interest, extends the mortgage's time frame (and term), or alters the type of mortgage to fixed rate from adjustable rate ARM. In some cases, two or even three of these changes may be approved together. The modifications can happen because the United States government backs them.

The Home Affordable Modification Program began as the Departments of Housing and Urban Development HUD combined forces with the Treasury in order to forge a new initiative that they named Making Homes Affordable. Though there were other parts to this ground breaking concept, the HAMP proved to be a key pillar of it. The government recognized in the wake of the Great Recession that many Americans were only one accident, job loss, or illness away from falling hopelessly behind on their mortgages and payments. This is why they decided to come up with their innovative program for modifying mortgages to make them more affordable for those who are in the most need of help.

Becoming eligible for this home modification assistance program requires an applicant be able to successfully meet a particular set of criteria. They must have bought and financed the house before or on January 1st of 2009. They have to be capable of proving a real financial hardship that makes them struggle to meet their monthly mortgage payments. At the same time, they have to show that they are already behind on the monthly payments or even at risk of sliding into foreclosure of their home. In order to successfully qualify, the property can not have been condemned. They may not owe more than $729,750 on the primary residence which is a single family home. Finally, applicants may not show any personal real estate fraud convictions from any time within the past ten years.

If they meet all of these exacting criteria, then interested parties are able to call their specific mortgage servicer to inquire about any additional requirements that could exist with their particular company. It is also important to inquire if the mortgage servicing company even participates with the Home Affordable Modification Program in the first place. If the provider does participate and the applicant actually meets all of the minimum requirements for participation, then the home owner will need to speak with his or her lender in order to obtain all of the necessary paperwork and forms to enroll.

These forms include first the Request for Mortgage Assistance Form, or RMA. There is also the Income Verification Form as well as the IRS' 4605T-EZ form to complete. It is important to note that the final application does not get submitted to the government, but instead to the mortgage servicer. They will require a tangible proof of financial hardship when the individual submits this application.

There are actually a number of key benefits which this Home Affordable Modification Program delivers for successful applicants. They are able to sidestep foreclosure of the home, reduce their costs for keeping the house, obtain a new start on the mortgage, and better their credit history and rating. The home loan will be made to work for the owners so that they can simply modify the mortgage instead of losing the house.

Though the program is one that has helped a number of Americans, it is not the foolproof answer to irresponsible home buying and borrowing. There have been a number of homeowners who availed themselves of the program in HAMP only to re-default a second time. Some of these have actually forfeited their homes in the foreclosure process. The program has been shown in a recently conducted study that it can help a number of the fully 20 percent of homeowners who are not saving money which they might be able to by taking advantage of either a loan modification program such as this one or through refinancing their home.

Home Equity Line of Credit (HELOC)

A home equity line of credit is also known by its acronym HELOC. It represents a viable alternative to the more commonly used home equity loan. Whereas home equity loans provide lump sum amounts, Home Equity Lines of Credit provide cash as and when the borrower needs it. The downside to a HELOC is that a bank can decide to reduce the amount of available credit or cancel the line altogether without warning. This can happen before a borrower has utilized the funds.

In a home equity line of credit, borrowers use the equity within the home to be their collateral with the bank. The lending institution decides on the maximum amount that the borrower can obtain. The home owner then determines how much of this they want to borrow for the amount of time the bank permits. This might be until the monthly payments reduce the line to a zero balance, or it could be for a certain number of months. This makes these HELOCs much like a credit card in the ability to draw on the resources only when and as they need them.

The main difference between a home equity line of credit and a home loan is that the former is a revolving loan instrument. Borrowers are able to use the money then pay it off. They can then draw on it once again. Home equity loans pay a single lump sum up front amount one time. HELOCs also feature variable interest rates that will change over time, while home equity loans come with interest rates that are fixed. The payment amounts on the home equity loans are also fixed every month, while the payment on the HELOC depends on how much of the line is used.

In order to be able to obtain a home equity line of credit, the home owner must have significant equity in the house itself. Banks will insist that owners keep at least 10% to 20% equity within the property all the time. This must be the case after the line is approved as well. The HELOC approval process will also require verifiable proof of income, consistent documented employment, and a high credit score that is generally more than 680.

It is important for prospective borrowers to determine what they will use the home equity line of credit money for before they draw on it. Home renovations lend themselves better to home equity loans. This is because the one time large amount would enable the borrower to finish the renovations and then repay the loan. A HELOC is a better fit for a revolving bill such as the children's college tuition. Borrowers can use them to cover the tuition, then pay them off hopefully before the next tuition payment become due. At this point they can re-utilize the HELOC for the next semester tuition.

The home equity line of credit can also be a good choice for individuals who wish to consolidate the balances on their credit cards which feature high interest rates. The rates for the HELOC are typically much lower. This strategy requires some discipline. Once the credit cards have been cleared, there is the danger that the home owner might be tempted to run them back up again while they are still making payments on the line of credit. This would put borrowers in a worse situation than before they chose to consolidate.

Home equity lines of credit can get a home owner into the bad habit of constantly borrowing and paying them back as with a credit card. This can be a problem if the borrowers take on more debt with the HELOC than they can afford to pay in monthly payments. Missing these payments would put their home at jeopardy of being seized by the bank.

Home Equity Loan

A home equity loan is a means for home owners to borrow money using the value of their house. Borrowers find these loans appealing because they can usually borrow significant sums of money. Besides this, they are much simpler to get approved for than with many competing kinds of loans. A home owner's house secures these home equity loans. The borrowers may utilize these funds for any purpose that they wish. They do not have to be spent on expenses related to the house that secures the loan.

Such a home equity loan is actually a kind of second mortgage on a house. The first mortgage allows the buyer to purchase the home. When sufficient equity is established in the house, owners can attach other loans to the property to borrow against it.

There are a number of benefits to obtaining a home equity loan. They appeal to both lenders and borrowers. Borrowers get better APRs or interest rates from them than with other loan types. Because they are secured by the value of the home, they can be easier to get approved for even with bad credit. The IRS allows home owners to deduct interest expenses from these home equity loans from their taxes. Finally, borrowers are able to obtain substantial loan amounts using these loan vehicles.

The lenders like these loans because they consider them to be safer loans. The house acts as collateral in the process. This means that banks are able to seize the house to liquidate it and regain unpaid balances if the owner fails to make the payments. Because of this, banks know that borrowers will make the payments of these loans a high priority so they do not lose their house.

Banks protect themselves in any case by not lending too much against the value of the property. In general, lenders will not allow borrowers to obtain a greater amount than 85% of the value of the house. This includes both the amount that remains on the first mortgage as well as the second mortgage home equity loan. This percentage is known as the loan to value ratio. It can vary somewhat from one bank to the next.

The way home equity loans work is relatively straightforward. Borrowers receive a one time cash payment. They then make fixed payments each month to pay back the loan over a pre-set amount of time. The interest rate will be set by the bank at the beginning of the loan. With every payment, the loan balance declines after part of the interest costs are covered. This makes these amortizing loans.

Sometimes borrowers do not require all of the money at one time. An alternative to the home equity loan in this case is the HELOC home equity line of credit. This delivers a set amount of money which home owners can draw on only when and if they require it. The borrowers only have to pay interest on money which they physically draw and borrow. It is possible for the interest rate to change on these HELOC loans. Banks may also cancel such a line of credit before the borrower has utilized all or part of the funds.

Home equity loans can be used for many different needs. It is wise to improve the value of the house with the money through renovating, remodeling, or increasing the appeal of the property. Other common uses borrowers employ them for are to help pay for a second home, to afford college tuition and expenses for family members, or to consolidate bills with high interest rates.

HSBC

HSBC stands for Hong Kong Shanghai Banking Corporation. This largest international bank in the world by balance sheet has over $1.63 trillion in total assets. The British London based banking giant counts more than 47 million customers as part of its international network spanning 71 countries and territories and 6,000 offices around the globe.

HSBC was founded by a British businessman in 1865 to finance the growing trade between the West and Asia, and especially China. Today HSBC remains among the largest and most impressive banking and financial services conglomerate groups in the world by any relevant measure. Their stated goal is to be recognized as the globe's foremost and best respected international bank.

HSBC is operated globally through four major divisions. These include its Commercial Banking, Global Banking and Markets, Private Banking, and Retail Banking and Wealth Management divisions. Among the banking group's many achievements over the centuries, the group was responsible for setting up the modern day Chinese currency and banking system back during the reign of the last Chinese imperial dynasty. This financial and currency system which HSBC established for China is still used today.

HSBC Commercial Banking operates throughout 55 different nations and territories. Their operation covers both developing and developed world markets that are most important to their many customers. The division serves a great variety of customer types, ranging from major multinational corporations to small outfits to medium sized companies. It offers them the financial tools they need to run their operations effectively.

One of the bank's most appealing features is that it can call upon its vast and multinational financial strength to support clients with term loans, project and acquisition finance, and daily working capital. The bank also offers its customers the financial and legal know how to assist them in engaging in effective stock and bond issues and offerings.

The commercial banking group supports specialist staff in four primary fields. Global Liquidity and Cash Management provides businesses with tools to effectively manage their liquidity. The online platform helps the customers to transact payments seamlessly between currencies and countries. Global Trade and Receivable Finance offers financing to suppliers and buyers in the trade cycle so that they can cover their supply chains.

Global Banking offers its commercial customers a variety of services such as capital financing via equity, debt, and advisory services. Insurance and Investments provides protection in the form of financial, business, and trade insurance. It also offers wealth management for corporations, employee benefits, and other commercial insurance products to protect against risk.

The Global Banking and Markets division works with customers to help them access commercial opportunities for developed and developing markets. This division operates in three groups including the corporate sector group, the resources and energy group, and the financial institutions group. Services and products are comprised of financing, advisory, research and analysis, prime services, trading and sales, securities services, and transaction banking.

HSBC Private Bank delivers global private banking services that include wealth management, investment, and private banking services to its individual, business, and executive clients. The division's goal is to become the world's foremost private bank for business owners who are high net worth individuals leveraging the group's longstanding globally leading commercial services and heritage.

Retail Banking and Wealth Management provides its tens of millions of customers with a broad range of products and services. These include personal banking, internet banking, loans, mortgages, savings, insurance, investments, and credit cards. They offer a variety of proprietary services and accounts that include HSBC Premier, HSBC Advance, personal online banking, financial planning, and wealth solutions.

Indemnity

Indemnity refers to financial compensation for loss or damages incurred by an individual or business. It comes from the original Latin word indemnis which translates to "without loss" and "undamaged" or "unhurt." The idea behind it springs from the premise of a contract between two groups, businesses, or individuals. One party will invariably promise to cover any possible damages or losses that they other party causes. When used in a legal setting, the word also pertains to the idea of gaining an exemption from being liable for damages. In the nation of Canada, the word means the salary which parliamentarians receive.

Insurance is a classic example of such indemnity. In these financial contracts, the insurer (who is the indemnitor) promises to provide compensation to the insured (who is the indemnitee) against any losses or damages. In exchange for this pledge, the insured will pay pre-arranged and agreed upon premiums to the insurer. Insurance contracts would not exist without such clauses.

These agreements will also feature a period of indemnity. This refers to the set time frame in which the guarantee is binding. There are also such contracts that provide letters of indemnity. These guarantee that the stipulations of the contract will be adhered to by both parties. If they are not, then indemnities have to be paid by the contract breaching party.

Clearly such indemnities are commonplace with contracts struck between businesses and individuals, as with insurance companies and their customers. On far grander scales, they are also prevalent in deals made between governments and companies, as well as in agreements made between governments of multiple nations.

There is also Indemnity Insurance. With such a policy, businesses and individuals are able to obtain protection in the event of any claims. Such a policy safeguards the policy holder from the necessity of having to pay out a large sum in indemnities. It does not matter if the policy holder is ultimately at fault or not. A great number of corporations require such insurance because of all the frivolous lawsuits in the United States.

There are countless examples of everyday insurance needs in this respect.

Malpractice insurance and E&O errors and omissions insurance are two of the most common. Malpractice insurance is issued to protect medical providers. E&O insurance protects corporations and employees of the company in case customers make any claims against them. Other companies are so concerned about this problem of being held responsible that they pay for Deferred Compensation Indemnity Insurance. This forward-thinking policy actually safeguards money which the firm anticipates earning at some point and time in the future.

These specific insurance policies provide for the various costs associated with such a claim. This includes such expenses as settlements, fees, and the legal and court costs. The insurance amount may not cover the entire costs though. The particular limitations in dollars and types of fees will be specified by the policy itself and is often based upon past claims.

There are also indemnity clauses where property leases are concerned. Tenants who obtain a rental property will be responsible for any damages which arise from their own negligence, fines they incur, and associated legal fees. Each agreement will specify the particulars.

The concept surrounding indemnities dates back hundreds of years. The New York Times revealed in an 1825 article entitled, "French President Makes Unprecedented State Visit to Haiti" that the country was being required to pay to France a debt to cover French plantation owner losses because of the destruction of their plantation lands and the emancipation of their slaves.

Winning nations also exact war indemnities from losing countries after the end of many conflicts. Some of these war reparations required from years to decades to pay. The best remembered example of such long-lasting indemnities is the one which Germany had to pay for its part in starting and prosecuting the First World War. It took until 2010 for Germany to finally finish paying the war reparation debt, as the New York Times told in its piece from that same year, "Ending the War to End All Wars." This was almost a century after they began paying it.

Institutional Investor

Institutional investors turn out to be organizations or occasionally individuals which buy and sell securities in huge enough quantities and currency totals. They benefit from lower fees and commissions as well as special treatment from the market makers.

These large and powerful deep pocketed investors experience fewer regulations from the regulatory agencies as well since they naturally assume that they have a larger knowledge base and are sophisticated enough to protect themselves in their investing strategies. There are many different kinds of investors who qualify as institutional investors. Some of them are life insurance firms and pension funds.

These entities derive their money from a variety of sources, but in all cases they pool the funds in order to buy and sell real estate, stock and bond securities, and other alternative types of investment classes such as loans, commodities, precious metals, and artwork.

There are many different kinds of institutional investors such as hedge funds, pension funds, insurance companies, sovereign wealth funds, commercial banks, investment advisors, Real Estate Investment Trusts, mutual funds, and university endowments. Other operating firms that choose to invest their extra capital in such asset classes are also covered by the term. Some institutional investors are activist. This means that they may interfere with the internal workings and governance of the firm by using their substantial voting rights in the companies in which they own larger stakes to influence corporate decisions, investments, and behavior.

Institutional investors act as intermediaries between smaller retail investors and corporations. They are also significant sources of critical capital for the financial markets. Since they pool together their member investment dollars or Euros, these larger and more powerful investors effectively lessen the cost of capital to entrepreneurs at the same time as the efficiently diversify their clients' portfolios. Since they can impact the behavior of companies as well, this helps to reduce agency costs.

Institutional investors have several significant and game changing advantages over smaller, weaker retail investors. They possess enormous resources to invest as well as specialty knowledge that pertains to a variety of different investment options. Many of these choices are not even available to traditional retail investors at all. They also have longer term investing horizons as they are not limited to accumulation and distribution requirements of individual investors who will want to transition to retirement at some point.

Such institutions turn out to be the biggest movers and shakers within both supply and demand segments in the securities markets. This means that they transact the overwhelming majority of all trades on the major stock and bond market exchanges. Their choices and actions substantially impact the prices and bid/asks of most securities on the various markets.

This has led a number of retail investors to attempt to level the proverbial playing field of investing by researching the various filings of holdings the institutions make with the SEC Securities and Exchange Commission to learn what different securities they ought to invest in for their own individual portfolios and trades.

Some of these institutional investors are critically important in specific types of countries. For example, those countries which are oil rich and exporting nations generally contain one or more massive sovereign wealth funds which possess a lion's share of the investable wealth of the nation. These are usually government controlled and administered institutional funds and investors.

They can amass even hundreds of billions of investable dollars, as have the Norwegian, Abu Dhabi, Saudi Arabian, Qatari, and Kuwaiti funds. In developed nations, it is the pension funds and insurance companies which control a substantial portion of the excess and readily deployable and investable capital.

Interest Rate

Interest rates are the levels at which interest is charged a borrower for using money that they obtain in the form of a loan from a bank or other lender. These are also the rates that individuals and businesses are paid for depositing their funds with a bank. Interest rates are central to the running of capitalist economies. They are commonly written out as percentage rates for a given time frame, most commonly per year.

As an example, a small business might require capital to purchase new assets for the company. To acquire these, they borrow money form a bank. In exchange for making them this loan, the bank is paid interest at a pre set and agreed upon rate of interest for lending it to the company and putting off their own use of the monies. They receive this interest in monthly payments along with repayments of the principal.

Interest rates are also used by government agencies in pursuing monetary policies. Central banks set them to influence their nation's economic performance. They impact many elements of an economy such as unemployment, inflation, and investment levels.

There are several different interest rates to consider. The most commonly expressed one is the nominal interest rate. This nominal interest rate proves to be the amount of interest that is payable in money terms. If a family deposits $1,000 in a bank for a year, and is paid $50 in interest, then their balance by the conclusion of the year will be $1,050. This would translate to a nominal interest rate amounting to five percent per year.

The real interest rate is another type of rate used to determine how much purchasing power is received. It is the interest rate after the level of inflation is subtracted. Determining the real interest rate is a matter of calculating the nominal rate and removing the amount of inflation from it. In the example above, supposed the economy's inflation level is measured at five percent for the year. This would mean that the $1,050 in the account at year end only buys what it did as $1,000 at the beginning of the year. This translates to a real interest rate of zero.

Interest rates change for many reasons. They are altered for political gains of parties in power. By reducing the interest rate, an economy gains a short term boost. The help to the economy will often influence the outcome of elections. Unfortunately, the short term advantage gained is often offset later by inflation. This reason for changing interest rates is eliminated with independent central banks.

Another main reason that interest rates change is because of expectations of inflation. Since the majority of economies demonstrate inflation, fixed amounts of money will purchase fewer goods a year from now than they will today. Lenders expect to be compensated for this. Central banks raise interest rates to fight this inflation as necessary.

Interim Financing

Interim financing is a way of obtaining funding on a short term basis for a project. It can also be called gap financing or bridge financing. People or companies elects for this kind of financing for a specific purpose.

They may be seeking to get funding so that a project can be finished and start creating revenues. This would keep them from having to take resources away from other projects. This concept generally refers to loans. There are also cases of interim financing where companies utilize grants or other types of financial assistance.

A short term loan proves to be among the most frequently employed types of interim financing. These kinds of loans can be crafted so that the borrower will pay back the entire principle of the loan along with all of its interest in twelve months or less from the loan issue date.

This is the opposite of long term financing. In the longer term variety, the borrower receives several years to repay the loan. Loan deals on gap financing often come with interest rates that are a little higher than with longer term loans. For individuals or companies with excellent credit, financing companies can often offer extremely competitive interest rates on these short term loans.

A common use of interim financing is with construction projects that need to be finished. On an individual level, a consumer may wish to renovate either a room in the house or the entire home. The borrower may decide to obtain a short term loan at a better interest rate to cover the costs of labor and materials at the beginning of the project. This can save the borrower on the more substantial interest rates and fees for using credit cards or store credit with the various vendors. The end result is that the consumer spends significantly less money on the improvement project than he or she would by not utilizing the interim financing.

Real estate deals are another common use for this interim financing. A home owner may wish to move forward and buy a new house. The owner may need their present house to sell first. Short term loans like these can prove to be an optimal answer to the problem. Using the bridge loan the owner buys the house. The borrower can then repay the loan once their original house sells. This kind of strategy will help to push through the sale of the original house as well. The previous owners have already moved, which means the new owners can occupy the property without delay.

The goal of interim financing is to offer a short term bridge loan for the individual or business concerned. Despite this, sometimes a situation develops where the borrower will not be able to repay the loan as quickly as hoped. In this case, longer term or additional financing becomes necessary. Many lenders will work with the borrower in such a case to come up with a longer term financing program.

This will completely pay off the short term original loan. Additional money will usually be provided so that the borrower has the funds necessary to complete the project. This is especially the case with construction companies. It works out better for the borrower to engage in a rollover longer term loan than to take out another short term loan. The reason for this is that the longer term loans' finance rates are nearly always lower than the most competitive rates lenders will offer borrowers for short term bridge loans.

Investment Value

Investment Value refers to an asset's specific value given a particular range of investment parameters. It can be defined as the property value to a given group of investors (or an individual investor) who have specific investment goals in mind. This makes it a subjective measurement of the asset or property's value.

Many times potential investors will employ the investment value metric when they have an interest in buying a certain real estate property with a particular group of investment goals and objectives. It might be they have a targeted return rate they are looking for in the investment. This is why such a value metric heavily involves motivations and beliefs in a particular investment strategy.

The reason that this investment value would have importance on a transaction concerns buyers contemplating buying a given asset when they want to compare the pricing of the real estate or asset in question to the anticipated rate of return. When they are able to use this value to consider their specific rate of return, they are able to measure up the investment final results with the projected price they will pay out for the property. This helps them to make an intelligent purchasing decision consistent with their investment objectives.

In contrast to the investment value, market value is the true value of the property (or asset) in question based on the supply and demand of the open market. It is typically determined by utilizing the appraisal process where Real Estate is concerned. This contrasts with the individual investors' value they may place on the property as it pertains to their unique goals, objectives, and needs for the property they are considering.

It is important to realize that investment value is not the same as market value in many cases. The investment values might be lower, higher, or the same to the market values. This would heavily depend on the property's specific scenario at the time. In fact the market values and investing values are typically approximately the same. Yet they can diverge.

For example, investment value might be greater than that of the market value. A certain buyer may place a higher value on the property than would a typical informed purchaser. This could happen in the real world when a firm decides to expand its premises into a larger newer building that has just gone on sale across the road from the current company offices. The company might be willing to pay a higher price than the market value so that it could ensure competitors stay out of the market and do not secure the building before they can conclude the transaction. In such a scenario, this extra value becomes derived from the strategic advantage that the firm will realize by having the property.

Where a single investor is concerned, it is also possible for investment value to exceed the market value. An example of this could be when the investors have a special tax status or situation that can not be transferred. They might also have some type of highly advantageous financing terms that do not apply to rival investors or buyers.

It is similarly possible for investment value to be under that of the market value on a property. This could happen when the given property is not a kind in which the investors normally specialize or concentrate their efforts. As an example, for multifamily developers, choosing to consider developing a hotel could cause the investment value for this particular situation to be lower than the traditional market value for the given site. This would be because of the greater costs involved in learning to develop the property. It might also be that the investors are seeking out and demand a higher than average return from a property thanks to their current portfolio diversification and allocation.

Investor

Strictly speaking, an investor is any person or entity that makes an investment. In the past, the word investors has acquired a far more specific meaning. In the world of business and finance, investors has come to characterize those individuals or companies that routinely buy debt instruments like bonds, or equity issues like stocks in an attempt to make financial profits. They hope to realize such gains in return for financing or providing capital to a company that is looking to expand.

Investors also relates to other types of individuals, businesses, or parties that put money into different types of investments. Although this is a less commonly used version of the word investors, it can relate to those engaging in currency, real estate, commodities, derivatives, or other personal property investments like art or antiques. An example of this would be a real estate investor. They purchase a piece of property or a house with the hopes of selling it for a greater amount of money than for what they purchased it. Similarly, commodities' investors are hoping to buy contracts or options on hard assets like gold, oil, or lumber cheaply to sell them later more dearly.

Investors are commonly buying such stocks, bonds, or other types of assets and holding on to them with the goal of realizing one of two types of returns, or in some unusual cases both types. These are capital gains or cash flow investments. Investors who are interested in capital gains are simply looking to sell an instrument or asset that they obtained at one price for a greater amount. When they do this, they realize a capital gain. Should they sell the investment for less than they purchased it, they would instead realize a capital loss. Capital gains can only be realized one time on an investment, as the investors will have sold the investment and have to look for another investment to begin the process anew once again.

Cash flow investors are alternatively looking for a repetitive income stream. They hope to achieve regular, smaller sums of passive income just from holding their investment. Dividends on a stock, royalties on an oil or gas investment, and rents from a residential or commercial realty property are all examples of cash flow investments and returns. So long as the investor owns the cash flow investment, he or she should be able to continuously count on a regular income stream.

The word investor commonly gives the connotation of a person who acquires these assets for the longer term. This stands in contrast to a day trader or even short term investor. Investors can be professional or self taught amateurs.

Investors also represent many entities other than individuals or even traditional businesses. They can be investment groups like clubs, venture capital investors who provide money to start up companies, investment banks, investment trusts such as REIT Real Estate Investment Trusts, hedge funds and mutual funds, and even sovereign wealth funds that invest on behalf of their respective nations.

JP Morgan Chase

JP Morgan Chase turns out to be among the oldest financial institutions or banks that are based in the United States. The firm's history hails back more than 200 years. Today, the company boasts assets that exceed $2.4 trillion, and it is a leading global banking and financial services outfit. JP Morgan Chase has a presence in over 100 countries and maintains more than 235,000 employees around the globe in over 450 corporate offices.

JP Morgan Chase counts millions of individuals and small businesses as customers of the banking group. They serve some of the most important governments, institutions, and corporations in the world. JP Morgan proves to be one of the global leaders in financial services for individuals and small businesses, investment banking, commercial banking, asset management, and financial transactions and processing. One of their proudest achievements as a testament to their importance in the United States is the fact that their company stock is one of the only 30 company components of the famed Dow Jones Industrial Average.

JP Morgan Chase & Company proves to be not only one of the oldest and biggest financial institutions in the world, but also among the best known such organizations on earth. The earliest predecessor of the banking group received its charter in New York City in 1799. The company has an aggressive history of mergers and acquisitions that have seen over 1,200 predecessor banking and financial institutions merged into the present day form of the banking behemoth.

Among its most important legacy firms are J.P. Morgan, Chase Manhattan Bank, Chemical Bank, and Manufacturers Hanover of New York City as well as Bank One, National Bank of Detroit, and First Chicago in the Midwest. These institutions each held important ties for their day and age to progress in finance and the expansion of both the American and world economies.

The mega mergers of the banking group began in 2000 when J.P. Morgan & Co. Inc. merged together with the Chase Manhattan Corporation. In this merger, J.P. Morgan, Chase, Manufacturers Hanover, and Chemical became one enormous financial conglomerate. This at last combined four of the biggest, most important, and oldest banking center groups of New

York City together under the single entity name and ownership of J.P. Morgan Chase & Co.

The activity continued in 2004. J.P. Morgan Chase & Company merged with Chicago's Bank One Corporation. At the time, the New York Times newspaper claimed that the combination would remake the competitive landscape of banking as it tied together the commercial and investment banking prowess of J.P. Morgan Chase with the significant consumer banking abilities of the Midwestern-based Bank One.

In 2008, JP Morgan Chase acquired the world's largest savings and loan Washington Mutual Bank as a result of the biggest bank failure in history. Gaining control of Washington Mutual's substantial banking operations meant that the banking group expanded its consumer branches into Florida, California, and Washington State for the first time. This formed the second biggest network of bank locations in the United States whose branches reached an astonishing 42% of all people living in the U.S.

That same year in the depths of the financial crisis, JP Morgan Chase took over the collapsing Wall Street firm The Bear Stearns Companies. This improved the group's swelling abilities in a wide variety of businesses such as global energy trading, cash clearing, and prime brokerage. The group rounded out its presence in the United Kingdom in 2010 by gaining full ownership of its original British joint venture J.P. Morgan Cazenove. This joint venture was among the most premier investment banks in Britain.

Jumbo Loan

Jumbo loans are specific types of loans made by banks for home mortgages. They are special because these loans are for larger sized house loans. In order for a loan to be qualified as a jumbo one, it must be larger than the conforming loan limits.

The government Federal Housing Finance Agency sets these conforming loan limits through regulation. They are the agency that oversees the mortgage buying government sponsored entities Freddie Mac and Fannie Mae. Both of these groups purchase mortgages from the traditional lenders like banks and credit unions.

For the majority of the United States, jumbo loan limits start at $417,000. There are several states and a few hundred counties that have different loan limit amounts. Some of these limits range as high as $625,000 for their loan limits in areas that are the most expensive property markets.

Counting Louisiana parishes, Alaska boroughs, and the District of Columbia like counties, the U.S. has 3,143 counties. This does not consider the Virgin Islands, Guam, or Puerto Rico. An overwhelming majority 2,916 of these counties have the traditional limit amount of $417,000 for jumbo loan minimums.

Another 115 counties have loan limits that are in between the typical $417,000 and $625,000 maximum. This would include higher than usual priced real estate markets but not the most expensive ones like Los Angeles. In Colorado Denver County is one such example with a jumbo loan minimum of $458,850. Another 108 counties contain higher jumbo loan limits that start at $625,500. Included in these are the most expensive housing markets. Among these are such pricey counties as those found in New York City, Los Angeles, and San Francisco.

Several states and their counties are allowed to have higher conforming loan limits than the maximum amounts set out by the government housing authority. This includes Hawaii, Alaska, the Virgin Islands, and Guam. These are all treated specially because of a long time exception to the regulation. In Hawaii for example, four of its five counties have the highest limits for jumbo loan cutoffs. They range from $657,800 to $721,050.

Obtaining a jumbo mortgage involves some extra paperwork and proofs. Underwriting for these jumbo types is much the same as with standard conforming mortgages. There are more requirements for appraisals and down payments than with smaller mortgages. Some jumbo mortgage lenders have a requirement for two appraisals rather than the standard single one.

Down payments are also often more demanding for jumbos than for the traditional mortgages. Usually these lenders will want a higher down payment to ensure the individual can really afford and is committed to the loan. The minimum down payments for these more expensive home purchases will vary with each lender. They might be as high as 30%, or they could be as low as 15% to 20%.

Only applicants with significant finances need apply for these jumbo loans. A great number of their lenders require a minimum high credit score of 700 or better. They also insist on a debt to income ratio that does not exceed 43%. These lenders will want to see minimally from six to twelve months' cash reserves in bank accounts as well.

Jumbo loans are not only made to individuals for their primary residences. Lenders will also issue them for vacation or second homes. Investment properties may also involve jumbo loans. They come with a wide range of terms and interest rates.

Jumbo loans can be issued as adjustable rate loans or fixed rate loans. They often come with higher interest rates than individuals would pay for conforming loans or for high balance conforming home loans. Sometimes in addition to the bigger down payment the underwriting standard will be stricter as well.

Lease

Leases are contracts made between an owner, or lessor, and a user, or lesee, covering the utilization of an asset. Leases can pertain to business or real estate. There are a variety of different types of leases that vary with the property in question being leased.

Tangible property and assets are leased under rental agreements. Intangible property leases are much like a license, only they have differing provisions. The utilization of a computer program or a cell phone service's radio frequency are two example of such an intangible lease.

A gross lease is another type of lease. In a gross lease, a tenant actually gives a certain defined dollar amount in rent. The landlord is then responsible for any and all property expenses that are routinely necessary in owning the asset. This includes everything from washing machines to lawnmowers.

You also encounter leases that are cancelable. Cancelable leases can be ended at the discretion of the end user or lessor. Other leases are non cancelable and may not be ended ahead of schedule. In daily conversation, a lease denotes a lease that can not be broken, while a rental agreement often can be canceled.

A lease contract typically lays out particular provisions concerning both rights and obligations of the lessor and the lessee. Otherwise, a local law code's provisions will apply. When the holder of the lease, also known as the tenant, pays the arranged fee to the owner of the property, the tenant gains exclusive use and possession of the property that is leased to the point that the owner and any other individuals may not utilize it without the tenant's specific invitation. By far the most typical type of hard property lease proves to be the residential types of rental agreements made between landlords and their tenants. This type of relationship that the two parties establish is also known as a tenancy. The tenant's right to possess the property is many times referred to as the leasehold interest. These leases may exist for pre arranged amounts of time, known as a lease term. In many cases though, they can be terminated in advance, although this does depend on the particular lease's terms and conditions.

Licenses are similar to leases, but not the same thing. The main difference between the two lies in the nature of the ongoing payments and termination. When keeping the property is only accomplished by making regular payments, and can not be terminated unless the money is not paid or some form of misconduct is discovered, then the agreement is a lease. One time uses of or entrances to property are licenses. The defining difference between the two proves to be that leases require routine payments in their term and come with a particular date of ending.

Lease-to-Own Purchase

A Lease-to-Own Purchase is a combination of a lease on a house with a purchase option on the home. This option is valid for a specific amount of time, typically for 3 years or less. The price for the purchase is agreed on in advance and is a part of the contract. These types of arrangements became far more common after the housing crisis and Great Recession. Many individuals who wanted to buy a house could no longer qualify for the stricter loan requirements. This also impacted sellers who could not obtain a selling price with which they were satisfied by any other means.

With a Lease-to-Own Purchase, the contract is typically designed and provided by the seller. The benefits of the arrangement can be set up to provide advantages to both buyer and seller parties. They might also be arranged so that the majority or even all of the benefits accrue to one side. This means that buyers should beware before entering such an agreement. It is wise for them to share the contract with a real estate attorney before they sign.

In a traditional Lease-to-Own Purchase contract, borrowers first pay an option fee that goes against the cost of buying the house. This generally amounts to from 1% to 5% of the home price. The renter will also pay a fair market value rent alongside a rent premium that also goes towards the price of buying the house. Everything is negotiable in these contracts, including option period, option fee, rent premium, rent, and the price of the house. Should the purchase option not be exercised by the renter, then he or she forfeits the rent premium and the option fee to the seller.

Buyers will naturally want a longer option period. This gives them a greater amount of time in which to repair their credit and save up money for a down payment. The downside to a longer option period in a Lease-to-Own Purchase comes into play if they can not exercise the option to buy. In this case, the renters forfeit both the option fee and the monthly rent premium which they have paid continuously. Sellers will want a shorter time period on the option. If they make it too short, they will be unable to sell the house to the renter.

It is possible for a Lease-to-Own Purchase to work out to be a win-win situation for both parties. The rent premium and option fee to the buyers represent equity they are paying into the house which they expect to buy. Such payments are compensation towards a guarantee for the seller that the house will sell. The seller will get to keep the additional payments as income if the buyer is unable to obtain the mortgage needed to purchase the property.

Some Lease-to-Own Purchase contracts will provide the renter with the ability to sell their option to another party. Such an option gives buyers additional confidence in the deal in the event that they are unable to personally exercise their buying option. This is a concession from sellers who would rather keep the house along with the fees they have collected. Some lease contracts will also have clauses that can cancel the buyer's option. These are often set as penalties for late rent payments.

One advantage to leasing the house before buying it lies in buyer awareness. The renters have time to consider any significant problems with the house, neighbors, or the neighborhood before they commit. If these are substantial issues, the buyers are able to cut their losses and not go through with the buying option.

Leasehold Estate

A Leasehold Estate relates to an official and legal interest that permits a company or individuals to assume temporary ownership of the land of another individual or company. They are able to use this land for business purposes, agricultural applications, or even as a dwelling. Property could include timber land, mineral land, oil land, farm land, or business and/or residence property. With such leasehold estates, landlords possess the title of the property at the same time as the tenant holds the rights to utilize said property. These estates range wildly in the format for the agreement and how it is set up, the amount of time the status exists, and the kind of property which is being leased.

A Leasehold Estate can be established orally or as a written agreement. Those agreements which are intended to endure over a year might have to be composed in a written document per the laws of the relevant state which has jurisdiction. These agreements provide either explicit or implicit permission for all the receiving end parties, who are called the lessees, to assume control of the said property of the other party, who is referred to as the lessor.

There are other various kinds of property agreements which exist. What separates leasehold agreements from these competing formats, such as purchase agreements, is the actual termination date. Every party which is involved with a leasehold agreement comprehends that the agreed upon ownership interests will eventually conclude. This is to say that they are not intended to last in perpetuity. Another distinctive feature of such estates lies with the lessee's right to possess the said property in question. Various other kinds of property agreements, like licenses or easements, actually provide the holder with the permanent rights to utilize the property as they see fit.

Leasehold Estates are quite specific. They comprise both land and any property on the land in question at a given address. Land in this sense of the word does not simply mean the physical land, but also includes any buildings which lie on the property. It also applies to any and all natural resources which occupy the land in question. These estates could also include other forms of personal property, like machinery or fixtures which are so permanently a part of the land that they become considered to be part and parcel of the property. Such fixtures could comprise things like fencing, lighting, wells, or windmills.

Estates are types of personal property. Applicable state laws commonly govern the legal definition of personal property. This means that they could supersede clauses within the Leasehold Estate agreement. An example of this is found in the state of California. The leasehold which pertains to agricultural purposes may not be extended past a maximum time frame of 51 years total.

This is why such leasehold agreements are established with a pre-determined and limited number of years in mind. This is articulated in the tenancy of years. Such a specified length of lease is determined by both lessor and lessee. The only exception is when state laws set the time span directly. It is possible to terminate such a leasehold tenancy ahead of the articulated time. The lessee must decide to surrender his or her possession of the property at the same time as the lessor agrees to resume control over his property and rights.

Four different classifications of these Leasehold Estates exist. They are fixed term, periodic, at will, and at sufferance. Fixed term tenancy refers to the number of years of the tenancy. It is states as an interest which is established to endure a particular amount of time.

Periodic tenancy relates to a set out amount of time, as with week to week, month to month, or even year to year. The leasehold can be ended by either tenant or landlord simply giving a notice to vacate the property. Usually a 30 days notice in writing must be provided to the owner of the property.

Tenancy at will refers to the lack of structure with these kinds of leasehold agreements. No date is given for the end of tenancy in such a form of leasehold estate. Tenancy at sufferance happens as a tenant decides to overstay the date of termination as spelled out in the applicable agreement. Landlords in these cases possess the legal rights to simply evict the tenant if they wish.

Lehman Brothers Collapse

The Lehman Brothers collapse occurred officially on September 15 of 2008 when the firm filed for bankruptcy. At the time it had $619 billion in debts and $639 billion in assets. This made it the biggest filing for bankruptcy in all of history. Its assets were massively higher than the ones that had preceded it in infamous collapses such as Enron and WorldCom.

When the Lehman Brothers collapse occurred, it held the distinction of being the fourth biggest American based investment bank. The bank boasted 25,000 employees located in financial centers around the world. Its untimely fall turned it into the biggest casualty of the financial crisis that began from the U.S. subprime mortgage collapse. This crisis ran like wildfire through financial markets around the globe in 2008.

The crisis became so much worse because of this turning point moment when the Lehman collapse occurred. It was a major contributing factor to the destruction of $10 trillion worth of market capitalization off of global stock markets in just October of 2008. This represented the largest recorded single month decline when it happened.

The investment bank had managed to successfully navigate and survive numerous challenges over the years before the Lehman Brothers collapse. Their origins dated back to a Montgomery, Alabama general store that German immigrant Henry Lehman opened in 1844. Six years later, Henry with his two brothers Mayer and Emmanuel established Lehman Brothers. The firm moved increasingly into investment banking in the subsequent decades.

As the U.S. economy expanded into a first rate power, Lehman prospered. Among the challenges it faced were the 1800s' railroad bankruptcies, the 1930's Great Depression, and the two world wars. The firm also navigated being acquired and then spun off by American Express in 1994 with a capital shortage. It survived both the collapse of Long Term Capital Management and the Russians defaulting on their debt in 1998.

Though it had survived world rocking disasters in the past, the catastrophic collapse of the housing market in the U.S. proved to be too much for the investment bank. This was primarily because it had rapidly embraced the subprime mortgage market in the early 2000s, a misstep that was to cost the bank and its employees everything.

It was in the years 2003 and 2004 that Lehman made the acquisitions that led to the Lehman Brothers collapse. It purchased five different mortgage lenders, among them the subprime lenders Aurora Loan Services and BNC Mortgage. These companies made loans to those borrowers who did not have complete documentation. Such mortgages were officially known as Alt-A loans but became nicknamed "liar loans."

At first the firm made enormous revenue gains in its real estate ventures. This capital markets division saw income roar up by 56% between 2004 and 2006. This massively outpaced growth in the asset management and investment banking divisions. From 2005 to 2007, the bank announced record profits. The year 2007 was the last one they could report such gains, with $4.2 billion in profits on $19.3 billion in revenues their best year ever.

When the housing market began to plunge and borrowers defaulted massively on their loans, the end approached for Lehman Brothers. Less than a year after their record 2007 profits, their failed mortgages, credit default swaps, and investments based on collateralized mortgage instruments brought them completely down.

Lender

Lenders are individuals or more commonly institutions that loan out money. The person who receives this money is a borrower. A number of different kinds of lending organizations exist. These include commercial, mutual organizations, educational, hard money, and lenders of last resort.

Commercial lenders are the most common of the traditional lenders. Commercial types are usually banks. Another kind of commercial lender would be a private financial organization. Commercial lenders provide offers on their loans to their borrowers at a set rate of loan terms. Such terms include time frame of the loan and the interest rate. Their goal is to make as much money as possible relative to the chances of the borrower not repaying the loan.

Mutual organizations are another type of lender. They are composed of members of the mutual who cooperate together to loan money to the membership. The members pool their money into the organization. From there it is loaned out to the members who need to borrow money. They do this with favorable terms and at advantageous rates.

Mutual organizations are not driven to make profits. This allows them to offer lower interest rates on the loans they make and higher interest rates on the deposits they take. Among these mutual groups are community based credit unions. Friendly Societies are another example of them.

Educational lenders provide loans to individuals who are looking to further their education at an institution of higher learning like a college or university. They offer borrowers subsidized or unsubsidized loans. When the loans are subsidized, the Federal Government guarantees the loans and ensures that the lender provides a low and often fixed interest rate.

Hard money lenders make special types of loans that are short term. These are loans principally secured by real estate collateral. The downside to this kind of a lender is that they often provide higher interest rates than a traditional commercial bank. The tradeoff is that they will often take on a larger variety of deals.

Typically these hard money lenders give terms that are more flexible to their borrowers. Some states have stricter laws on interest rates that may be charged than does the Federal government. This forces hard money lenders to operate under different rules and with lower interest rates when they are in conflict with usury laws in give states.

Many times these loans that lenders make to individuals become brokered loans. In such cases, third parties consider the borrower's case then send the loan request out to a variety of lenders. This is often done over the Internet. They pick these different lenders because of their chance of approving the borrower in question. Sometimes the terms can be improved by one or more of these competing lenders in order to win over the borrower's business.

Lenders of last resort are an interesting final category. They are often governmental organizations whose goal is to save national economies and important banks from failure. These types of organizations loan money out to too big to fail banks which are close to collapse. They do this to safeguard the bank's depositors and to prevent panic from pushing the nation's economy into a downward spiral.

Lenders of last resort can also be private organizations that make loans to individuals. These groups loan out money to borrowers who present great risks of default or who have extremely low credit scores. Interest rates with these lenders are substantially higher than with traditional lenders. They charge these rates in order to make up for the losses they suffer from their borrower's greater default rates. Such lenders that charge even higher rates are sometimes known as loan sharks.

Lien

A lien is a claim on one individual's property by another person or entity. The party that holds the lien is able to recover the property if a debtor will not follow through with making payments. There are also other circumstances in which liens would allow the lien holder to take the property. Mortgages on houses or buildings prove to be one kind these. Vehicle loans for a business or individual represent other types that are put on the value of the vehicle. When the obligation is paid off, the lien becomes discharged.

Before individuals are able to receive their money after the sale of an asset like a car or house, the lien must be paid off first. With a vehicle, this means that the lender will not send out the title until they receive complete repayment of the principal.

The majority of liens allow for the individuals or businesses to utilize the property as they are paying it. There are scenarios where the lender or creditor physically holds the property while the borrower is making payments. These are a part of bankruptcy procedures as well because they are secured loans with debt repayment rules that have to be addressed in a case.

While there are a number of different types of liens, the most typical one is on a vehicle. Individuals buy a car from the dealer. The bank loans the money and secures the loan. They do this by placing a vehicle lien which allows them to hold on to the automobile's title. The lender files a UCC-1 form to record this. So long as the debtor continues to make payments, the loan will be paid off finally. The bank would then release to the individual the title.

If the individuals stop making their payments, the bank is able to take possession of the vehicle back while still holding the title. If the vehicle owners choose to sell the automobile when they still owe principal, they must clear the bank loan in order to obtain the title. Without the title, a person can not sell the vehicle.

There are a variety of different types of liens in the world. Consensual ones are those which individuals voluntarily accept when they buy something.

Non consensual ones are also known as statutory. These come from a court process where an entity places a lien on assets because bills have not been paid. Three of these are fairly common.

A tax lien occurs when individuals do not pay local, state, or federal income taxes. These are put on the offender's property. A judgment lien comes as a result of a case in a small claims court. When a court gives a judgment to one party, the offending party might refuse to pay. In this case the court will place a judgment lien on the offender's property.

A mechanic or contractor lien happens when a contractor performs a job for a home owner. If the owner refuses to pay, the contractor can ask a court to place a lien on the property in question. This would have to be paid off along with other security interests before the property owner is able to sell.

Lloyds Banking Group

Lloyds Banking Group represents the biggest financial services consortium in the United Kingdom. As a financial services provider that concentrates on business and retail clients, they count millions of customers throughout the country. They have a presence in practically every community of the U.K.

Part of the impressive size and strength of Lloyds Banking Group centers on its major household name brands. Among the most important of these are Lloyds Bank, Bank of Scotland, Halifax, and Scottish Widows.

The main businesses of the Lloyds Banking Group help it to touch so many customers in their daily lives. They provide retail, business, and corporate banking. The group also delivers general and life insurance. They provide investment opportunities and pension plans as well.

The shares of the Lloyds Banking Group trade on the London Stock Exchange as well as the New York Stock Exchange. The company is one of the biggest in the main British stock market benchmark index the FTSE 100. It also ranks among the largest banks in the world.

Lloyds Banking Group also runs the biggest retail bank in the United Kingdom. This was formerly known as Lloyds TSB but is now simply called Lloyds Bank. It claims the highest number of bank branches in the country. This gives them access to a diversified and massive base of customers. It helps them to cross sell products and services so that they are able to offer a total package of financial services and products for their clients. Their mobile, telephone, and digital services are comprehensive.

The history of this leading member in the Lloyds Banking Group, Lloyds Bank, goes back three centuries. Founded in 1765, the bank celebrated its 250 year anniversary back in 2015. This also makes it among the oldest of the largest banks in the world.

Lloyds Bank started its first branch in Birmingham where it operated as a single branch for a hundred years. In the twentieth century, it pursued decades of mergers to grow into first a national and then an international bank. The 1995 merger with TSB changed its name to Lloyds TSB Bank for a time. In the process of its expansion, the bank gained control of the company which invented Travelers Checks, opened the first British ATM machine, and had a foremost part in launching among the first credit cards in the United Kingdom.

Bank of Scotland is headquartered in Edinburgh. It turns out to be the oldest bank in Scotland. The Scottish Parliament founded it in 1695. It has remained a cornerstone of Scottish business since the act created it. The Parliament originally established the bank to increase the trade of Scotland with nearby trading partners. These included neighboring England and the Low Countries (now Belgium, the Netherlands, and Luxembourg).

The Bank of Scotland also claims a number of pioneering firsts in the industry. It became the very first European commercial bank to issue banknotes with success. It continues to do this today. The bank became the first in the U.K. to put in a computer for processing accounts in 1959. In 2009 the bank joined the Lloyds Group.

The banking group also owns the Halifax brand. This is a building society that arose in 1852. A little group set it up in meetings at the Halifax based Old Cock Inn. They created this investment and loan society to benefit the area working people. Individuals with extra money were able to invest it while others could borrow these funds to build or buy their own house. Eventually Halifax grew into the largest building society around the globe. It counts over 18 million customers today.

Loan Modification

A loan modification proves to be a set of changes on the original terms and conditions of a mortgage loan agreement. These must be agreed to by both the borrower and the lender. The housing crisis of 2007 caused many American homeowners to be on the verge of foreclosure. The numbers of imminent and in process foreclosures increased dramatically.

Loan modifications were amended to be a means for home owners to stay out of foreclosure and keep their houses. The process is not simple or quick, and it can be time consuming. Consumers also have to watch out for scams that prey on the vulnerable owners of homes.

Before the financial crisis erupted, a loan modification turned out to be a means for borrowers to ask for better interest rates on their mortgages without having to undergo an entire refinancing ordeal. Every mortgage company did not offer them. The ones that featured these would provide them for a cost to borrowers on the condition that their mortgage had not been resold to another firm. Now they are far more commonplace since lenders needed unorthodox solutions to help homeowners who were struggling to keep up with their payments and avoid foreclosure.

For the process of a loan modification to begin, the borrower must first request such a change to the loan terms. These changes once only affected the interest rate and made them lower. The more recent packages offered since the Great Recession are even able to change adjustable rate mortgages into standard fixed rate types. It is possible that a lender could suggest such a change to its borrowers as a possibility. Usually the borrowers initiate the process by determining they can not keep up with their loan payments and asking for help and a modification.

The next step is for the lender to consider the borrower's request. They are not required to agree to these petitions. A great number of lenders have very strict guidelines on which borrowers they will approve for modifications and which they will not. This is the case even when the homeowner has foreclosure looming. It is partly because such modification programs were not created to save home owners from rising adjustable interest rates or payments they could not handle. They were made to create a cheaper way of refinancing down to better interest rates. Each lender makes its own rules for which modifications they will accept and which they will reject.

Finally the lender will decide whether to approve or reject the modification request. They will then notify the borrower in writing. Many borrowers are rejected because they have been late with their mortgage payments frequently or too recently. Other lenders might not be in possession of the original loan any more. Whatever the reason is, the lender will state this in the letter.

If the request for modification gains approval, the request goes through to the department that handles loan servicing. There the loan will be modified to the new terms and conditions. Usually this will only reduce the interest rate and not change the loan's amortization. It may require several payment periods before these changes take effect. This is why borrowers should always keep making the payments in the amount and time for which they are scheduled.

Loan to Cost Ratio

Loan to Cost Ratio, or LTC, proves to be a measurement utilized by finance companies in extending loans for commercial real estate projects. It is employed ultimately to make comparisons of the offered financing for a given building project versus the expenses of completing said project. With the LTC ratio, lenders of commercial real estate loans are able to decide on the risks involved in backing a particular construction project via loans. The LTC ratio is similar to the LTV loan to value ratio. They both compare the amount of the construction loan to the value in fair market terms of the project in question.

Lenders work with the Loan to Cost Ratio in order to decide what loan percentage or dollar amount the financier is agreeable to finance. They do this with a basis on the firm costs stated in the construction project budget. After construction completes, these projects then possess a new and often times significantly higher value. Future values can often be double what the construction costs prove to be. This means that on a loan for $200,000 in construction, the future value of the project is likely to be $400,000 once it is fully concluded.

Consider how LTC will look in this example. With $200,000 in construction costs, and an 80% LTC ratio, the lender would be willing to loan out $160,000 on the total project. Using a similar 80% LTV ratio metric instead would significantly change the amount of money the lender is wiling to extend to $400,000 x 80% for $320,000.

Lenders never completely finance 100% of construction costs. This is because they feel that the builders also need to have significant exposure to the project in order to guarantee they will give their all to see them succeed. This is what is meant by the colloquial expression "skin in the game." It prevents a builder from simply getting up and walking away from a project gone bad. It is why the majority of lenders will require a builder to kick in minimally 10% to 20% of the construction costs to secure a financing deal.

Loan to value ratios are not the same as the Loan to Cost Ratio, though they have much in common up to a point. LTV evaluates the loan issued versus the project value once it will be fully completed. Since most banks assume that construction projects will double in value once they are finished, this is why an identical LTV percentage to the LTC ratio will yield twice the loan amount.

Lenders hold firmly to the LTC ratio. It helps them to clearly express the levels of risk in a given financing project for commercial construction. In the end, using a greater Loan to Cost Ratio will entail a significantly riskier project from the lender's perspective. This is why the overwhelming majority of reputable mainstream lenders will not surpass a pre-determined percentage when they consider any given project. They usually limit this amount strictly to a maximum of 80% of the project's LTV or LTC. When lenders are willing to become involved at a higher percentage and ratio, they will most always insist on a substantially greater project and loan interest rate to compensate them for the additional level of risk to which they are consenting.

Lenders will also have to consider other information and circumstances beyond simply Loan to Cost Ratio and Loan to value ratios when extending such financing. They take into consideration the value of the property and its location for where the project will be constructed. They also contemplate how much creditworthiness and experience the commercial builders in the application possess. Finally, they consult both the borrowers' loan payment histories on other loans and their credit record as demonstrated in their company credit report.

Loan-to-Value-Ratio (LTV)

The Loan to Value Ratio is commonly known by its acronym LTV. This loan to value ratio states the total value of the first mortgage against the full real estate property's appraised value. The formula for figuring this ratio is simply the amount of the loan divided by the property value. It is expressed as a percent. So if a borrower is seeking $180,000 with which to buy a $200,000 house, then the Loan to Value Ratio is ninety percent.

The loan to value ratio proves to be among the most critical risk factors that lenders consider when they are deciding whether to qualify borrowers for a mortgage loan on a house. The dangers of a default occurring most influence the loan officers in their lending decisions. The chances of an institution having to take a hit in a foreclosure procedure only goes up as the dollar amount of the property equity goes down. Because of this, as the Loan to Value ratio goes up, the qualification tests for many mortgage programs get significantly stricter. Some lenders will insist on a borrower who comes with a high loan to value ratio on the property in question to purchase mortgage insurance. This safe guards the lender from any default realized by the borrower, but it also raises the mortgage's total costs.

Property values used in the loan to value ratio are generally set by appraisers. Still, the most accurate value of a piece of real estate is undoubtedly that determined when a willing seller and willing buyer come together to agree on a sale. Usually, banks decide to go with the lower number when they are offered choices of a purchase price that is fairly recent or an appraisal value. Recent sales are commonly deemed to be those that happened from a year to two years ago, although every bank makes its own rules in this regard.

When a borrower selects a property that he or she will purchase with a lower loan to value ratio that is less than eighty percent, lower interest rates can many times be obtained by borrowers who are low risk. Higher risk borrowers will also be considered in such a scenario, meaning those who have prior histories of late payments on mortgages, who have lower credit scores, who have high loan requirements or higher debt to income ratios, and who have neither sufficient cash reserves nor requested income documentation. Generally, higher loan to value ratios are only permitted for those borrowers who have a reliable mortgage payment history and who possess greater credit scores. Only those buyers with the greatest credit worthiness are considered for one hundred percent financing that translates to a one hundred percent loan to value ratio.

Loans that are made to the standards of lending giants Freddie Mac and Fannie Mae and their guidelines can not have loan to value ratios that exceed or are equal to eighty percent. Any loans higher than this percentage of eighty percent must come with attached private mortgage insurance. The private mortgage insurance premiums simply go on top of the existing mortgage principal and interest payments.

London Interbank Offered Rate (LIBOR)

LIBOR is a main global benchmark interest rate. It stands for London InterBank Offered Rate. This rate represents how much banks actually charge each other for loans based on one year, six months, three months, one month, and overnight timeframes. Banks all over the world use this benchmark rate. Reuters news service publishes this critical rate every day at 11 am. They do this in five different currencies of the U.S. dollar, the Euro, British Pound, Swiss franc, and Japanese yen.

Historically the BBA British Bankers Association oversaw and compiled this rate. The IBA ICE Benchmark Administration assumed this responsibility on August 1st of 2014. They figure up this rate using contributor bank submissions. In every currency for which they calculate it there are between 11 and 18 contributing banks who act as an oversight board.

LIBOR does more than provide a rate for the interbank loans. It is utilized as a bank guide for their setting of credit card rates, interest only mortgages, and adjustable rate loans. Bank lenders add in between one and two points to make money. An incredible $10 trillion in loans are determined at least in part by this interbank rate.

Besides these uses, this rate also serves as a base price for credit default swaps and interest rate swaps. These contracts are a type of insurance in case loans default. The swaps also created the 2008 financial crisis. Hedge funds and banks believed that risk did not exist in the mortgage backed securities because they were protected by this insurance.

The problem arose as the subprime mortgages that underlay the mortgage backed securities started defaulting. AIG and other insurance companies discovered they did not have enough cash available to pay off the swaps. In order to save all swap holders from bankruptcy, the Federal Reserve was forced to rescue AIG with a bailout. Despite the fact that these swaps were supposed to be dispersed after the financial crisis, the LIBOR rate remains the basis on over $350 trillion of such credit default swaps.

Banks created LIBOR in the 1980s in response to a demand for a standard interest rate to establish derivatives. The original rate came out in 1986 in the three currencies the U.S. dollar, British pound, and Japanese yen. The

BBA later expanded it to include the additional currencies of Swiss franc and Euro.

A scandal plagued the LIBOR rate starting in 2012. The British Bankers' Association figured out the rate using its panel of banks that acted as representatives from every one of the currencies involved. BBA queried the banks about the rate they would charge in the set currencies for different amounts of time. The BBA's downfall was that they believed the rates the banks provided them with were true.

This unraveled in 2012 as British bank Barclays became charged with deliberately providing lower rates to the BBA then the ones they actually received from 2005 to 2009. They suffered a $450 million fine and the CEO Bob Diamond had to resign. When Diamond went down he told authorities the majority of other banks engaged in the same practice and that the Bank of England was aware.

The reasons that Barclays and others were lying about their rate was for better profits. Lower rates made the banks look stronger and more attractive to borrowers than banks with higher rates. The end result had three bankers found guilty of manipulating rates in 2015 while six others were acquitted of their charges in 2016. The guilty bankers all worked for Rabobank. The rate was taken away from the British Bankers Association and given over to the care of the ICE Benchmark Administration because of the scandal.

Loss Mitigation Program

Loss Mitigation Program refers to a special vehicle which arose during the latter years of the global financial crisis and preceding subprime mortgage crisis. This happened because of the 2008 subprime mortgage crisis which the American economy suffered from at that time.

It started because of an enormous bursting of the housing prices bubble that caused a substantial rise in delinquencies and foreclosures of mortgages. Next a collapse in the value of all home-backed securities occurred, including in the now-infamous MBS mortgage backed securities.

The economy continued to struggle to recover even four years later in 2012. Banks had been bailed out of their poorly made loans by the United States Treasury and Federal Government. Homeowners received no real such help at first though. They had no recourse but to try to manage their higher interest rates at the same time as their home prices had declined substantially.

Fortunately for homeowners across the United States, one court intervened on behalf of consumers in the Western part of the state of Pennsylvania. It was this Bankruptcy Court for the Western District of Pennsylvania that took great initiative and developed the Loss Mitigation Program late in the year 2012. The program finally offered beaten down homeowners the ability to modify their mortgages in a court-overseen program which the banks administered directly.

This Loss Mitigation Program began in an effort to offer clarity on failing mortgages. The idea was to fast track the process of loan modification for both the lenders and the borrowers who were involved. It is true that many mortgage and finance companies had already developed their own internal programs for mortgage modification after the mortgage meltdown happened in 2008. Still the process for obtaining such a modification was overwhelming as homeowners dealt with tedious procedures and often saw little to no end results.

The Loss Mitigation Program became necessary because the HAMP Home Affordable Modification Program which the federal government had sponsored had not prevented defaults at what the Special Inspector

General for the TARP called an "alarming rate." HAMP had been created originally to assist homeowners who needed to modify their government FHA insured mortgages, to stay out of foreclosure, and to lower their high monthly payments.

Yet according to this watchdog group, by the conclusion of March in 2013, more than 312,000 participants in the program had realized default on their mortgages. The U.S. Treasury could not come up with any one reason to explain why these default rates had grown so egregiously. Some participants in the program revealed that they only benefited from a modification which was temporary in the initial trial period of the mortgage modification program.

This is why the Loss Mitigation Program began. It was an effort to help the homeowners obtain real and lasting relief so that they could stay in their homes. The program worked according to a simple process which involved four steps. First homeowners had to file for bankruptcy protection in order to safeguard all of their assets and reduce or eliminate their other debts. This allowed them to concentrate their available income on keeping the residential property.

Next the homeowner would engage a bankruptcy attorney to file motions that enrolled the individual into this Loss Mitigation Program. In other words, the modification program existed beneath the umbrella of the bankruptcy protection. Third, the court would approve the application then sign an order that laid out strict procedural guidelines for both lender and borrowers. Clear deadlines were spelled out for both borrowers and lender. It ensured the process became instantly transparent for borrowers since the mortgage modification package and mortgage status had to be treated in good faith by the mortgage company.

Finally, the program set up an electronic portal through which all relevant correspondence on the process had to pass. The court's representatives would monitor the correspondence to be certain that the two parties were carrying out their responsibilities and roles in good faith.

Thanks to this portal, the Loss Mitigation Program process became streamlined, time saving, and cost reducing for all of the concerned parties. The entire process had to be completed in 60 days unless either the lender or borrower sought out and explained a valid reason for requiring extra time. Serious consequences were mandated for either party delaying the process unnecessarily.

Loss to Lease

Loss to lease is a phrase that is used in real estate property leasing, particularly pertaining to apartment complexes or senior assisted living facilities. Loss to lease is also an accounting line in the books of rental properties and apartment complexes. In both cases, it refers to income on leases that is potentially lost through making incentive offers to prospective tenants whom you hope to lease a unit in a property.

Examples of loss to lease are helpful to understand the concept. Some apartments will offer one free month's rent with a six or twelve month lease contract. The amount of this lost month's rent would be the loss to lease figure for the leasing property and the leasing property's books. Other examples involve loss to lease figured up on a monthly basis. Should the potential revenue from rent amount to only $500 when the market rate for rental is $550, then the loss to lease comes out to be $50 per month.

Cash flow is the part of a rental property books where loss to lease most commonly appears. When required, it can be figured up using a simple formula. The scheduled base rental revenue is determined. This figure has the potential market rent subtracted from it to come up with the Loss to Lease result.

The interesting thing about loss to lease is that it has no meaningful impact on a rental property or apartment complex's cash flow bottom line. Instead, it only represents an accounting number. Loss to lease does not offer any advantages to a company or individual when they are figuring up and filing their taxes either, since it does not represent any actual real or tangible loss in income, only loss in potential income, or hoped for income.

Margin

Margin refers to a term used by companies and corporations in business. It is the spread between the firm's product or service sales price and the cost to make it. Another way of putting this is the ratio of firm's revenue to expenses. Margin can be utilized to refer to profit margins, operating margins, net margins, pretax profit margins, and gross profit margins.

Profit margin is the larger catch all category for many of these margins. Analysts and businesses figure it as the total net income divided by the firm's revenues. Another way of deriving it is through net profits divided by sales. Coming up with the net income is not hard. It requires that individuals subtract out the total of a firm's given expenses. This means that all material costs, operating costs, interest expenses, and taxes costs will have to be deducted from the total revenue. Such profit margins become expressed in percentage terms. In practice they measure the amount from each dollar in sales that the corporation gets to keep as earnings.

The other business margins are not difficult to understand and are simply variations on profit margins. With gross profit margins, the phrase displays the connection between firms' total sales revenues and their COGS cost of goods sold. Conversely, operating profit margins consider the cost of goods sold along with the operating expenses. They compare these against the revenues. Finally, net profit margins gather all of these expenses, interest paid on loans and bonds, and taxes to compare them to total sales revenues.

It is always useful to look at practical examples to better understand complex concepts. Consider a company like Burger King. They might claim an 18 percent profit margin. This would mean that after they paid their expenses, labor costs, material costs, any interest on debt, and taxes, they would have left 18 cents on every dollar of sales revenues they realized. Margin can have several other meanings as well.

A common one has to do with investor accounts. Many stock or options' account holders will have what industry personnel call a margin account. This permits the investors to be able to purchase their securities on margin. They may buy a stock or option by only having to pay a certain set and predetermined percentage of the cost of the investment. The remaining cost they simply borrow from the brokerage firm or the associated bank of the firm.

In most cases, the broker becomes the lender and carries out these functions as expected. This means that they enforce the collateral requirement and minimum maintenance requirements. The securities which the investor purchased using the margin account become the collateral for the balance of the loan. This will commonly be expressed using a percentage.

Consider an example of this to better understand the idea. Investors may purchase $10,000 in stocks with margin. As the rate is set by the brokerage firm at 25 percent, they will have to deposit and pay $2,500 of their own cash. The remainder $7,500 they simply borrow from the brokerage company (or bank). This makes great sense for those investors who predict that the return they will realize on the investments will significantly outweigh the cost of the loans.

Margins are also utilized as a concept with regards to mortgages. Some particular mortgages are called ARMs, or adjustable rate mortgages. They provide a fixed interest rate during some type of introductory time frame. At that point, the rate adjusts up (sometimes dramatically). Banks figure up this new rate by simply adding margins on to the pre-established index. Such margins typically remain fixed during the remainder of the loan's life span. Yet the rate of the index can and will change.

Market Value

With regards to real estate, market value is the price which a real property seller can anticipate obtaining from the property purchaser in normal open and fair market negotiations. In general, appraisers value a home or other piece of real estate property utilizing a number of critical factors. When markets are volatile, such prices will vary significantly. Real estate agents may place one value on a home or other piece of real estate, yet in the end, the true property value is only what an able and willing buyer will actually pay to acquire it.

It is crucial to be aware of the market value of a piece of property individuals or businesses are selling as this ultimately sets the asking price of the real estate in question. Those sellers who are not intimately aware of this will either overprice their houses or under price them. Either of these actions will often lead to poor financial results. Not being aware of a property's true value can cause homeowners to become victims to practices of predatory lending. In this unscrupulous lending behavior, the bank or other lending financial institution will prevail upon a borrower to take out a greater amount of money than their property is really worth.

It is real estate agents or better still professional appraisers who determine most accurately the market value of a house or piece of real estate through measuring it up to other properties in the area or neighborhood which share similarities with the one in question. Real estate agents and appraisers call such recently sold area properties "comparables." They will always seek to find houses which are as alike in style, size, and location to the one they are appraising as possible.

Such properties must have sold within the prior six months to a year. According to this strategy, the professionals will similarly discern what the typical price per square foot of the houses in the area actually is. This practice by itself will not set the market price of a house, but it will give the professionals a good starting point from which to set a reasonable and viable asking price for the property.

There are also various other factors which influence a property's market value. These include the condition of the property in question as well as any improvements which the seller makes. Where a home is concerned, bathroom and kitchen renovations and updates are the main ones which will boost the selling price. Other more cosmetic appearance improvements like new carpet, fresh paint, updated light fixtures, and special window treatments will help a house to show better and perhaps sell faster, yet they will not increase the all around value of the home.

Yet it is absolutely true that the overall condition of any piece of real estate will impact its total value. Houses that boast more current and better maintained appliances and systems, roofs, windows, and even entry doors will realize a significantly better final selling price than those which offer flawed structures or outdated appliances, systems, entry doors, and mechanics.

In corporations and investments, market value is the price for which a given asset will sell in the open market. This measure of value can often be applied to the market capitalization of any company which is publically traded. Determining the market cap value is a matter of multiplying out the current price per share by the quantity of total outstanding shares.

This measure of market value is simplest to calculate for those instruments which are traded on exchanges, like futures and stocks. This is because their market prices are readily available and commonly disseminated. With over the counter securities such as fixed income securities, it can be far harder to ascertain. Yet the most difficult to determine market values are those commonly associated with less liquid assets such as businesses and real estate. This is why business valuation experts and real estate appraisers determine the market values for such assets as these.

MERS

MERS stands for the Mortgage Electronic Registration Systems. It is also a privately owned and operated company that maintains this electronic database and registry whose purpose is to follow the ownership of and servicing rights to American mortgage loans.

This MERS represents a revolutionary way of vastly simplifying the means of keeping track of how both mortgage servicing and ownership rights can be originated, sold, and followed. The Real Estate finance industry actually created it. MERS boasts that it does away with the requirement to create and record assignments as both commercial and residential loans are being exchanged.

The mortgage banking industry got together to come up with a way to simplify the process of working with mortgages through utilizing e-commerce to reduce and even eliminate paper. The mission of the company and its database lies in registering literally all mortgage loans within the U.S. on the MERS system.

MERS actually performs its role on behalf of the servicer and the lender in handling county land records. Loans that are registered on the MERS system can not have problems with future assignments since MERS is always the nominal mortgagee, regardless of the number of times that a mortgage servicing is sold. MERS is approved to be original mortgagee by all of the major lending outfits, including Freddie Mac, Fannie Mae, Ginnie Mae, the VA, the FHA, and both Utah and California Housing Finance Agencies, along with each of the Wall Street ratings agencies.

Many groups benefit from the existence of the MERS registry. This includes mortgage servicers, originators, wholesale lenders, warehouse lenders, retail lenders, settlement agents, document custodians, title companies, investors, insurers, and country recorders. MERS claims that the consumer benefit as well, though this has been in question until recently.

Ironically, a recent situation has arisen surrounding MERS that may actually benefit many consumers in the end. They are embroiled in the middle of a scandal surrounding original titles and signed promissory notes. Part of what they accomplished in their paperless process led to the loss of such critical original signature documents that the majority of states require for enacting mortgage foreclosures. MERS is now right in the middle of a number of legal challenges resulting from the sub prime crisis and going on in most states around the country. Their right to begin the process of foreclosure has been called into account, since they lack these required original signed documents.

This means that their role in the early days of setting up the system that helped with the buying and selling of mortgages may come back to haunt them and the entire mortgage industry as a whole in the end. Should judges rule these legal suits in favor of the homeowners who took out the mortgages, then it is widely believed that the losses that the banking industry in America suffers from will be so great that they will require substantial amounts of re-capitalization.

Mortgage

Mortgages are loans made on commercial or residential properties. They commonly use the house or the property itself as collateral. These mortgages are paid off in monthly installments over the course of a pre determined amount of time. Mortgages commonly come in fifteen, twenty, and thirty year periods, though both longer ones and shorter ones are available.

A variety of differing mortgages exist. All of them have their own terms and conditions that translate into advantages and disadvantages. Among the various mortgage types are fixed rate mortgages, adjustable rate mortgages, and balloon payment mortgages.

The most common kinds or mortgages, especially for first time home buyers, prove to be fixed rate mortgages. This is the case because they are both simple to understand and extremely stable. With such a mortgage, the regular monthly payments will be the same during the entire life of the loan. This makes them very predictable and manageable. Fixed rate mortgages have the advantages of protection against inflation, since the interest rate is locked in and can not go up with the floating interest rates. They allow for longer term planning. They come with very low risk, since you are always aware of both the payment and interest rate.

Adjustable rate mortgages, also known as ARM's, have become more popular since they begin with lower, more manageable interest rates that result in a lower initial monthly payment. The downside to them is that the interest rate can and likely will go up and down in the loan's life time. Factors to consider with ARM's are the adjustment periods, the indexes and margins, and the caps ceilings, and floors. The adjustment period is the one in which the interest rate is allowed to reset, commonly starting anywhere from six months to ten years after the mortgage begins.

The interest rates change based on the index and margin. The interest rates are actually based on an index that is published, whether it is the London Interbank Offered Rate, or LIBOR, or the U.S. Constant Maturity Treasury, or CMT. The margin is added to this index to determine the total new interest rate on your mortgage. The amount that these ARM rates are capable of going up or down in a single adjustment period and for the life of the loan is called a cap, a ceiling or a floor.

The third common type of mortgages is balloon reset mortgages. They come with thirty year schedules for repayment, with a caveat. Unless you pay are willing to allow the mortgage to reset to then current interest rates at the end of either a five year or seven year term, then your entire balance will be due at this point. This gives you the benefits of the low monthly payment plan as a person with a thirty year loan would have, yet you will have to be willing to pay off the whole mortgage if you do not take the reset option when the term is up. Because of this, many people refer to this type of a mortgage as a two step mortgage.

Mortgage Backed Obligations (MBO)

Mortgage Backed Obligations are also called mortgage backed securities, or MBS. These are real estate-based financial instruments. They represent an ownership stake in a pool of mortgages. They can also be called a financial security or obligation for which mortgages underlie the instrument.

Such a security offers one of three different means for the investor getting paid. It might be that the loan becomes paid back utilizing principal and interest payments that come in on the pool of mortgages which back the instrument. This would make them pass through securities. A second option is that the security issuer could provide payments to the investing party independently of the incoming cash flow off of the borrowers. This would then be a non-pass through security. The third type of security is sometimes referred to as a modified-pass through security. These securities provide the security owners with a guaranteed interest payment each month. This happens whether or not the underlying incoming principal and interest payments prove to be sufficient to cover them or not.

Pass-through securities are not like non-pass through securities in key ways. The pass through ones do not stay on the issuer of the securities' or originators' balance sheets. Non-pass through securities do stay on the relevant balance sheet. With these non pass through variants, the securities are most frequently bonds. These became mortgage backed bonds. Investors in the non-pass through types often receive extra collateral as a letter of credit, guarantees, or more equity capital. This type of credit enhancement is delivered by the insurer of the mortgage backed obligation. The holder of the MBO will be able to count on the security which underlies the instruments in the event that the repayments the pools of mortgages make are not enough to cover the payments (or fail altogether) for the bond holder investors.

These offerings of Mortgage Backed Obligations, Mortgage Backed Bonds, or Mortgage Backed Securities are all ultimately backed up by mortgage pools. Analysts and investors usually call these securitized mortgage offerings. When such types of investments are instead backed up by different kinds of assets and collateral then they have another name. An example of this is the Asset Backed Securities or Asset Backed Bonds. They are backed up with such collateral as car loans, credit card receivables, or even mobile home loans. Sometimes they are referred to as Asset Backed Commercial Paper when the loans that underlie them are short term loan pools.

With these Mortgage Backed Obligations, they are often grouped together by both risk level and maturity dates. Issuers, investors, and analysts refer to this grouping as tranches, which are the risk profile-organized groups of mortgages. These complicated financial instrument tranches come with various interest rates, mortgage principle balances, dates of maturity, and possibilities of defaulting on their repayments. They are also highly sensitive to any changes in the market interest rates. Other economic scenarios can dramatically impact them as well. This is particularly true of refinance rates, rates of foreclosure, and the home selling rates.

It helps to look at a real world example to understand the complexity of Mortgage Backed Obligations and Collateralized Mortgage Obligations like these. If John buys an MBO or CMO that is comprised of literally thousands of different mortgages, then he has real potential for profit. This comes down to whether or not the various mortgage holders pay back their mortgages. If just a couple of the mortgage-paying homeowners do not pay their mortgages while the rest cover their payments as expected, then John will recover not only his principal but also interest. On the other hand, if hundreds or even thousands of mortgage holders default on their payments and then fall into foreclosure, the MBO will sustain heavy losses and will be unable to pay out the promised returns of interest and even the original principal to John.

Mortgage Backed Securities (MBS)

Mortgage backed securities turn out to be a special kind of asset which have underlying collections of mortgages or individual mortgages that back them. To be qualified as an MBS, the security also has to be qualified as rated in one of two top tier ratings. Credit ratings agencies determine these ratings levels.

These securities generally pay out set payments from time to time which are much like coupon payments. Another requirement of MBS is that the mortgages underlying them have to come from an authorized and regulated bank or financial institution.

Sometimes mortgage backed securities are called by other names. These include mortgage pass through or mortgage related securities. Interested investors buy or sell them via brokers. The investments have fairly steep minimums. These are generally $10,000. There is some variation in minimum amounts depending on which entity issues them.

Issuers are either a GSE Government Sponsored Enterprise, an agency company of the federal government, or an independent financial company. Some people believe that government sponsored enterprise MBS come with less risk. The truth is that default and credit risks are always prevalent. The government has no obligation to bail out the GSEs when they are in danger of default.

Investors who put their money into these mortgage backed securities lend their money to a business or home buyer. Using an MBS, regional banks which are smaller may confidently lend money to their clients without being concerned whether the customers can cover the loan itself. Thanks to the mortgage backed securities, banks are only serving as middlemen between investment markets and actual home buyers.

These MBS securities are a way for shareholders to obtain principal and interest payments out of mortgage pools. The payments themselves can be distinguished as different securities classes. This all depends on how risky the various underlying mortgages are rated within the MBS.

The two most frequent kinds of mortgage backed securities turn out to be collateralized mortgage obligations (CMOs) and pass throughs. Collateralized mortgage obligations are comprised of many different pools of securities. These are referred to as tranches, or pieces. Tranches receive credit ratings. It is these credit ratings which decide what rates the investors will receive. The securities within a senior secured tranche will generally feature lesser interest rates than others which comprise the non secured tranche. This is because there is little actual risk involved with senior secured tranches.

Pass throughs on the other hand are set up like a trust. These trust structures collect and then pass on the mortgage payments to the investors. The maturities with these kinds of pass throughs commonly are 30, 15, or five years. Both fixed rate mortgages and adjustable rate ones can be pooled together to make a pass through MBS.

The pass throughs average life spans may end up being less than the maturity which they state. This all depends on the amount of principal payments which the underlying mortgage holders in the pool make. If they pay larger payments than required on their monthly mortgages, then these pass through mortgages could mature faster.

Mortgage Costs

Mortgage costs are fees that real estate transactions incur when it is time for them to close. The point for closing comes as the seller transfers the title to the property over to the buyer. Mortgage costs can be absorbed by the seller or the buyer. A number of different expenses go into these overall costs.

The amount for mortgage costs ranges dramatically based on the property the individuals are buying and where they live. They cover many different expenses. There are fees for such things as credit reports, attorney costs, and appraisals. A survey fee pays for the expense of confirming where the property lines are. Pest inspection fees pay to check for termites and other home damaging insects.

Credit report fees pay for running the borrower's credit. Inspections may be requested by the lender or the buyer, and there is a fee for these. With the loan origination fee, lenders receive their compensation for handling all of the loan paperwork on behalf of the borrower. They receive a separate amount called an underwriting fee when they evaluate the application for the mortgage loan.

Other mortgage costs have to do with discounts, titles, and escrows. Discount points turn out to be optional fees that borrowers pay to receive a more favorable interest rate on the loan. A title search fee pays to have a background check performed on the title to ensure that there are no problems like tax liens or unpaid mortgages attached to the property.

Lenders also insist on title insurance. This insurance protects them against a title that turns out not to be clear. The recording fee goes to the county or city to compensate them for adding the update to the land records. There could also be an escrow deposit. This provides for several months of the private mortgage insurance and property tax costs.

Even though mortgage costs vary wildly from one region to another, it is still possible to estimate how high they will be. Home buyers can anticipate commonly paying somewhere between two percent and five percent of the final price of the house in closing fees. This means that if a house costs $200,000, the mortgage costs could run from $4,000 to $10,000.

The law requires that lenders provide home buyers with a Loan Estimate that covers the amount that these fees will approximately be. They must do this in three days or less of accepting the loan application. These are estimates that will change on a number of the fees.

Three business days or more before the closing occurs, the lender will provide borrowers with a Closing Disclosure statement. This covers the actual closing fees. It is a good idea to hold this up to the original Loan Estimate to contrast the expenses. The lender should explain every item on the fees, why they are important, and why they differed from the original estimate.

In many cases, a significant number of these costs can be negotiated. Some of them can even be removed as unnecessary. This includes fees such as courier, mailing, and administrative costs that the lender is attempting to collect. Borrowers always have the option of walking away from this particular loan if the fees seem high and unreasonable. Other lenders will be agreeable to provide competitive loans with more reasonable fees.

There are also no closing cost mortgages. In these, borrowers are able to sidestep the fees upfront when they close on the loan. Lenders still make money by exacting a higher interest rate or by rolling the costs into the whole mortgage. This last method causes borrowers to pay interest for the mortgage costs as well. Sellers can occasionally be persuaded to absorb the fees at closing.

Mortgage Modification Package

Mortgage Modification Package refers to an agreement that reduces the homeowners' mortgage payments and possibly overall mortgage debt when they are suffering from significant financial struggles. The idea is to help the borrowers become capable of making their loan payments. This way they can keep their home and not forfeit it in costly foreclosure proceedings.

This does not mean that it is easy to get approved on a Mortgage Modification Package. The mortgage company ultimately will determine if they will allow for such a modification. These changes to the mortgage agreements really are to the advantage of the lender and are often in their best interest. Through helping borrowers to make their payments in a timely fashion, the financial institutions get to keep performing loans and sidestep the tremendous costs, time, and hassle of foreclosing on the property.

The name Mortgage Modification Package describes precisely what occurs in these arrangements. Current mortgage terms become modified so that the interest rate, payments, and overall final balance of the loan are manageable for the borrowers' in question. Amounts which are past due can be paid down either utilizing installments or otherwise can be deferred to the end point of the mortgage. The repayment timeframe of the loan can be extended as well. This lowers the principle payments which are due each month. There are cases where the financial institution will even consent to writing down the remaining loan principle to a manageable amount the borrower can truly afford.

Sometimes these modifications will be temporary. This is often the case where interest rates alone are lowered. They may provide a several year break in the rate that will finally rise back to its original amount. Other times, the lender will permit the borrowers additional time to catch up the late payments without incurring additional fines and fees.

In other scenarios, these modifications can be permanent. This is more common when the financial institutions opt to push out the loan repayment schedule or agree to write down some of the principle which borrowers owe on the mortgage. Without a doubt, such permanent changes to a mortgage are not as easy to receive as are the more temporary in nature ones.

It is not necessarily the financial institution which issued the mortgage loan in the first place which has to approve such a Mortgage Modification Package. Rather the loan servicer is the entity responsible for changing the terms of the loan. This is often another company from the one which extended the mortgage loan upfront.

Loan modifications should never be confused with refinancing, even though they have some similar end results. Both routes will make the payments more affordable in most cases. Yet in order to successfully achieve refinancing, the borrowers will require solid credit and dependable finances. In fact the majority of applicants for loan modifications do not enjoy these significant advantages.

Refinancing is instead actually closing out the existing loan and re-making a new mortgage with which to replace it. The new terms will be more beneficial. Even as borrowers had to qualify for the first mortgage, they must re-qualify for the new one. For some borrowers who are late on or are missing payments altogether (because finances are no longer sufficient to cover the obligations of the mortgage), this will practically rule out qualifying for a traditional refinancing offer.

Mortgage Modification Packages alternatively were purposefully established for those individuals who find themselves in financial straights. They will change the existing mortgage terms in order to help the borrower catch up on late payments and possibly to help make the mortgage terms overall more manageable. This arrangement can be either permanent or temporary.

Mortgage Servicing

Mortgage servicing refers to the organization that handles the administration of a given mortgage loan. When many individuals obtain a mortgage, they mistakenly believe that their lender is going to keep and service this loan until they repay it in full or alternatively sell the house. This is not true much of the time, if not most of the time. In the competitive mortgage market of today, the loans a bank makes and its rights to service them it will commonly sell or buy. This simply means that in many instances, individuals send their payments in to a different company than the one which actually holds their loan.

It is useful to understand the definition of a mortgage servicer. These entities carry the responsibility of managing the daily needs for a given account on a mortgage loan. This includes a number of different services which they perform for the loan. The mortgage servicing model includes receiving and applying the every-month loan installment payments. Servicers also manage the escrow account for any mortgage that possesses one. It is this servicer who homeowners will call or email if they have questions regarding the mortgage itself or any particulars of the loan account.

This administration involved in mortgage servicing revolves around administering the loan from the time the loan proceeds are paid out all the way through the repayment of the loan in full. Besides the obvious tasks that a servicer will perform on a mortgage account, there are several other critically important ones. The servicer must collect and make payments on both insurance and taxes for the borrower. They have to deliver the received funds to the holder of the mortgage. Finally, they have the unpleasant but necessary task of dealing with any delinquencies on the mortgage accounts.

The mortgage servicers receive their compensation for these services in a particular way. They get to keep a fairly small percentage of every loan installment payment. This is called the servicing strip or servicing fee. It typically amounts to between .25% and .5% of the amount of the periodic interest payment.

Looking at an example of how this compensation works out in practice is helpful. When a remaining balance on a given mortgage proves to be $200,000 and there is a servicing fee amounting to .50%, the mortgage servicer will keep .005 divided by 12 months times $200,000 to arrive at a servicing amount of $80. They will retain this $80 from the coming periodic payment and then turn in the rest of the payment amount to the holder of the mortgage.

These mortgage servicing rights can be bought and sold on the secondary market. This happens in a similar fashion to the MBS mortgage backed securities trading. In fact, the mortgage loan servicing value works out to be much like the MBS IO strips value. This is referred to as MSR Mortgage Servicing Rights. Such servicing rights are actually contracted. They provide the rights to service the original mortgage. The initial lender will often sell these off to another firm that specializes in servicing mortgages. The contract will then specify what percentage amount the servicer will keep from each payment.

Though it is hard to believe, the United States national banking laws permit these lending institutions to sell their mortgages and/or servicing rights to any other institution they wish without having to first obtain the consent of the borrower or even to alert them of the change. This is because the interest rate, payment amount, kind of loan, and other terms will stay the same regardless of who services the mortgage. The only difference is that the company and address where the borrower sends the payments will be different.

Lenders might choose to sell these mortgage servicing rights in order to make available additional funds to more borrowers who wish to obtain mortgages. This is necessary as the majority of loans on homes take from 15 to 30 years (or even longer) to repay. Banks would requires billions of dollars in funds to loan out in order to meet the mortgage market demand if they had to keep all of their loans on the books ad infinitum. By selling the loans and/or servicing rights, they are able to help more individuals into homes.

Net Present Value (NPV)

Net Present Value refers to a principal profitability measure that companies utilize in their corporate budget planning process. It helps them to analyze the possible ROI return on investment for a particular proposed or working project. Thanks to the involvement of time value and its depreciating effect on dollars, the NPV is forced to consider a discount rate and its compounding effect throughout the term of the entire project.

The actual Net Present Value in an investment or business project considers the point where revenue (or cash inflow) is equal to or greater than the total investment capital that funds the project or asset in the first place. This is particularly useful for businesses when they are comparing and contrasting a number of different projects or potential projects. It allows them to draw a valuable comparison of their comparative profitability levels to make sure that they only spend their limited resources, time, and management skills on the most valuable ventures. The higher the NPV proves to be, the more profitable it is as an investment, property, or project in the end.

Another way of thinking about the Net Present Value is as a measurement of how well an investment is meeting a targeted yield considering the upfront investment that the firm made. Using this NPV, companies can also determine precisely what adjustment they need in the initial investment in order to reach the hoped for yield. This assumes that all else remains constant.

Net Present Value can also be utilized to effectively visualize and quantify investments in real estate and other asset purchases in a simple formulaic expression. This is that the NPV is equal to the Current value minus the cost. In this iteration of the NPV, the current value of all anticipated future cash flow is discounted to today utilizing the relevant discount rate minus the cost of acquiring said cash flow. This makes NPV essentially the value of the project less the cost. When analysts or corporate accountants examine the NPV in this light, it becomes easy to understand how the value explains if the item being purchased (or project being funded) is more or less valuable than the cost of it in the first place.

Only three total categories of NPV ultimate values are possible for any property purchase or project funding. NPV could be a positive Net Present Value. This means that the buyers will pay less than the true value of the asset. The NPV might also be a Zero NPV. This simply means that the buyer or project funder is paying precisely the value of the asset or project worth. With a negative NPV in the final categorization, the buyer will be paying too much for the asset technically. This will be more than the asset is actually worth. There are cases where companies or buyers might be willing to pursue a project or acquire an asset with a negative NPV when other factors come into play.

For example, they might be interested in purchasing a property for a new corporate headquarters whose NPV is negative. The reasoning behind such a decision could be the unquantifiable and intangible value of the location of the property either for visibility purposes or because it is next to the present company headquarter premises.

It is always helpful to look at a concrete example to de-mystify difficult concepts like Net Present Value. Consider a corporation that wishes to fully analyze the anticipated profits in a project. This given project might need an upfront $10,000 investment to get it off the ground. In three years time, the project is forecast to create revenues amounting to $2,000, $8,000, and $12,000. This means that the project is expected to provide $22,000 on the initial $10,000 outlay.

It would appear that the return will amount to 120 percent for a gain greater than the initial investment. There is a reason why this is not the case though. The discount rate for the time value of money has to be factored in, and this means a percentage of several points per year at least. The figure of 4.5 percent is often utilized on a three year project like this. This takes into consideration the fact that dollars earned three years from now will not be so valuable as today's earned dollars. This is why the corporate accountants will use business calculators in order to plug in the discount time value rates to figure the true NPV. Discounting by the 4.5 percent means that the project actually will return somewhere near $21,000 in terms of today's dollar value.

Origination Fees

Origination fees are also known as activation fees. These are the costs pertaining to setting up an account with a mortgage broker, bank, or other firm that will go through the tasks of collecting and processing all documents and requirements for getting a loan, in particular a mortgage on a house.

These origination fees are generally amounts that are pre determined for any new account. Origination fees can range from half a percentage point to two percentage points of the entire loan total. This variance has to do with where the loans come from, off of either the prime or the subprime loan market. On a subprime mortgage for $200,000, the origination fee would likely amount to two percent, equaling four thousand dollars in this particular case.

The average origination fee comes in at approximately one percent of the total mortgage loan dollar amount. This fee goes to the firm that originates and processes your loan. It defrays their expenses that arise from developing, putting together, and finally closing on your mortgage.

The rise of the Internet has allowed for an alternative compensation scheme for companies that put together and originate mortgages. While the vast majority of mortgage brokers and banks still charge these loan origination fees, there are some Internet based brokers who use a different model. These entities do no charge origination fees at all; instead they pass the savings directly on to you the customer. The way that they get paid is by selling your loan to an investor once it is closed. The investor pays them a premium for the packaged loan, which covers the origination fees, and the online mortgage broker is compensated for his or her work and time.

The origination fees can be deducted from taxes. The year that the transaction closed and the origination fees were charged, they can be used to reduce actual income on income tax forms. The Internal Revenue Service permits this reduction to income no matter who pays the origination fees, meaning that a person who employs a broker that does not charge them origination fees will still be able to deduct the fees that the investors who later buy the loan are subsequently paying to the mortgage broker. This means that if you take out a $200,000 mortgage, then you are able to deduct the $2,000 in loan origination fees, even if you did not have to pay them, but an investor in the loan did instead.

Origination fees are listed on the HUD-1 Settlement form. They are tallied beneath the sub-heading of lender charges. Discount points that are used to bring down interest rates either permanently or temporarily are also listed on this form under the category.

Passive Income

Passive income refers to money that, once it is arranged and established, does not require additional work from the person getting it. A variety of different types of passive income exist. Among them are movie, music, book, screenplay, television, and patent royalties. Other samples of passive income include click through income, rental income, and revenue from online advertising.

Activities that lead to passive income have something in common. They usually need a great amount of money, time, or both invested in them upfront to get them started. There are financial means to establishing passive income as well. You could purchase a rental property or choose to invest in a partnership or other form of company where you are a silent partner. The income that you derive from these investment activities is deemed to be passive.

Various other kinds of passive income do not need a great deal of financial investment made in them, but instead require great amounts of effort, time, and even creativity to achieve. More than a year can be required to either build up a popular website that can contribute passive income from advertising or to write a great novel. Making money from such passive income that is actually profit may take longer.

Books are a good example of how long it can take to actually make money from passive income. Publishers generally get to recover all of their printing and promoting costs, as well as any advance monies given to authors, before royalties are created and paid. Books that sell poorly could turn out to pay the author little to nothing.

Websites have a different set of challenges for their creators. There has to be more than simply good content to make money from them. They must similarly rank high in the search engine results for the necessary amount of visitors to find and go to the website. Unless a great number of visitor hits are recorded on a website, the passive income that is generated will be negligible or even none.

People are willing to put in such a huge amount of time with little assurance of results because they know that the passive income generating activity will create money for them around the clock for years to come, if it is successful. This means that passive income money is constantly being made, even when the person is asleep or on vacation. If you are able to get one passive income project up and running well, then you can attempt others. This way, you might hope to develop a few different income streams that result in a significant annual revenue which can even support you.

Many investors believe that passive income is the most superior kind that you can achieve. This is why rental properties can be so popular. Even though they can require a significant amount of maintenance work and tenant management, they can provide substantial income once several such properties are owned and made profitable.

Personal Assets

Personal assets are items of value that belong to an individual. There are many examples of such tangible personal assets. Among these are houses, real estate, cars, and jewelry. Personal assets can also be any other thing with cash value.

When individuals go to a bank or other institution to apply for loans, such personal assets and their values are often considered. These assets are also the bedrock of the formula for net worth for consumers. The value of people's personal assets can be higher than they expect and surprise them as so many different items can be included under this label.

There are many personal assets that are material and easy to measure. These include such financial assets as savings accounts, checking accounts, and retirement accounts. Assets that have a value that can not be easily accessed are also included in the personal assets category. This includes life insurance policies and annuities that have cash values. Other items of value which would be included in a list of personal assets cover such items as antiques, art collections, electronics, personally owned businesses, and other valuable items.

Personal assets can do more than simply help people get loans and count towards net worth. They are also sometimes able to create income for their owners. Bank accounts and savings accounts accrue interest. Holders of real estate are able to lease or rent it out. This brings in rent or lease fees. Individuals who have personal assets should educate themselves in the best practices for managing them so that they are able to increase their total wealth by generating the highest income possible from them.

It is important to keep a careful track of rent or other income obtained from personal assets as the money will be taxable. Income that is not properly reported to the government on the correct tax forms can incur penalties from the Internal Revenue Service.

It is also important to know the value of an individual's personal assets. There are two different methods of learning this. In the first method, individuals examine the item's market value. This is the value for which the asset would sell if a person were to put it straight on the market. Another way to determine the value of these assets is to have a personal asset appraised.

Appraised values can be substantially greater than market values. This is because an appraisal value relies on the possible future price of the item in question. This difference matter significantly, particularly when having an item insured. Individuals generally have to obtain appraised value insurance coverage. This means that they will likely have to pay for a greater amount of insurance.

When properly managed, personal assets can greatly contribute to an individual's personal financial situation. It is also true that these assets can prove to be a liability if they are not well taken care of or managed. Part of managing assets well involves asset allocation.

Financial experts warn against placing all or the majority of personal assets into a single asset type or location. This type of practice causes people to take on additional risk than is prudent. Instead, it is better to spread around an individual's wealth into a variety of different assets so that if one suffers or decreases in value, some of the other assets may offset this by outperforming or increasing in value.

Taking care of personal assets is also an important part of maintaining their value. Individuals can break expensive electronics if they are not careful. Not engaging in proper maintenance for works of art can also lead to their value declining over time.

Portfolio

In the world of business and finance, a portfolio stands for an investment collection that a person or institution holds. People and other entities put together portfolios in order to diversify their holdings to reduce risk to a manageable level. A number of different kinds of risk are mitigated through the acquisition of a few varying types of assets. A portfolio's assets might be comprised of stocks, options, bonds, bank accounts, gold certificates, warrants, futures contracts, real estate, facilities of production, and other assets that tend to hold their value.

Investment portfolios may be constructed in various ways. Financial entities will commonly do their own careful analysis of investments in putting together a portfolio. Individuals might work with the either financial firms or financial advisors that manage portfolios. Alternatively, they could put together a self directed portfolio through working with a self directed online broker such as TD Ameritrade, eTrade, or Scott Trade.

A whole field of portfolio management has arisen to help with the allocation of investment money. This management pertains to determining the types of assets that are appropriate for an individual's risk tolerance and ultimate goals. Choosing the instruments that will comprise a portfolio has much to do with knowing the kinds of instruments to buy and sell, how many of each to obtain, and the time that is most appropriate to purchase or sell them.

Such decisions are rooted in a measurement for the investments' performance. This usually pertains to risk versus return on investments and anticipated returns of the entire portfolio. With portfolio returns, various types of assets are understood to commonly return amounts of differing ranges. Portfolio management has to factor in an individual investor's own precise situation and desired results as well. There are investors who are more fearful of risk than are other investors. These kinds of investors are termed risk averse. Risk averse portfolios are significantly different in their composition than are typical portfolios.

Mutual funds have evolved the act of portfolio management almost to a science. Their fund managers came up with techniques that allow them to prioritize and ideally set their portfolio holdings. This fund management reduces risk and increases returns to maximum levels. Strategies that these managers have created for running portfolios include designing equally weighted portfolios, price weighted portfolios, capitalization weighted portfolios, and optimal portfolios in which the risk adjusted return proves to be the highest possible.

Well diversified portfolios will contain many different asset classes. These will include far more than just stocks, bonds, and mutual funds. They will feature international stocks and bonds to provide diversification away from the U.S. dollar, as well as foreign currencies and hard asset commodities such as real estate investments, and gold and silver holdings.

Power of Attorney

A power of attorney is an agreement in writing that grants another individual the authority to make some choices if the grantor is not available. This person who receives the power does not have to be an attorney. Attorneys are typically only involved in drafting up or potentially witnessing such an agreement. The phrase comes from an individual receiving status as an agent or attorney in fact.

When people implement such a power of attorney they do not lose the ability to make their own decisions. Instead they are allowing another individual to act for them in matters specified within the written text. This can be very helpful if people are out of the country or in the hospital as an example. Someone else with this authority would be able to cash checks at the bank or pay bills on their behalf. It is simply a matter of sharing power with another person. The agent is only carrying out the grantor's wishes, not actually making choices for them, so long as they are coherent and mentally capable.

People who will be out of town for an extended period of time might find these arrangements particularly useful. With a power of attorney, the agent could carry out major decisions such as selling cars or other personal assets. The Internet has eliminated the need for some of these functions as computers and mobile devices make it possible for people to buy and sell stocks and handle many financial transactions from anywhere they have an online connection. There are still cases where a transaction will require an in person agent to handle them.

There is also a special kind of power of attorney that is used by individuals who lose their ability to handle decisions for their personal financial affairs. This is known as a durable power of attorney. In this case, the word durable refers to the ability of the agent to make the choices on the grantor's behalf when he or she can not mentally do them. This type of arrangement grants the agent the legal authority and responsibility to make the best possible physical and financial decisions for the grantor.

It means that the agent is able to spend the individual's money as appropriate, cash checks, deposit checks, and even withdraw money from the personal bank accounts. The agent further gains the authority to sign contracts, sell personal property, take legal actions, and file and follow up on insurance claims.

When people decide to enter a durable power of attorney arrangement, a notary public or lawyer should witness the document before they sign and execute it. If such individuals need to have a durable agreement established and are not mentally able to do it, courts can do this for them as they deem necessary.

Agents who become appointed to this position are expected to keep correct and segregated records on each transaction they perform. The records must also be easily available at all times. When the individual dies, his or her power of attorney becomes null and void. The will is responsible for the dispensation of the deceased person's estate.

Powers of attorney can be rescinded. If individuals feel unhappy in the ways that their agent is managing their personal affairs, they can simply revoke the authority back at any point. It is always wise for people to choose an individual to be agent whom they know and implicitly trust.

Prime Rate

The Prime Rate is the most typically utilized shorter term interest rate for the United State banking system. All kinds of lending institutions in the United States employ this U.S. benchmark interest rate as a basis or index rate to price their medium term to short term loans and products. This includes credit unions, thrifts, savings and loans, and commercial banks.

This makes the Prime Rate consistent around the country as banks strive to be competitive and profitable in their lending rates which they provide to both consumers and businesses. A universal rate like this simplifies the task for businesses and consumers as they shop around comparable loan products that competing banks offer. Every state in the country does not maintain its own benchmark rate. This makes a California Prime or New York Prime identical to the U.S. Prime.

Commercial and other banks charge this benchmark rate to their best customers. These are those clients who have the best credit ratings and loan history with the bank. Most of the time banks' best clients are made up of large companies.

The prime interest rate is also known as the prime lending rate. Banks typically base it on the Federal Reserve's federal funds rate. This is actually the rate that banks loan money to each other for overnight purposes. Retail customers also need to be aware of the prime lending rate. It directly impacts the lending rates that they can access for personal and small business loans as well as for home mortgages.

The federal government and Federal Reserve Bank do not set the prime lending rates. The individual banks set it. They then utilize this base rate or reference rate to set the prices for a great number of loans such as credit card loans and small business loans.

The Federal Reserve Board releases a statistics called "Selected Interest Rates." This is their survey of the prime interest rate as the majority of the twenty-five biggest banks set it. It is this publication which reveals the Prime Rate periodically. This is why the Federal Reserve does not directly set this important benchmark rate. The banks more or less base it on the target level of the federal funds rate that the Federal Open Market Committee sets and changes at their monthly meetings.

Different banks adjust their prime lending rate at the same time. The point where they change it is generally when the Federal Open Market Committee adjusts their own important Fed Funds Rate. Many publications refer to this periodically changing reference rate as the Wall Street Prime Rate.

A great number of consumer loans as well as commercial loans and credit card rates find their basis in the prime lending rate. Among these are car loans, home equity loans, personal and home lines of credit, and various kinds of personal loans.

The rates above the prime lending rate that banks charge their less then prime (or subprime) customers depend on the credit worthiness of the borrower in question. The banks attempt to correctly ascertain the risk of default for the borrower. For the best credit customers who have lower chances of defaulting, banks can afford to assess them a lower interest rate than others. Customers with higher chances of defaulting on their loans pay larger interest rates because of the risk associated with their loans not being repaid.

As of June 15, 2016, the Federal Open Market Committee voted to maintain its target fed funds rate in a range of from .25% to .5%. As a result of this, the U.S. prime lending rate stayed at 3.5%. Once per month the Federal Reserve committee meets to determine if they will change the fed funds rate.

Private Mortgage Insurance (PMI)

PMI is the acronym for Private Mortgage Insurance, also known sometimes as Lenders Mortgage Insurance. PMI proves to be insurance that is paid to a lending institution that is required much of the time when an individual gets a mortgage loan. Such insurance is used to cover any losses that arise if a person is not capable of paying back their mortgage loan.

Should the lender not be able to recoup all of its costs in foreclosing on and selling the mortgaged property, then PMI insurance covers the remaining losses that exist on the balance sheet of the bank or other lender. The general rates for this Private Mortgage Insurance turn out to be around $55 each month for every $100,000 that is actually financed. On a $250,000 loan, this amounts to $1,875 each year in premiums.

Private Mortgage insurance yearly costs range though. They are usually given out in comparison against the entire loan's value. This depends on a number of factors, such as loan type, loan term, actual coverage amount, amount of home value that the person finances, the premium payment frequency that might be monthly or yearly, and the individual's credit score. While PMI can be paid in advance with closing costs, it can also be worked into the loan payments with single premium PMI.

Private Mortgage Insurance is generally only necessary when the down payment proves to be smaller than twenty percent of either the appraised value of the property or alternatively of the sales price. When then loan to value ratio is greater than eighty percent, you can expect to be required to carry it. As the principal is reduced with monthly payments, or the home value rises through real estate appreciation, or a combination of the two occurs, then this Private Mortgage Insurance might not be required any longer. At this point, the home owner is allowed to discontinue paying for the PMI insurance.

There are some banks and lenders who will insist that PMI be paid for minimally for a pre fixed period of time, such as two to three years. This is regardless of whether the principal value of the property exceeds eighty percent in a shorter amount of time. Banks do not have to permit a person to cancel this insurance legally until the loan has amortized down to a Loan to Value ratio of seventy-eight percent of the original price for which the house is purchased.

A cancellation request must originate from the mortgage servicer. They must send it to the issuing company that made the PMI policy in the first place. Many times, such a mortgage servicer will insist on a current home value appraisal being done in order to ascertain the actual loan to value ratio.

Premiums paid for mortgage insurance were not tax deductible according to the Internal Revenue Service in the past. In 2007 this changed. Now all PMI premiums are considered to be fully reducing of your income for the year in question.

Promissory Note

Promissory notes are negotiable instruments that are called notes payable in accounting circles. In such promissory notes, an issuer writes an unlimited promise that he or she will pay a certain amount of money to the payee. This can be set up either on demand of the payee, or at a pre arranged future point in time. Specific terms are always arranged for the repayment of the debt in the promissory note.

Promissory notes are somewhat like IOU's and yet quite different. Unlike an IOU that only agrees that there is a debt in question, promissory notes are made up of a particular promise to pay the debt. In conversational vernacular, loan contract, loan agreement, or loan are often utilized in place of promissory note, even though such terms do not mean the same things legally. While a promissory note does provide proof of a loan in existence, it is not the loan contract. A loan contract instead has all of the conditions and terms of the particular loan arrangement within it.

Promissory notes contain a variety of term elements in them. Among these are the amount of principal, the rate of interest, the parties involved, the repayment terms, the date, and the date of maturity. From time to time, provisions may be included pertaining to the payee's rights should the issuer default. These rights could include the ability to foreclose on the issuer's assets.

A particular type of promissory note is a Demand Promissory note. This specific kind does not come with an exact date of maturity. Instead, it is due when the lender demands repayment. Generally, in these cases lenders only allow several days advance notice before the payment must be made.

Within the U.S., the Article 3 of the Uniform Commercial Code regulates most promissory notes. These negotiable forms of promissory notes are heavily used along with other documents in mortgages that involve financing purchases of real estate properties. When people make loans in between each other, the making and signing of promissory notes are commonly critical for the purposes of record keeping and paying taxes. Businesses also receive capital via the use of promissory notes that are sometimes referred to as commercial papers. These promissory notes became a finance source for the creditors of the firm receiving money.

Promissory notes have functioned like currency that proved to be privately issued in the past. Because of this, such promissory notes that are bearer negotiable have mostly been made illegal, since they represent an alternative to the officially sanctioned currency. Promissory notes go back to well before the 1500's in Western Europe. Tradition claims that the very first one ever signed existed in Milan in 1325. Reference is made to some being issued between Barcelona and Genoa back in 1384, even though we no longer have the promissory notes themselves. The first one that we still have dates back to 1553 where Ginaldo Giovanni Battista Stroxxi issued one that he created in Medina del Campo, Spain against the city of Besancon.

Rabobank

Rabobank refers to the Dutch banking giant whose full name is the Coöperatieve Rabobank. This Dutch international banking giant is a full-scale financial services organization whose headquarters today lies in the city of Utrecht in the Netherlands. The banking group is a world leader for agriculture and food production financing as well as in banking based on sustainability. Their motto is "as large as necessary, as small as possible."

The group Rabobank is a unique form of banking organization and structure in many ways. It is made up of 120 fully independent local Rabobanks in the Netherlands as of 2013. These banks actually own the parent central organization called Rabobank Nederland. They also operate a significant number of subsidiaries and specialized international operations and offices. The main international concentration of the Rabobank Group proves to be agribusiness and food-related.

By their assets, this bank remains the second biggest Dutch bank. When measured by their Tier 1 Capital, the bank proves to be in the top 30 biggest financial institutions on earth. Current as of December 2014, their aggregate assets equaled 681 billion (Euros) while they claimed a net profit amount of 1.8 billion. The banking and finance industry publication Global Finance ranks Rabobank at an impressive number 25 for "world's safest banks."

The bank's historical and current day roots remain in agriculture. As a confederation of local credit union banks which deliver banking and financial services to their local markets, the company operates on a bottom up model which is most unusual in banking. This means that the central organization and all of its countless subsidiaries and international offices throughout the world are a huge subsidiary of the local Dutch branches. With the overwhelming majority of commercial banks in the world today, the central organization proves to be the owning parent entity.

The roots of the bank came from the founder of the credit union cooperative movement Friedrich Wilhelm Raiffeisen, whose name is today immortalized in the enormous central and Eastern European, Austrian-based Raiffeisen Bank. He was the one who started the original farmers' bank within Germany. The local countryside town mayor was aghast at the dire poverty he saw in the local farmers, their families, and communities. Though he attempted to deliver charity to alleviate their suffering, he soon discovered that helping them to be more self-reliant would yield better results over the long term. He did this by establishing his farmers' banks which gathered up the countryside residents' savings in order to offer them out as loans to enterprising farmers who needed capital to expand. Among his early followers was Father Gerlacus van den Elsen. He founded and inspired many of the local farmers' banks throughout the south of the Netherlands.

The bank had traditional dual headquarters in both Utrecht and Eindhoven. It was in the year 1898 that two different cooperative banking conglomerates formed as the Utrecht- based Coöperatieve Centrale Raiffeisen-Bank and the Eindhoven-based Coöperatieve Centrale Boerenleenbank. The former proved to be a co-op of six different area banks, while the latter existed when 22 local banks formed their co-op. Even though the two banks were largely the same, they still operated as separate competitors alongside one another for around 75 years. It was ironically the differing Christian religious bents of the two banks that kept them apart for so long. While the Eindhoven co-op was strongly Catholic, the Utrecht based Raiffeisen-Bank had Protestant roots. It explained why the Catholic based-bank was heavily centralized while the Protestant-based bank encouraged local autonomy of its branches.

The two were cooperating by 1940 and merged together in 1972 as Rabobank. The name changed to Rabobank Nederland in 1980. Overseas expansion came through many acquisitions in farming-oriented countries. They bought Primary Industry Bank of Australia in 1994 and reformed this as Rabobank Australia Limited by 2003. In 1997 they acquired Wrightson Farmers Finance Limited of New Zealand and converted this in 1999 to Rabobank New Zealand. They entered Indonesia decisively with the buyout of Bank Haga and Bank Hagakita. In 2011 and 2012, they opened online banks in Poland and then Germany. A savings business in Ireland followed. They also expanded into the Western U.S. with the purchase of Mid-State Bank & Trust in 2007 and Pacific State Bank in 2010.

Real Estate

Real estate turns out to be a phrase that is used legally to describe property and the structures on such property. It refers to the land and the residential, commercial, or industrial structures on the land. Other improvements to the property can also be covered by the term, such as wells, fences, and other immobile objects fixed on the property. The natural features of the property are also included in the phrase, like lakes, streams, and trees. Real estate can be natural land, residential property, commercial property, and even industrial property.

Real Estate is governed by real estate law. This represents the legal codes and regulations that have to do with real estate in a given jurisdiction. It covers such elements as the specifics of transactions of residential and commercial real estate. Real estate attorneys practice this form of law.

Realtors are the principal professionals who work in the field of selling real estate. Realty is the term that pertains to realtors and their firms. Real estate and realty companies are often equated with real property. This stands in contrast to personal property and personal property law.

As real estate property has developed and become more complex, it has evolved into an important part of business. This is referred to as commercial real estate. Commercial real estate can be buildings and office spaces used by businesses. Buying real estate is an expensive proposition requiring large investments. As every type and zoning of land has its own characteristics, the real estate industry has developed into a variety of different fields. There are people who specialize in valuing different kinds of real estate and helping the transactions to come together.

Many different types of real estate related businesses have developed as a result. Brokers are third parties who collect a fee in exchange for mediating real estate transactions between two different entities or individuals. Appraisers perform professional level evaluations of properties. Developers improve a land's value, typically by building or rebuilding structures on it.

Property managers handle the management of a given property on behalf of the owner. Real estate investors handle real estate investments. Real estate marketers handle the promotion and sales aspects of any property business. Corporate real estate people deal with the real estate portfolios of a company in support of its main businesses. Relocation servicers function to move businesses or individuals to a different part of the country or internationally from one real estate property to another.

The different types of real estate involve specialists in the various branches of real estate. In each of the different fields, real estate businesses commonly focus on a single type of real estate. This might be residential realty, commercial property realty, or industrial property realty. Construction businesses are involved significantly with sometimes either one branch, or sometimes even two or all three branches of real estate. They develop and build real estate to an end user's specifications.

Real Estate Appraisal

Real estate appraisal refers to the procedure where an expert real estate appraiser creates a professional opinion on the value of a house, land, or other real property. It is also called land valuation and property valuation. The value the appraiser comes up with is typically the market value for the house or land in question. Many times real estate purchases and sales need an expert to perform an appraisal since they do not otherwise happen very often. Besides this, each property is totally unique, as is there location and condition.

Properties can not change their location, however they may benefit from improvements and upgrades. Real estate appraisal takes such modifications into consideration when formulating a value. The resulting appraisal report is what they produce in the end. Such reports prove to be the underlying basis for mortgage and property loans, some forms of taxes, divorce and estate settlements, and other important legal and financial transactions. Appraisal reports can even be (and often are) utilized to set the property's ultimate sale price.

The majority of countries mandate that their professionals who perform real estate appraisals must be certified, licensed, or both. These appraisers have a number of titles in different nations and jurisdictions, including "land valuers" and "property valuers." British English calls them "valuation surveyors." Real estate appraisals within the U.S. report on Uniform Residential Appraisal Reports. For those appraisals of commercial properties such as land or income producing ones, Certified General Appraisers complete and report these in a running narrative version.

Real estate appraisals can produce a few different kinds of value. The most typical of these are the market value, investment value, use value, insurable value, and liquidation value. Market value is also called fair value or open market value. It is the approximate amount at which the real estate should change hands between willing sellers and buyers on a given valuation date in an official and legally binding transaction.

Investment value is the value of the property in question for a certain investor. This could be or might not be greater than the market value for the house, land, or commercial property. It is the difference between the market value and investment value that offers an incentive for people to buy or sell their property in the first place.

Use value refers to the NPV or net present value for cash flow of the asset. This is the revenue it creates from a particular use for the specific owner. It could be higher or lower than the given home or property's market value.

Insurable value will be the one that relates to the insurance policy coverage on a given piece of real property such as a house or commercial office building. This will typically not include any site value for the land and/or location. It is also a form of replacement cost value.

Liquidation value relates to the price of a property typically when it is sold during bankruptcy proceedings. It might be determined as either a part of an orderly liquidation or a forced liquidation. The price will reflect the fact that the seller is made to sell the property in a shorter than typical market time frame. This means that the liquidation value on a given house, building, or piece of land is commonly lower than the market value. At times it can be substantially lower because of the desperate circumstances which warrant a near-immediate sale. This gives rise to the phrase a "fire sale" of property or assets.

It is worth noting that there are often significant differences in the relevant market value and purchase price. Sometimes buyers are able to obtain the property for less than the market value. This could be because of a personal connection between the buyer and seller or other mitigating factors. When the price given for a property is not the fair market value as shown by the real estate appraisal, then this value is referred to as the market price.

Real Estate Bubble

A Real Estate bubble occurs as housing prices rise because of increased speculation, actual legitimate demand, and irrational exuberance all working in concert. These bubbles generally begin because of a legitimate rise in demand for housing and Real Estate at the same time as the housing supply is quite limited.

Because of this limit in supplies, it needs quite a significant amount of time in order for the available housing stock to be replenished and grow. In such a climate, speculators appear on the market and begin to really encourage demand. Finally, demand will stagnate and even decrease as the supply is finally increasing to catch up to the prior demand. This results in a catastrophic bursting of the bubble in the form of disorderly, rapid, and sharply decreasing prices that finally become a self-fulfilling prophecy.

In the past, housing markets did not suffer as often from such bubble phenomenon as did other kinds of financial markets like stocks and bonds. This was because the carrying costs and purchasing prices of homes are significant barriers to investment entry for smaller and medium sized investors. Thanks in large part to historically low interest rates and an unfathomable loosening of credit standards, borrowers were able to enter the market in record demand and drive massive orders for houses. Conversely, raising interest rates and tightening up on standards for credit reduces demand effectively, which leads to the Real Estate bubble bursting quickly.

These Real Estate bubbles are also referred to commonly as housing bubbles or property market bubbles. These economic bubbles can inflate either in worldwide real estate markets or only on small local markets. They generally come after the buildup of a land boom. Land booms prove to be the quick growth in market price of houses and land to the point when they attain levels which are ultimately unsustainable and then lead to a sharp decline in said bubble.

The financial crisis and Great Recession of 2007-2009 evolved out of the Real Estate bubble bursting that had inflated from the early 2000s in all major countries of the world. It took years for this bubble to rise as investors abandoned the global stock markets in record numbers following the bursting of the dotcom bubble and resulting 2000 stock market crash. They poured their capital instead into real estate and house properties during the following six years. The craze which surrounded homeownership rose to frightening levels while interest rates were crashing and responsible lending underwriting all but disappeared.

Analysts have estimated as many as 56% of all house purchases in those six years came from individuals who could not have afforded to buy a house under traditional lending requirements. These people became known as the infamous and economy-wrecking subprime borrowers. The overwhelming majority of such loans were issued as adjustable rate mortgages, or ARMs, that carried an upfront lower interest rate with a punishing schedule set to adjust the prevailing interest rate massively upward after from three to five years passed.

The government was much to blame for the irresponsible encouragement of universal homeownership which they pressed banks to allow in those years. Banks responded to the directives by slashing their interest rates and tough requirements. This encouraged a home purchasing bonanza that had not been witnessed in American history heretofore. Prices increased by as much as from 50 percent to 100 percent in various parts of the nation. The bubble sucked in financial speculators who started flipping houses in order to earn even tens of thousands of dollars of profits with only two weeks of holding such properties. Analysts have further estimated after the fact that fully 30 percent of the housing prices were based on purely speculative endeavors from the zenith of the Real Estate bubble in 2005 to 2007.

As the interest rates began to gradually rise while stocks finally rebounded, adjustable rate mortgages started resetting at massively higher interest rates in a show that the economy was beginning to slow down by 2007. Home prices already sat at impossible to justify and sustain levels and the risk premium had finally risen to be too high for the speculators who suddenly ceased buying houses without warning.

Home prices started to plummet after home buyers realized that the prices could in fact drop. This led to an enormous sell off in the associated and now-infamous mortgage backed securities, or MBS market. The home prices finally dropped by over 40 percent in parts of the country that had been the most overheated, like Florida, Nevada, Arizona, Colorado, and California. This led to incredible default rates on mortgages that caused as many as tens of millions of homes to be foreclosed upon by the banks in the following several years.

Real Estate Investment Trusts (REIT)

Real Estate Investment Trusts are also known as REITs. These turn out to be investment companies which finance or outright own real estate that produces income. REITs were created along the model of mutual funds. They give all levels of investors the access to the benefits that real estate typically provides.

This includes diversification, income streams, and capital appreciation longer term. Usually these REITs pay their investors 100% of their taxable income in the form of dividends. The shareholders are responsible for paying taxes on the dividends as income tax.

The beauty of Real Estate Investment Trusts lies in the ability for any investor to participate in major properties. They are able to do this by buying shares of stock to become involved as they would with any other industry Just as a shareholder obtains benefits through stock ownership in companies, the stock holders in a REIT gain a percentage of the income that the underlying real estate produces. They do not have to locate, purchase, or finance any of the properties in the process.

The majority of Real Estate Investment Trusts trade on the bigger stock exchanges. Despite this, some of them are privately held or public companies that are not exchange listed. With these REITs there are two principle types, Mortgage and Equity REITs.

The mortgage REITs buy mortgage instruments or outright mortgages that are connected to residential or commercial properties. The Equity REITs produce their income by collecting rent from and selling properties they hold over longer time frames.

Real Estate Investment Trusts have expanded into practically every part of the economy today. There are REITs connected to timberlands, student housing, storage centers, shopping malls, company offices, nursing homes, infrastructure projects, industrial facilities, hotels and resorts, hospitals, and apartments. Every state in the United States has properties which are owned by REITs. Ernest and Young has funded a study that shows REITs provide for around 1.8 million jobs in the United States every year.

These American REITs have become so successful that they are now a model for other countries. Over 30 nations throughout the globe have approved legislation that allows the Real Estate Investment Trust.

Real Estate Investment Trusts offer diversification that does not correspond to the overall stock market and its performance measured longer term. Their dividends give investors a reliable stream of income. They are so liquid because these stock exchange based ones may be simply and quickly purchased and sold.

Their performance is standout. REITs which are publically listed and traded have outperformed the Dow Jones Industrial Average, the S&P 500, and the NASDAQ Composite when measured over the longer term. Like publically traded companies, they offer the transparency and oversight of quarterly financial reporting and commonplace regulatory standards.

There are many qualifications a company must meet to be considered a Real Estate Investment Trust. They have to place minimally 75% of all assets they possess into real estate. They also must obtain 75% or more of their gross income from sales of real estate, rents on property, or interest on mortgage holdings that finance property. These companies have to pay out a minimum of 90 % of their taxable income as dividends to shareholders every year.

The prospective REIT must have the status of corporation that is taxable. It must also have either trustees or a board of directors that manage it. They can not have over 50% of their entity shares owned by less than six individuals. The REITs also must possess at least 100 different shareholders.

Refinance

When the word refinance is used, it is referring to the act of refinancing, or canceling out a currently existing debt with another debt that a bank or refinance company issues under alternative terms. By far and away the most popular refinancing that pertains to consumers is for mortgages on houses. Debt replacements that are performed in conditions of financial distress are also known as debt restructuring.

Home owners might choose to refinance their mortgage for a variety of reasons. It can assist them in meeting a range of end goals. You as a home owner might be interested in lowering your monthly payments on the mortgage through attaining a better interest rate or lengthening the terms of the loan.

You could lessen the amount of interest that you pay during the loan's term and expand the equity build up by going through a refinance to get a loan with a shorter life. You could also decrease your exposure to the risk of rising interest rates through obtaining a fixed term loan in place of a balloon mortgage or adjustable rate mortgage. Finally, you might be interested in drawing out home equity in order to do debt consolidation or to cover the costs of major expenses that you are encountering elsewhere.

The act of refinancing eliminates the original mortgage loan. This is then replaced with a new loan. There are many factors that you will have to decide in obtaining this new loan. This includes what type of loan is most ideal for the circumstances, which lender you will utilize, which term and rate are most advantageous, and the fees that you feel are reasonable. Because of these complicated decisions that must be made, consumers should seek out advice in their refinancing. If you do not possess a clear comprehension of all that is involved with the refinancing procedure, then you could accidentally put your house or your finances in danger.

There are risks associated with refinancing. These are principally penalty clauses that are also known as call provisions. When you pay off a mortgage loan early, these penalties would be triggered along with closing fees. The refinancing itself will entail transaction fees. All of these fees should be figured up and considered before you begin a project to refinance your home loan. This is especially the case since all of the fees together may eliminate any potential savings that you hoped to realize through the refinancing.

Another possible downside to refinancing loans is that they may provide you with lower payments every month on the same amount of money to be repaid. In this case, you will pay a greater amount of interest throughout the loan term. You would also pay on the debt for a great number of additional years over the original mortgage's terms. This is why it is so important to determine not only the upfront charges, but also the variable and ongoing costs involved in refinancing as a factor in the decision on whether to pursue it or not.

Refinancing Boom

A refinancing boom refers to the points in the market where the share of the refinance mortgage applications is greater than 50% of the total applications. This is the definition that home lending agency giant Freddie Mac employs. They determine both the start and the end of ref booms based on this 50% of MBA's survey figure for the weekly applications. This information provides data for both government and nonconforming loans alongside the traditional loans making it a good all inclusive basis.

Under this Freddie definition, the refinancing boom began in 2008 in the third quarter. It lasted almost six years into 2014. This made it the longest lasting refi boom since Freddie Mac began issuing its quarterly report on refinance activity back in 1990. It was actually during the week of May 2nd that the share of refi applications declined under 50%.

The week before this gave a warning that volume would drop below that critical level as total application volume reached its lowest level since December in 2000. Even though refi applications rose above 50% the following week May 9th, this still represented a break in the statistics that Freddie Mac utilizes. This explains why they described the end of the long lasting refi boom in May of 2014.

Because of this it is not easy to concretely define when these refi booms start and finish as the market share of loan volume that is refinancing can fluctuate. Besides this overall mortgage activity volume can be down in total, and yet the market still can be called a refi boom if the refi percentages exceed 50%. This is why there are other competing definitions of what constitutes a refi boom.

Another popular rival definition that has gained some traction on defining refi booms has to do with the volume of overall originations. When the all around origination volume rises on a year over year basis and this happens because of a boom in refinance activity, this better signifies that a refi boom is underway. This can still be somewhat misleading. There could be a seemingly greater number of refinance applications at a given time if home sales are less than impressive. This would lead to a decline in mortgage purchase applications.

Despite these alternative definitions, Freddie Mac continues to use the one it pioneered on refi booms. According to this traditional definition of the booms, Freddie Mac called the end to the longest refinance boom in history during 2014 in the second quarter. This happened in part because the market shifted to one that was dominated by purchases that exceeded 50% of total applications for the first time since the year 2000.

Freddie Mac compiled interesting statistics on this longest refi boom in American history. They saw more than 25 million different American homeowners engage in refinancing their mortgages during the boom. This equated to the total savings in interest payments of more than $70 billion.

A number of industry observers felt that the refi boom actually ended a year earlier than Freddie Mac's official call. Many watchers claimed that cooling of refinance and origination loan activity in 2013 in the spring signaled the end of the refi boom. By that point the market had already taken hits to refinance applications and activity because of the quick increase in the mortgage interest rates.

The higher interest rates removed the incentive for homeowners to continue refinancing their mortgages. This is why many economists called the end of the refi boom a full year before Freddie Mac did.

Repayment Penalty

A repayment penalty is commonly associated with paying back a loan before the end of its term. If you are contemplating paying off your loan balance in advance of its due date, then you should be aware that a number of loans come with these repayment penalties for liquidating the balance early. Different types of loans utilize different names for these same fees. Repayment penalties can also be called redemption charges, early redemption fees, prepayment penalties, or financial penalties.

The fees associated with repayment penalties vary depending on the loan in question. These repayment penalties are commonly stated as a percentage of the balance that is outstanding when prepayment is offered. Alternatively, they might be figured up as a certain number of months of interest charges. In general, when they are figured up using months of interest, they are comprised of one to two months' interest in fees. The sooner in the loan's life that you choose to repay the loan, the greater amount of charge you can expect to pay. This is because the anticipated interest portion of the loan comprises a great part of the repayment earlier in the loan's time frame. Early repayment penalties might increase the total cost of your loan significantly.

If you wish to avoid a repayment penalty in paying off your loan in advance of the term's end, then you will have to be aware of the loans that come with these fees and the ones that do not. Even if you change a currently existing loan into a loan for debt consolidation, you will have to cover the early repayment penalty if one is in the terms. The only way to avoid early repayment penalties is by selecting loans that specifically do not have ones attached to them. It is ironic that some of the least expensive loans out there do not include repayment penalties for early pay off actions.

Another factor of repayment penalties involves a gradual disappearance of the provision over time. With many mortgages, these repayment penalties gradually go down over the years of the mortgage. After the fifth year, the majority of repayment penalties no longer even apply. In many cases, repayments of as much as twenty percent of the original balance are permitted in a given year without you having to be penalized.

Besides this, there are different kinds of penalties for repayments. Penalties that only apply to your refinancing of the mortgage are called soft penalties. Penalties that include the sale of the house and a refinancing are known as hard penalties.

Repayment Split

A repayment split refers to the ways that payments are allocated on a split mortgage. These repayment splits might allow you to take out a mortgage where part of the loan is a fixed rate loan, while the remainder of the loan is a variable rate, set against a tracking rate for the life of the loan. Home buying borrowers are able to fix their rate at twenty-five percent, fifty percent, or even seventy-five percent of the total mortgage amount. The balance of the loan then tracks a certain rate, like the Prime Rate or Bank of England base rate alongside the fixed part of the loan.

The interest rate charged varies along with the percentage of the mortgage balance that is at a fixed rate. For example, with only twenty-five percent of the home loan balance fixed, the fixed part of the rate might amount to 3.49% interest. If the split is done at a fifty percent rate of split, then the interest rate might instead be at 3.69% on the fixed rate. With seventy-five percent of the mortgage total fixed, the interest rate on the fixed portion could come in at 3.99% instead. These sample rates assume a loan to value ratio of only seventy percent, meaning that a thirty percent down payment would be expected. With only a twenty percent down payment made, the rates would likely be a half percentage point higher. The interest rate on the balance of the loan total is variable and is adjusted periodically. The repayment split then determines which portion of the payments applies to which interest rate balance. This form of repayment split and split mortgage is most commonly seen in Great Britain.

A second way that repayment splits are used has to do with split mortgages that involve first and second mortgages. This split mortgage technique is commonly used in America to reduce the amount of the principal mortgage to no more than eighty percent of the purchase price so that Private Mortgage Insurance will not be required. With this technique, a second mortgage or home equity line of credit to the amount of five to ten percent of the home purchase price is used to come up with enough cash to keep the first mortgage to eighty percent or less. In this version of the split mortgage, the repayment split refers to which portion of the payments goes against the first mortgage and which against the second mortgage.

Residual

Residual refers to residual income. Residual income can have several different meanings depending on the context that you use. For an individual, residual income proves to be the money that remains at the end of a month after all financial responsibilities for the month are covered.

These include living costs, taxes, and housing costs. Where business is concerned, residual incomes are the operating income that is additional as compared to the typical minimum amount of operating assets that are controlled. Residual income furthermore refers to passive income that is earned. In this form of the term, it relates to all income that is created as a result of activities that are indirect. These might include royalties, rental income, investment portfolio returns, website revenues, or passively managed businesses, all of which qualify as residual income.

The word residual is a variation on the word residue. Residue means anything that stays behind because of some other substance or cause. So, residual income proves to be additional money made because of another activity like penning a novel and collecting royalties for the sale of every book.

Rental incomes are residual as they remain from the action of buying a house and then renting it to a tenant who pays you a monthly rental fee. Work is involved in this activity, although a property management company can do it on your behalf. The rewards for this rental project can be significant, as you enjoy the continuous rental stream as well as any increases in the value of the real estate property underlying it. Rental income can be utilized to pay for potentially an entire mortgage.

Income from investment portfolios is similarly considered to be residual income. Both dividends and interest are acquired as an additional, passive benefit of possessing stocks, bonds, mutual funds, and other instruments. This residual income is not guaranteed from these investments, but it is common for investors.

A form of residual income that is growing in popularity these days is website, or Internet based, revenues. Internet revenues are commonly those that you make from having advertising on a given website. The dollar value of the advertising is mostly based on the number of visitors to the page. A significant amount of start up work is required to create the website and get it highly ranked on the major search engines. After this, you can see continuous monthly profits that you earn as a result of the advertising, which builds up a residual income. This amount of money could be as little as a few dollars a month to possibly thousands of dollars per month.

A last form of residual income can result from a business. If your company becomes large enough, you may be able to hire a manager to run it. The income that supports you while the manager runs the business is then considered residual income.

Resource Holdings

Resource Holdings, also known as Resource Land Holdings and RLH, is a private equity firm which focuses on purchasing huge pieces of real estate which are rich in natural resources. The company's ultimate goal with these acquisitions is to sell off those parts of the properties that do not generate cash flow so that they can reduce the cost basis of the property to as nearly zero as they can. At the same time, the work to maintain and improve the cash flow of the remaining piece of property to share this out to their investors. They also enter a number of partnership arrangements with original owners so that these parties remain actively involved in the management and success of the operations. The company is headquartered in Colorado Springs, Colorado in the United States.

Resource Holdings arose in 1998 because its founders wished to provide opportunities for and to invest themselves in timber, agricultural, and mining properties and operations throughout the United States. They work with a variety of local operators, brokers, and entrepreneurs in order to invest in this range of land parcels across a wide range of asset classes which are rich in resources. As of time of publication of this article, RLH had created and managed two individually funded entities along with four different private equity funds.

The first Resource Land Fund I they capitalized with $20 million worth of committed equity. It entered its first investment back in December, 2001. Their second Resource Land Fund II they established using $51 million in equity. It purchased its initial investment in July, 2003. Their Resource Land Fund III received a larger $175 million. It obtained its first investment March of 2006. Each of these investment funds received full investment and then was closed in turn. The Resource Land Fund IV closed with $316 million in committed funds back in August of 2010.

The firm seeks out investments in land across a range of asset classes. Their primary focus has always been on regional timber, agriculture, quarry, mining, and other resource rich properties which have typically been ignored or overlooked by the massive institutional investment world. Such regional entrepreneurs that require significant capital intense investment have found that the needed funds are often not available to them as economic cycles create financial and funding challenges for these medium sized operations. In these particular scenarios, Resource Holdings appears on the scene as a life saving potential source of capital. They often invest right along with local entrepreneurs and partners.

As part of their specific portfolio of investments and property holdings, Resource Holdings owns or invests in properties across 20 different states in the U.S. spanning from Florida, to Texas, to California. At time of publication, they had 46 different properties within their various funds and portfolios. Among these were a limestone quarry in Texas, a citrus operation in Florida, timber operations in California, sand quarrying in Alabama, a large coal surface mine in the Midwest, and apple orchards in Washington state.

As an example, Resource Holdings saw that there were positively growing trends within the building stone market. They used this basis to seek out and invest with two long standing operator-owner partners of two different limestone quarries found in the center of Texas. The owners continue operating the limestone quarrying firm with RLH as the capital partner.

In another instance, the investment firm saw an opportunity to become involved in a successful Florida citrus business a few years ago. They arranged a unique sale-leaseback with the owners which guaranteed the investment company both a minimum yearly return and a profit split with the operating partner-owners. Thanks to their sympathizing and working with the various concerns of the owners, they were able to obtain a high quality property that the markets never had an opportunity to seize. The final arrangement which the company struck with the owner operators allowed both of them to sit on one side of the table to share economic objectives and interests.

Retail Banking

Retail banking is also called consumer banking. This form of banking is most easily described as the common everyday activities of financial service firms. In this definition their individual clientele utilize the local area branches of the more significant and bigger commercial banks. They provide a wide range of services to their customers through this division of financial services. These include checking and savings accounts, personal loans, mortgages for homes, lines of credit, credit cards and debit cards, and CDs certificates of deposits investment opportunities for customers. The main concentration is on the one on one consumer relationship.

Within the United States, the phrase commercial bank refers to a traditional bank. This term distinguishes it from the competing concept of investment bank. Following the Great Depression of the 1930s, the American Congress mandated that banks were only allowed to participate in traditional deposit and lending banking activities as opposed to investment activities. This Glass Steagall Act similarly required that investment banks could only participate in activities pertaining to the capital markets.

This important separation prevented another severe financial crisis like the Great Depression from erupting. Unfortunately for Americans everywhere, the Congress chose to repeal these protections afforded to markets and individuals by Glass Steagall when they canceled out the act in the 1990s. This allowed commercial banks to once again dabble in investment bank activities with depositors' money. It was considered to be a main factor which led to the financial collapse of the Great Recession in the years 2007-2009.

Commercial banking also relates to a division of a bank, or even an entire bank, that focuses on larger businesses and corporations. They handle these huge entities' loans and deposits. This would separate the concept from retail banking which only addresses the ordinary individuals along with their banking needs and accounts.

The idea behind retail banking is to be a one size fits all, single stop shop which provides all the financial services which they possibly can to their retail customers. Bank clients demand a full lineup of essential banking services from these retail operations. Included in this are such expected products as savings and checking accounts, lines of credit, personal loans, home loans, credit cards, debit cards, and CDs. The majority of retail banking customers visits their local bank branch in order to receive these services. Such centers deliver the consumer demanded onsite client service to provide for each of these retail customer requirements.

Financial representatives also work in these local area branches. They offer their clients of the bank both financial advice and customer service. Such financial reps prove to be the primary contact for garnering credit related applications for these products which help the banks to generate their revenues and profits.

These types of banks have begun to offer expanded retail services so that they can capture more business from their retail customers. Besides the typical bank accounts and accompanying customer service that the in branch financial reps deliver, banking centers have added various combinations of financial advisors. They provide a wide array of product offerings. Some of these are investment services like stock brokerage accounts, wealth management services, retirement planning, and even private banking for High Net Worth Individual clients and families.

There are occasionally insurance products and services offered through the in-branch retail banking network as well. Sometimes, such ancillary products and services will be provided out of third party affiliated institutions like insurance companies and investment firms. The idea behind such broadened offerings is to both provide customers greater convenience and to develop more points of financial interaction between them and the bank. This allows for clients of the bank to have greater and more convenient access to their funds and to engage in personal banking transactions both faster and easier.

The Internet has also made possible online retail banking. Many banks now offer partial banking services online. A few are actually banks which are entirely structured to provide banking services over the Internet alone. Among these are GoBank, Moven, and Simple. They offer lower fees as they have significantly smaller overheads with no in-branch personnel, buildings, and networks to support.

The top five biggest American commercial banks possessed more than half of the retail bank customer deposits for the entire country in the year 2015. These five largest institutions were JPMorgan, Bank of America/Merrill Lynch, Wells Fargo, Citibank, and U.S. Bank.

Reverse Annuity Mortgage

A reverse annuity mortgage has several different names. Industry insiders call them reverse mortgages or home conversion loans. The government and finance companies created them to assist retirees who find themselves in a condition of being rich in assets but poor in cash. There has become a greater need for this type of product as more and more individuals find themselves increasingly retiring with only the significant asset of their house.

A greater number of individuals now only receive social security payments after they retire. This amounts to less than $20,000 for an individual or perhaps around $30,000 for married couples. It means that there usually will be a massive need for more money coming in during the retirement years. This gave rise to the concept of the reverse annuity mortgage.

This specially tailored reverse annuity mortgage allows homeowners to sell part or all of their house now but to remain in it until they die. It provides money that retirees are able to utilize for a variety of needs. This could be to supplement the monthly income. It might also be used for medical expenses, long term care, home maintenance, or even the overseas trip of a lifetime.

The way these reverse mortgages work is fairly straight forward. Finance companies provide a set dollar amount of money. Homeowners can receive monthly income as with the reverse annuity mortgage. They might also get a lump sum amount from the option for home equity conversion. The borrowers do repay the loan principle along with interest. What makes these vehicles unique is that there is no physical repaying of the funds. The debt accrues to be paid back after the owners sell the house. This is usually after the retirees have passed away or gone into a permanent care facility.

When retirees choose the annuity option, they utilize the funds from the house to purchase a lump sum annuity. This pays out every month so that they can count on monthly payments that continue until they die. It provides tremendous security for struggling retirees who have only their house to help out their situations.

Scams are a significant and real concern with a reverse annuity mortgage.

Retirees are often taken advantage of and cheated. There are companies that charge even thousands of dollars in exchange for information which the HUD provides for free. They disguise these fees under their estate planning service contracts. Fees can amount to from six to ten percent of the full amount the retirees borrow. This can cost even tens of thousands of dollars depending on the reverse mortgage amount. HUD has advised reverse mortgage lenders to not work with such companies.

Other companies are using reverse mortgages as a way for retirees to pay for a significant purchase such as insurance or annuities which they sell. They often hide unethical and exorbitant fees or unfair terms in their contracts. Some lenders will include share appreciation or share equity terms. This can ravage the retirees' equity position and not give them any benefits in return.

Individuals are able to protect themselves from such scams in the reverse mortgage field. The simplest and most effective means is to work with a reverse annuity mortgage counselor that the HUD has approved. They will evaluate the retiree's scenario as well as the contracts on a reverse mortgage. These specialists will find any possible problems and make it clear what needs to be changed or avoided.

Reverse Mortgages

Reverse mortgages are special types of loans. They are limited to homeowners who are at least 62 years old. These mortgages permit the owners to take a portion of their home equity and convert it to cash. The seniors may use these mortgage proceeds in any way that they like.

The government came up with these unique products because they were looking for a way to help out retired individuals who did not have enough income. The idea was that they might unlock the wealth they had built up in their houses to provide for health care, outside home care, or ordinary monthly costs of living.

These loans are referred to as reverse mortgages because the home owners do not send a lender monthly payments. These are the opposite of traditional mortgages. Lenders provide the borrower with payments instead. The home owners have several advantages. They do not have to repay the loan until they either no longer live in the home or sell it. They also do not make any regular monthly payments against the balance of the loan. The borrowers are required to keep up with their homeowners insurance, property taxes, and any association or homeowner fees.

The most common type of reverse mortgages are known as HECM Home Equity Conversion Mortgages. The U.S. HUD Housing and Urban Development designed and oversees these. These are not loans from the government. Rather they are mortgage loans that lenders provide with insurance from the FHA Federal Housing Administration. In these particular types, borrowers accrue a 1.25% insurance fee as part of the balance on the loan. This increases the loan balance annually.

This insurance is useful for two protections. In case the lender can not make the monthly payment, it provides for it. Should the house resale value be insufficient to pay back the final loan balance at the end, it makes the lender whole. The government and its insurance fund would then clear any balance that remained.

These HECMs comprise the majority of such reverse mortgages in the United States. Included in their regulations is that the senior borrowers must undergo third party counseling to help them with all of the documents and agreements.

The other type of reverse mortgage is a Proprietary Reverse Mortgage. The mortgage lenders that provide these also insure them privately. This means that they do not have to follow the regulations as with the HECMs. The majority of firms that offer these mortgages choose to honor the identical consumer protections featured in the HECM program. This means that mandatory counseling is usually a part of their programs.

These types are also known as jumbo reverse mortgages. Seniors with larger value houses go with these kinds since there is a $625,500 maximum loan limit on the government's HECMs. Two companies in the country presently offer these types of PRMs. These are the Orange, California based American Advisors Group and the Tulsa, Oklahoma based America Reverse Mortgage.

Regardless of the type of reverse mortgage, the lenders have to put potential borrowers through a financial assessment before making the loan. This is so that they can be certain the seniors will be able to pay the future homeowners insurance and taxes and afford to live in the house for the loan's life. To do this, lenders consider all of the income streams of the borrower. This includes their Social Security, investments, and any pensions. The home owners are also required to give the lender their tax returns and bank statements so that expenses and income may be properly documented.

Right of First Refusal

Right of First Refusal refers to a right, but not an obligation, to enact a transaction regarding an asset with another party ahead of any competitors. It is similar to possessing a particular call option on the asset in question. Such a contractual right will typically be negotiated after a party to a transaction wishes to first see how its business will go. The participant could easily decide it is better to have the option to become involved in the asset or opportunity later on instead of having to commit to and pay for it in advance.

There are some significant advantages and benefits to having a Right of First Refusal. It represents a true insurance policy for the contract holder to not lose the possibility of later acquiring the valuable asset which may help to build up the business. It is always helpful to consider a concrete example to better understand this. The commercial tenant of a building might wish to lease or re-lease their office space. It might be willing to purchase the space if the alternative was to be thrown out in favor of a new tenant. This is a good instance when a tenant would want to obtain a first right of refusal as part of the lease contract.

At the same time, such a Right of First Refusal is an inconvenience for the owner of the office building and property. This is because it restricts the capability of seeking out buyers for the building or selling it off. The landlord for the building in this example will discover how hard it is to entice buyers for the property when they learn that the present tenant has the right to match any offer which they decide to make on the property. Yet for building owners, getting the right tenant can be worth providing the first right of refusal incentive in order to secure the lease deal.

There are many cases in the business world where such Rights of First Refusal are in evidence. This is especially the case with joint venture scenarios. Joint venture partners will usually have a true Right of First Refusal to buy out their partners' interests in the venture when the partners wish to exit the business. Private companies also have common scenarios with their stockholder agreements that permit the pre-existing stake holders to buy out the ones who wish for an exit event before any new stock holders are created.

There are a wide range of other cases where these Rights of First Refusal apply in business and entertainment. This goes well beyond the world of corporate deals and boardrooms or even partnerships. In avenues as wide ranging as sports, real estate, or even arts and entertainment they are quite common elements of the business models and contract traditions. There are countless examples of this to consider.

With Real Estate, buyers of land may obtain a first right of refusal from a property holder on the future sale of any adjacent land next to that which they are acquiring. In this case, the property holder would have to offer the original buyer the opportunity to add to their existing holdings by purchasing the adjacent property.

In entertainment, large publishing houses sometimes require a new author to provide them with a Right of First Refusal on additional books they may write and seek to have published. The author would likely have to go along with this, as the publisher could simply refuse to take a chance on the unknown author if he or she is unwilling to accommodate the company. Publishers who put up significant resources into new authors look for this financial incentive of having sequels or additional hit books to help justify their risk.

On the one hand, this likely guarantees the author will have subsequent books published by the same publishing house (unless the first book is a commercial failure). At the same time, the author may not be able to accept a more lucrative competing offer from a rival publishing house. This is because the original publisher will likely not have to meet competitors' offers as part of the first right of refusal clause.

Securities Markets

Securities Markets refer to either literal physical or virtual online places for traders and investors to buy and sell securities. These markets have been dramatically changing in the last several decades in order to best meet the requirements and wishes of investors and traders alike. Traders must have such markets which are easy to access, highly liquid, and that levy the most competitive transaction costs possible. These three core needs of traders have combined to create several different kinds of market structures around the globe. Among these are markets which are order driven, quote driven, hybrid, and brokered.

Many Securities Markets are order driven. With these markets, the sellers and buyers on the exchanges match directly up, typically using a computer system. The middle man is eliminated in such a market structure. This makes them the opposite of markets which are quote driven. Price discovery is accomplished thanks to the traders' limit orders on every security. The majority of such order-based markets utilize an auction system. Naturally sellers will be seeking the highest possible price while buyers are on the hunt for the best possible bargain. When they match, execution of trades happens.

The two kinds of such markets are the continuous auction and the call auction markets. The greatest advantage to this style of market is the massive quantities of investors and traders who will offer to sell and buy a security. This means that prices are competitive and provides superior prices for all traders. It does have a downside. When a security has only a few members trading, then liquidity is often weak. The TSX Toronto Stock Exchange of Canada represents a market that is order driven.

Securities Markets which are quote driven are also referred to as dealer markets. In such market structures, the sellers and buyers have a transacting middle man in between them in the form of a dealer or market maker. It is up to the market makers to provide the ask and bid quotes on stocks for which they are willing to sell and purchase shares. These market makers have exclusivity in their market functions (many times) and receive special privileges. Among these are low to no exchange fees, specific order book and order flow information, and the unique ability to post the stock quotes. Such markets are most common with OTC over the counter markets like the NASDAQ and London's SEAQ, the FOREX market, and the bond markets. Nowadays NASDAQ has become more of a hybrid type with elements of order-driven structures in place.

The greatest advantage to such quote-driven securities markets appears when stocks or markets are illiquid. Dealers are able to boost the traders' liquidity with their intervention, as they often keep a security inventory on hand. They get to enjoy the spread between the bids and ask as a compensation for this accommodation.

Hybrid markets are also popular structures with many Securities Markets. They are sometimes called mixed markets. The NYSE New York Stock Exchange is a well-known example of this category. Naturally this system will utilize characteristics from the two order-driven and quote-driven arrangements. When they have low liquidity periods, these markets are able to fall back on the dealer-provided liquidity to improve transactions.

A final type of Securities Markets is the brokered markets. Brokers represent middle men who engage in discovering counterparties for any trade. As customers request of a broker to help them complete an order, the brokers will go through their extensive networks in an effort to locate an appropriately matching client. These types of markets are mainly for those securities which do not have a traditional public market. Illiquid and unique securities fall into this category. Where huge block trades of highly illiquid stocks or bonds are concerned, brokered markets are employed. Direct real estate is another classic example of such a brokered type of market. Real estate brokers are the ones who fill the service of matching up a unique seller and interested buyer in this case.

Securitization

Securitization is a financial engineering procedure. In this process, sponsors take an asset or group of assets that is illiquid and turn them into a saleable security. Mortgage backed securities are common instruments that result from securitization. These MBS products are backed by assets. The security that underlies them are a group of mortgages.

The securitization process works in a series of steps. It begins with a bank or other financial institution originating a number of mortgages. The mortgages themselves are backed up by the specific properties the home buyers purchase. Next, these single mortgages become combined together into what is known as a mortgage pool. The pool of mortgages remains in trust for the MBS collateral.

MBS are sometimes put together in the securitization process by an investment bank or other third party independent financial firm. They could also be issued by the original bank that underwrote the mortgages in the beginning. Large aggregators like the government sponsored entities Freddie Mac, Fannie Mae, and Ginnie Mae put together many of these mortgage backed securities themselves.

Whichever group undertakes the effort, the end result is identical. Securitization creates a new financial security that is underpinned by the legal and financial claims on the assets of the mortgagors. Sponsors then take the new security and sell it investors or other interested parties in the secondary mortgage market. This proves to be a very large and liquid market. It offers substantial tradability to the securitized mortgages that would have little to no liquidity as stand alone investments.

When these mortgage backed securities are being created through the securitization procedure, issuers have options. Many times they decide to break up their pool of mortgages into a group of different components. They call these tranches. With tranches the issuers are able to put together the security however they would like.

This means they can craft one MBS into a range of tolerance for risk. Some buyers like pension funds are only interested in investing in mortgage backed securities with high credit ratings. Other investors like hedge funds have a higher tolerance for risk. They will be willing to take on tranches with lower credit ratings in exchange for higher returns.

Individual investors who want to participate in these mortgages have several choices. They can take a participation certificate share in a pool of mortgages. This pass through participation provides a pro rated share of interest and principal payments that come back into the pool when the issuers obtain the borrowers' monthly payments. There are also pools of such pass through mortgages called CMOs collateralized mortgage obligations.

Many individuals would like to become involved in mortgage investing but are unsure of all the research involved with the various kinds of MBS. An ideal way to participate without having to understand the detailed mechanics is through mortgage mutual funds. These funds could invest in a single kind of MBS like a Ginnie Mae issued one.

Still other funds are comprised of a range of mortgage backed securities as part of a group of holdings in government bonds. Mutual funds provide a better diversification in loan holdings than individuals might afford on their own. They also offer the ability to reinvest all payments of principal and interest into other MBS. This helps to reduce the risks of changing interest rates and prepayments. It also permits investors to receive yields that vary with current interest rates.

Seller Financing

Seller Financing turns out to be a loan that a business or property seller offers to the buyer. When seller financing is provided, the buyer generally gives a down payment amount to the seller. The balance of the purchase price is paid to them using installment payments that are typically monthly. This is accomplished at a certain time of the month and for an interest rate that the two parties agree to, until the loan itself has been completely paid back.

Seller provided financing is not governed by any regulatory body or set of laws. Because this is the case, for a seller and a buyer both to protect their interests, a purchase agreement that is legally enforceable in a court of law needs to be drafted by an attorney. The two parties, buyer and seller, can then sign this agreement to make the transaction fully legal.

There are many benefits offered in pursuing seller financing. Both the seller and the buyer of a real estate property can realize significant closing cost savings that typically amount to thousands of dollars. The interest rate, loan conditions, and repayment schedule may also be negotiated with seller financing. Borrowers are not forced to go through a loan qualification process via a loan officer or underwriter either. Private Mortgage Insurance is also not required to be paid. Buyers are able to make specific requests as part of the condition of buying the property too, like having the appliances included in the sale.

Sellers also receive benefits when they provide seller financing. They might end up with a better return on the investment if they get their equity payments with interest. They similarly might be capable of obtaining a better selling price and interest rate. They could choose to sell the property in "as is" condition, meaning that they will not be required to cover the costs of any repairs that the property needs. Finally, the seller is capable of picking out the security documents that he or she believes best serve the interests of getting the loan paid off, such as deeds of trust, mortgages, or land sales documents.

There are some downsides to seller financing that should be carefully considered as well. While the buyer might make the payments on time, the seller could choose to not pay off more senior financing on the property, which would cause the property to be foreclosed on. Besides this, the buyer might not be given the title to the property if there are problems tying up the property title, even when he or she paid off the loan as per the agreement. The buyer also does not benefit from the safeguards offered by mortgage insurance, home inspections, or appraisals that will ensure that he or she is not paying too high a price for the house.

The seller also encounters risks with seller financing. If the seller does not get an accurate picture of the buyer's ability to pay for the property, then he or she might suffer through a foreclosure. This foreclosure can require as long as a year to complete. Finally, the seller might accept a smaller down payment and then find that the buyer later abandons the property and payments since he or she puts a limited investment into the property.

Short Sale

Short sales are real estate sales where the money received from the sale is not sufficient to cover the balance that is owed on the property loan. This commonly happens as a result of borrowers being unable to keep up with the mortgage payments for their home loan. In this case, the bank or other lending institution will likely determine that it is in their best interest to take a reasonable loss on the sale of the property instead of pressuring the borrower to make the payments that he or she can not afford.

Both parties come together and agree on the short sale process, since it permits them both to stay out of foreclosure. Foreclosure is a negative outcome for the two parties, as it lowers credit scores of borrowers and costs banks in expensive fees. Borrowers must be careful, since a short sale agreement does not always absolve the borrower from having to cover the additional balance left on the loan. This remaining balance is called the deficiency.

The process of a short sale starts with the two parties concurring on a short sale being the best option to resolve a mortgage that the borrower is unable to keep up with as a result of financial or economic difficulties. The home owner actually sells the house in question for an amount that he or she is able to realize, even though it is less than the remaining loan balance. They give the money to the bank or lender. This is really the most economical answer for the problem in this scenario, since short sales are less costly and quicker than foreclosures that damage both lender and borrower.

Banks commonly employ loss mitigation departments. Their job is to contemplate the short sales that are possible or likely. Most of them work with criteria that they have set up in advance. In the difficult days following the financial crisis of 2007-2010, they have become more flexible and willing to entertain offers from borrowers. The banks will usually decide on how much equity is in the house by ascertaining the likely selling price that they will be able to receive either through a Broker Price Opinion, appraisal, or Broker Opinion of Value.

Even when Notice of Defaults have been sent out to borrowers beginning a foreclosure process, many banks will still consent to short sale requests and offers. They have become more understanding and accepting of short sales in the wake of the financial crisis than they ever were before. This means that for the countless borrowers who own houses on which they owe more than they are worth and who can not sell them, there is a better option open to them than foreclosure.

Sub-prime Borrower

A sub-prime borrower is an individual who has credit that is considered to be less than perfect. This is the opposite of a prime borrower. Bankers call prime borrowers those who possess higher and better credit scores, low debt ratios, and significant incomes which are more than enough to cover their monthly bills and expenses.

Sub-prime borrowers often are only able to obtain sub-prime loans. These types of loans received the blame for causing the 2008 mortgage crisis. Despite this fact, the loans continue to exist today. They are an important part of post crisis lending, though so far they have not caused another financial crisis or global meltdown.

Those called sub-prime borrowers have many characteristics in common. These imply that the individuals are more likely to default on their mortgage loans than other individuals. Poor credit is the first element they share. This could be because they did not receive any opportunities to create a sufficient credit history.

It might also be from problems they had with making payments in the past. The dilemma for these borrowers is that they do not have many choices other than sub-prime lenders. This often traps them in a cycle of debt from which is difficult to escape. An under 640 credit score is considered to be sub-prime, though some lenders set the defining limit lower to even 580.

The sub-prime borrowers also have problems with their monthly payments. These payments are so large that they consume a significant part of the monthly income for the borrowers. This is determined in how high the debt to income ratio proves to be. A higher DTI ratio means that the borrowers do not have enough money to cover bills if they suffer a drop in income or have unanticipated expenses arise. Loans can still be approved in some scenarios when the borrowers' present debt load is significant.

The cost for a sub-prime loan is another thing these borrowers share together. These forms of mortgage loans usually cost more since lenders do not want to assume additional risk without higher compensation. Predatory lenders have used this limited ability to receive loan approvals in order to prey on borrowers with no other choices. These higher expenses manifest in a few different ways. It might be junk application and processing fees, greater interest rates, and penalties for early prepayment which prime borrowers seldom pay.

Risk is the dominant theme for sub-prime borrowers, lenders, and loans. Because the loans have a lower chance of being paid back, the lenders exact more in fees and higher rates. These greater costs cause the loans to be riskier for the borrowers as well. Debt is difficult to retire when higher interest rates and costs come with it.

Sub-prime borrowers should try to avoid these expensive and debt trapping loans whenever they can. Staying out of such costly credit is essential for individuals to not drown in debt. This is easier said than done when people are put into the sub-prime category. There are not as many options to comparison shop for the loans. There are also fewer options for alternative kinds of loans to use for the needed financing.

If these borrowers are able to make themselves look less risky to the various lenders, it will improve their chances of escaping from these types of loans. This may mean some credit repair work needs to be done before individuals with credit challenges make applications for loans.

Sub-prime Lender

A sub-prime lender makes loans to customers who fall into the sub-prime borrower category. These products often include loans which are normally considered to be standard. They are structured for and marketed to borrowers who possess inadequate income, lower credit scores, and a higher debt to income ratio. These borrowers can not qualify with lenders regarded as traditional.

Sub-prime lenders are often willing to issue loans to customers with special circumstances. These include those who possess less documentation of income, high LTV loan to value ratios, and sometimes a combination of the two. This type of lending is considered to be aggressive and overly risky for most traditional financial institutions.

Where mortgages are concerned, sub-prime lenders are still providing basically the same product in the form of a 5/1 ARM adjustable rate mortgage or a 30 year fixed rate mortgage. The main difference is that the rate which accompanies such a product will be considerably higher.

There are other types of mortgage loans that some observers include in this category as well. Among these are negative amortization loans, interest only loans, and non fixed interest rate mortgages. A great number of analysts consider FHA loans to be in the subprime category. This is because their highest allowable LTV is 96.5% while they accept a credit score minimum of 500.

Sub-prime lenders will also make loans for other assets and in other categories besides housing and mortgages. In fact they issue them for practically all financing needs. This includes credit cards, car loans, unsecured personal loans, and student loans.

After the financial crisis that started with sub-prime mortgages, the government enacted a number of laws protecting consumers from these predatory types of finance. It has made it more difficult to find sub-prime house loans since then. There are a great many of the original loans from before the crisis still in existence. Besides this, sub-prime lenders have found means of circumventing them and giving approval to loans that fall into this category.

Borrowers can take many actions to avoid being a victim of a sub-prime lender. Managing credit carefully is among the most important. It is free to check all credit reports for accuracy. Borrowers can fix errors. Consumers should also deal with any defaults or missed payments if they can. Rebuilding credit requires some time, but going through the process will help borrowers to be considered more prime to lenders.

There are many newer lenders these days that are considered to be legitimate. Online searches and online lenders have opened a whole new avenue to consumers trying to avoid sub-prime loans. Some of these online lenders appeal to those with poor credit and still provide acceptable rates.

There are also peer to peer lending services. They can be more flexible with borrowers than the traditional credit unions and banks often are. It is always a good idea to research any lenders which consumers consider before providing them with important personal information or paying any fees.

Borrowers who are struggling to avoid these sub-prime lenders can also look into a co-signer on a loan. It can help credit challenged borrowers to receive approval from a lender which is traditional and offers better rates. These co-signers put their own credit at stake and take a big risk in doing so.

Sub-prime Mortgage

A sub-prime mortgage is one where the home loan that the bank or lending institution makes is offered to the category of consumers who are considered to possess the riskiest credit. Sub prime mortgages are actually sold on a different market than are prime mortgage loans. Sub prime mortgage borrowers are determined through a combination of factors, such as the credit rating of the borrower, the documentation offered for the loans, and the borrower's debt to assets ratio. Besides this, sub-prime mortgage are also deemed to be those that do not fulfill the prime mortgages' standards and guide lines offered by Fannie Mae and Freddie Mac, the two biggest issuers of mortgages within the United States.

A universally agreed upon definition for sub-prime mortgages does not exist today. In the U.S., sub-prime mortgages are commonly considered to be those where the associated borrower possesses a FICO credit rating score that is less than 640. This phrase became a part of pop culture in the credit crunch that occurred in 2007.

The original sub-prime mortgage program began in 1993. At this time, some lenders started offering sub-prime mortgages to borrowers classified as high risk, who possessed credit that was less than ideal. Traditional lenders showed wariness towards sub-prime mortgages and borrowers. They tended to shy away from people who had impaired credit histories. Sub-prime mortgage borrowers commonly have information on their credit reports that argue for greater percentages of defaults. These include too much debt, a track record of not paying debts or missing payments, recorded bankruptcies, and low amounts of experience with debt.

Around twenty-five percent of the American population is grouped into this category of sub-prime borrowers who qualify for the category of sub-prime mortgages. Because of this, proponents of sub-prime mortgages argued that they allowed a large number of people to gain access to credit who would not otherwise have experienced the opportunity to purchase and own a home. Borrowers with less than perfect credit who can demonstrate enough income are able to qualify for sub-prime mortgages. This proves to be the case even if their credit scores are lower than 640.

The lenders who participate in sub-prime mortgages take significant risks in so doing. This is because people who have a credit score of less than 620 statistically possess a significantly greater rate of defaulting on their mortgages than do those people with much higher scores over 720. Lenders compensate for the risks associated with offering sub-prime mortgages through several different means. One of these is by charging higher rates of interest. They also collect late fees for any customers who do not keep up with their payments. These greater interest rates and fees help to reward lenders who take the risks of the higher default rates, and who also incur costs for collecting and keeping up with these -mortgage accounts. As an example of their potential danger, sub-prime mortgages proved to be among the main causes of the Financial Crisis of 2007-2010.

Sub-prime Mortgage Crisis

The sub-prime mortgage crisis proves to be a still going financial and real estate crisis. It continues to revolve around the steep decline that you saw in American housing prices, the resulting increase in numbers of mortgage delinquencies and finally foreclosures, and the ultimate fall of securities that are backed up by these sub-prime mortgages.

The problems began with the fact that around eighty percent of all United States mortgages that banks gave out to sub-prime borrowers, or people with less than perfect credit, turned out to be adjustable rate types of mortgages. Housing prices actually reached their highest point in the middle of 2006 and then began sharply falling. This caused refinancing of interest rates on mortgages to be harder to obtain. The double edged sword of adjustable rate mortgages resetting at their higher rates started, causing an enormous number of delinquencies and finally foreclosures in mortgages.

The greater problem came as these mortgages underlay a number of financial securities that many financial firms held in huge numbers. They saw most of their value disappear in the following months. Investors around the world then began to dramatically cut back on the quantities of collateralized debt obligations and other mortgage securities that they bought. Besides the damage that increasing sub-prime mortgage delinquencies and foreclosures created themselves and for the investments based on them, this sub-prime mortgage crisis led to a fall in the ability of the banking system to engage in lending. This caused significantly tighter credit and lower rates of growth throughout the developed world, in particular in Europe and the United States,that are still plaguing the industrial countries.

Ultimately, the sub-prime mortgage crisis arose as a result of easy up front loan terms which banks made to borrowers. Both the borrowers and the banks felt confident that the loans could be easily refinanced into better terms as needed, since housing prices were steadily rising over a long term trend. Financial incentives were provided to sub-prime mortgage originators.

This coupled, with fraud that borrowers and lenders engaged in, significantly boosted the quantities of sub-prime mortgages to customers who should have received standard conforming loans or who should not have received loans at all. When the easy interest rate terms expired, the majority of sub-prime loan holding consumers could not refinance at the better rates in which they had believed. The interest rates reset higher, dramatically increasing the monthly mortgage payments.

Home prices started falling to the point that homes were no longer even worth as much as the original mortgage, meaning that they could not be sold to pay off the mortgage obligation. Instead, the borrowers' best interest lay in going through foreclosure and walking away from the hopelessly underwater homes. This continuous epidemic of foreclosures that began with the sub-prime mortgage crisis is still a major continuous part of the world wide financial and economic crisis. The foreclosures are still taking away wealth from consumers and sapping away at the damaged banks' balance sheets.

Subordinate Financing

Subordinate financing refers to that type of debt finance which ranks behind the primary finance. It is second in importance and position to debt that senior or secured lenders hold. This is important when a default occurs, as it determines who gets repaid first from any bankruptcy proceedings or foreclosure. The term signifies that senior lenders who are secured will be repaid before the debt holders that are subordinate.

Lenders who participate in this subordinate financing take on greater risk than the lenders considered to be senior. This is because they have a lower claim on the business or property assets. Sometimes this type of corporate finance is comprised of both equity and debt financing. A lender would be interested in this because it would offer them potential stock options or warrants that would reward them with extra yield as a means of compensating for the greater risk they take.

Where consumer borrowers and loans are concerned, subordinate financing would be a second mortgage. It takes second priority below the original first mortgage. First mortgages have the property to secure their loan and the debt. While nearly every mortgage is backed by the underlying property, first mortgages receive special seniority ahead of subordinated mortgages. This means the senior mortgage lender is repaid first in a foreclosure. With mortgages, subordinate financing could be a mortgage that is 80/20. In this case, the first mortgage would be 80 percent while the second mortgage that was subordinated represents 20 percent.

This means that only the lenders which are first mortgage holders are likely to get at least a portion of their money back if a borrower defaults in general. Should a borrower only default on the subordinate mortgage, this lender is able to foreclose on the property to regain its principal. Subordinated lenders could work to make their mortgage the senior one and then foreclose. They could do this by buying out their borrower's first mortgage. Afterwards, they could choose to subordinate the original first mortgage so that their once second mortgage became senior in the foreclosure.

Consumers should think carefully before participating in subordinate financing to obtain their houses. There are several disadvantages involved.

Home owners will usually have to write two different mortgage payments each month if they do. They will also typically pay a higher interest rate on the second mortgage since these rates are usually greater than the first mortgage rates. There are also often two different loan fees, costs, and even discount points when first and second mortgages are used. Finally, this type of finance will often lead to a greater monthly payment when the two are combined than only one mortgage payment would.

The main reason that a home buyer would be interested in employing subordinated financing to purchase a home is because an 80/20 mortgage would not require them to come up with any down payment. It might also eliminate the need to pay for PMI private mortgage insurance which can be a substantial component of the monthly mortgage payment. This would depend on how the mortgage financing was originally structured.

Consumers will generally require a high credit score of minimally 700 in order to qualify for this subordinated financing. When borrowers have two mortgages, it will likely be impossible to obtain a home equity loan or line of credit at a later time.

Systemic Risk

Systemic Risk refers to those dangers that threaten the entire financial sector, another segment of the market, or the entire market. Analysts and economists also call this volatility, "undiversifiable" risk, and market risk. Such risk is especially dangerous because it can not be entirely avoided nor accurately predicted or forecast. There is no practical way to mitigate such risks to the entire system by diversifying assets. Instead, it can only be managed (though never perfectly) via effective hedging strategies or through the optimal allocation of assets.

Another way of considering such Systemic Risk is that it entails the very real possibility that a company-level or bank-level failure could set off serious volatility and instability. It might begin a chain reaction that leads to collapse in a whole industry, market segment, or even entire national or multinational economy. This risk to the system caused much of the Global Financial Crisis of 2008. At this tumultuous time in American and Western economic and geopolitical history, there were a number of financial companies in particular that were labeled too big to fail simply because they posed a real risk to the entire system.

This is the case because institutions like these are extremely large and systemically important in their own market industries. In extreme cases they might represent a dangerously large portion of the entire economy of a nation. Firms that are highly entangled with a number of other ones also prove to be systemically risky.

The federal government of the United States engages in the study of systemic risk so that it can justify becoming involved in the national economy from time to time. They do this with the idealism that they can lessen the impacts of company-centered events that cause sometimes severe ripples. The Feds feel with surgically- and precisely-targeted actions or regulations that they can reduce the severity of the consequences of these failures on a macroeconomic level. One example of this was the Dodd-Frank Act of 2010. This massive package of additional rules, regulations, and laws was intended to stop another Global Financial Crisis and Great Recession from happening. The heavy-handed regulation of important banks and other financial companies is supposed to reduce risk to the system.

It is instructive to look at the historical real-world examples of which companies posed such Systemic Risk in the middle of this greatest financial crisis since the Great Depression of the 1930s. It was the so-called "Lehman Brothers moment" that nearly brought down the entire Western-based financial and banking system in 2009. The size and scope of Lehman Brothers and its connectedness to the entire American economy caused it to be a massive source of risk to the system.

As the company collapsed the effect of this spread far and wide through the entire national and even international financial system. In the United States first, the capital markets froze. This meant that companies and individuals were no longer able to access loans. In some cases, they still could obtain them, but only if they had the highest standard of creditworthiness so they would not entail any risk of default for the embattled banks and other lenders.

At the same time, AIG the American International Group insurance company experienced intense and insurmountable financial problems. As the world's largest insurance company, they were overly connected to the other banks and financial companies of the globe. This made them a serious Systemic Risk not only to the American financial system, but also to the British, European, and Asian financial systems.

Their own portfolio of highly toxic assets connected with subprime mortgages and residential MBS mortgage backed securities meant it suffered from repeated calls for collateral, a downgrade of its credit rating, and an evaporation of liquidity. This only worsened and became a vicious downward spiral as the values of these poisonous assets declined further every month.

For some unknown reason, the same U.S. government that would not prop up Lehman Brothers intervened dramatically to save the AIG by loaning them over $180 billion. It may have been because various regulators, analysts, and economists, were convinced that the failure of AIG would have led to many additional banks, insurance companies, and financial firms collapsing.

Tax Abatement

Tax abatement represents a taxation level reduction. It can be for either individual consumers or companies. There are many examples of this type of tax break. They could be in the form of a rebate, reduction in tax penalties, or an actual tax decrease. Sometimes people or firms pay too many taxes or get a tax bill that is higher than it should be. In this case, they have the right to ask for an abatement from the IRS or state taxing agency.

Among the different types of tax abatement is the property tax kind. Owners of property might feel that their property value is assessed too highly. They would be able to appeal to the area tax assessor to receive a tax abatement. Businesses that are not for profit can obtain them on their property because of their special tax exempt status.

Tax abatement on property is a major savings. Most owners of houses will be required to pay property taxes that are commonly from 1% to 3% of the value of the house every year. This annual expense does not disappear when the mortgage is completely paid. It represents part of the ongoing cost of owning a home.

There are cities that offer special programs of real estate tax abatement. Such a package assists consumers dramatically. It could help them to purchase a nicer house for the same payment. It might also allow them to be able to obtain a mortgage that they might not otherwise. This is the case if the monthly house payment drops to a level they can afford through such abatement. This type of abatement on property can also help to boost the resale value of the house if it is still in effect when the owner sells.

Some cities in the U.S. offer tax abatement's to massively lower or even completely eliminate tax payments on houses for not only years but even decades. The idea behind such a program is to bring in buyers to neighborhoods that are in poor demand. This could be part of the inner city which the city is attempting to revitalize. Cities can offer these abatement's throughout the entire limits. Others provide them for specific areas. Authorities can choose to restrict such programs to middle or low income owners of property as well. A great number of these abatement programs do not carry such an income restriction.

It is possible to purchase properties that are already under abatement. Individuals may also buy properties that are eligible and go through with the necessary improvements. They then apply for this program. It is far easier to buy a property with an abatement than to go through the hassle of bureaucracy and construction.

For abatement's on improvements to a property, there are special rules. The improvement, rehabilitation, or construction property taxes can be reduced or eliminated. This does not mean that the entire property tax is gone. The pre-improved value of the property will still have taxes owed for it in this particular case.

It is often necessary for a house to be occupied by the owner for the abatement to continue. Renting the house out would cause the special status to disappear. When an owner sells a home to another owner who will occupy it, the property tax abatement will stay with the house. Abatement periods never restart just because the property transfers ownership. If a 10 year program eliminates or reduces the taxes on a home and the seller has enjoyed seven of these years, then the new owner will have the three years left of the status.

Title Deed

Title deeds are a form of legal documents. They are utilized to demonstrate that a person owns a certain property. Title deeds are used most often to provide proof of home or vehicle ownership. Title deeds might also be given out on other kinds of property. Title deeds give owners privileges and legal rights. To transfer a property's ownership to another individual, a title deed is required.

Title deeds generally come with detailed descriptions of the property to which they are attached. They are made specific enough so that they can not be mixed up with other properties. They also include the individual's name who owns the piece of property. More than one person can be named as an owner on a title deed. Proof that the title deed is recorded with the appropriate office is provided by the presence of an official seal. Title deeds are commonly signed by the property owner and a person who witnesses the signature, such as a clerk or area government official.

Having a title deed does not mean that a person keeps the car in his or her possession. You can loan a car to a relative to use, even though they are not on the title. If you purchase a car using a loan, then the bank will have the title for its security, even though you would keep the car. You might purchase a house and rent it to a tenant. Although the tenant would not have the title deed, he or she would still possess and occupy the house. The title deed is useful for forcefully retaking possession in any of these scenarios.

When you sell a property, the old title deed is invalidated and a new one is given out that has the new owner's name on it. You might also add another person to a title deed by working with a title company for a property, or the Department of Motor Vehicles for vehicle titles. You have to fill in a request in writing before you receive a new title deed with the other names added to it. Once a person's name has been added to a title deed, they legally control the property along with the original title deed owner.

Title deeds have to be kept safe. As official legal documents, they are not easy to replace when stolen or lost. It is a smart idea to keep title deed copies separate from the original to have proof of ownership while an official replacement title deed is being issued. Physical possession of title deeds allows a person to start a transfer of ownership, so they must be kept where they will not be stolen and then subsequently utilized to transfer your property to another individual.

Too Big To Fail

Too Big To Fail refers to the disturbing but proven concept that some businesses have become so enormous and systemically important that the jurisdictional government has no choice but to save them from failing with whatever means necessary. The governments feel they must deliver material assistance to the firms in order to prevent a catastrophic rogue wave effect from reverberating across the entire economy.

The simple explanation for how a company can be so important to an entire economy is this. When such an enormous firm fails, all of the companies that count on it for parts of their revenue can also be compromised and fail, as well as its debt holders and ancillary services providing companies that work with the failing massive firm. Jobs then become eliminated en masse. For this reason, the expenses involved with a simple bailout or government backed guarantees of the mega corporation are significantly less than the cost of overall widespread economic failures. It explains why governments will often opt for the bailout as the less expensive answer to the moral problem.

Too Big To Fail especially pertains to commercial banks and financial services firms. These financial companies are so critical for the United States' and other Western economies that it would create havoc and spread financial ruin if they declared bankruptcy. Because of this, the American and British governments especially opted in the Global Financial Crisis of 2008-2009 to spare the banks and other financial service firms.

They saved the bank creditors and holders of counter party risk. As an unwished for side effect, they allowed the managers and company board members to keep their enormous salaries and incredible bonuses. Throughout the last years of the 2000's, the United States' Federal Government doled out approximately $700 billion in order to shore up such critical failing corporations as Bear Stearns, AIG, and the major banks which stood on the edge of financial ruin.

It was investors' total evaporation in confidence of the major financial institutions that led to their near-downfall back in the years 2008 and 2009. Especially the investment banks ran into trouble as they had become unbelievably leveraged (to the tune of from forty to one and eighty to one) when suddenly their mortgage loan-based assets and derivatives plunged in value as the subprime mortgage crisis spiraled out of control. Both stake holders and creditors quickly began to have doubts in their financial solvency as their balance sheets crumbled.

The defining moment in the Too Big To Fail crisis erupted when the government did not step in to prevent Lehman Brothers investment bank from failing. This has become widely known as the "Lehman moment." As widespread chaos erupted in the financial markets, regulators suddenly became painfully aware that these largest companies were so intricately connected that it would take enormous financial bailouts in order to stop literally half of the U.S. financial sector from collapsing.

Once the bailouts had intervened to save the major Too Big To Fail investment banks, only two remained standing. Even the survivors Morgan Stanley and Goldman Sachs were both forced to convert to traditional commercial banks so that they could be backstopped by the FDIC. Bear Stearns was effectively wound down, Lehman's skeleton was bought out by Barclays of Great Britain, and once-mighty Merrill Lynch became a subsidiary of Bank of America. The shadow banking industry had all but disappeared overnight.

The government then attempted to address the issues of Too Big To Fail financial firms. The U.S. Congress passed the Dodd-Frank Wall Street Reform and Consumer Protection Act of 2010. The idea was to create restrictions which would make it far more difficult for such conditions to flourish again. They hoped to sidestep having to extend other bailouts in the future.

The Act made the financial institutions create forms of "living wills" so that their plans are in place in order to rapidly liquidate assets if they have to file for bankruptcy. An internationally based consortium of financial regulators came up with a new set of rules in November of 2015 to force the major global banks to raise their capital by $1.2 trillion more in additional debt funding which they are able to convert into equity or write off if they suffer catastrophic losses again.

Toxic Assets

Toxic Assets is a coined phrase for those financial assets which saw their actual value plummet. Toxic assets do not have well working markets anymore, making them difficult or impossible to sell for a price on which the owner will agree. The term arose as a popularly coined phrase during the financial crisis of 2007-2010. Toxic assets proved to have a major part in causing the financial crisis.

As toxic assets' markets seize up, they are called frozen markets. Many markets for these toxic assets froze up starting in 2007. The problem only continued to grow exponentially worse in the second half of the following year 2008. A number of elements combined to lock up the markets for toxic assets. These assets had values that proved to be extremely vulnerable to the worsening economic situation. As uncertainty only grew in this scenario, finding a value for toxic assets became more difficult. In the resulting frozen markets, banks and similar lending institutions chose not to unload these assets for greatly diminished prices. The reason for it lay in their fear that such drastically lower prices would force them to mark down all of their holdings, so that they became insolvent or bankrupt.

Typically, toxic assets are able to clear when the supply and demand of them reach the point that buyers and sellers will come together. This did not occur in the financial crisis starting in 2007. As a number of the financial assets simply hung around on banks' balance sheets, experts declared that the markets had broken down.

Another way of putting this is that because banks would not write down the prices on the assets, the price of them proved to be overly high. Buyers knew that these assets were now worth far less than the selling banks hoped to realize for them. This kept the sellers' price expectations far higher than buyers were willing to pay.

Toxic assets mostly arose as a result of banks and other investment banks deciding to pour enormous sums of money into new and complex financial assets like credit default swaps and collateralized debt obligations. These highly leveraged assets had values that turned out to be extremely vulnerable to a variety of economic conditions like the rates of default, prices of houses, and liquidity of financial markets. These toxic assets threatened to destroy the entire financial system and did manage to take down a number of venerable institutions like Bear Stearns, Lehman Brothers, and Washington Mutual Bank, the country's largest savings and loan institution. As a result of the carnage created by these highly leveraged, speculative investments in toxic assets, experts have named them financial weapons of mass destruction.

Tranches

Tranches refer to a French word that means a portion or a slice. In the world of investing, it relates to securities which may be subdivided into tinier parts and then sold off to various interested investors. These securities typically represent structured financing. Every part of the tranche is a portion of a few correlated securities that specific banks called investment banks offer all at once. Yet each of the tranches comes with its own set of rewards, risks, and maturities.

MBS Mortgage backed securities are often represented in tranches. There are different types of these MBS. One of them is the CMO collateralized mortgage obligation. Such securities will be subdivided up according to their maturity dates. At this point, the offering firm will sell them to investors who buy them according to the maturity date they prefer. Looking at an example helps to clarify the concept as it pertains to CMOs. An investment bank might offer a tranche or several of them made up of mortgages. The maturity dates on these could vary according to twenty year, ten year, five year, two year, and single year maturities. Each of these would offer a range of returns versus risks. Every maturity would be its own tranche in this example.

There are particular reasons why various investors would prefer different types. In one scenario, the investors might require shorter term cash flows yet not wish to have any in the longer term future. Still other investors might wish for longer term cash flow but not need it today. Because of these different needs from investors, investment banks might decide to split up their assets in the CMOs. They could assign them to different parts, or tranches. This way the former investor is able to obtain his initial cash flow from an underlying group of mortgages while the latter investor can obtain the later period cash flows. Thanks to the investment banks forming such tranches, the CMO securities which might not have attracted sufficient investor interest can acquire a new lease on life through a variety of investors with different needs.

Tranches find a great deal of use in numerous mortgage pools which contain many different types of mortgages. There would usually be riskier loans in the pool that came with greater interest rates. At the same time, more conservative loans that come with lower interest rates will be in most pools. Every pool of mortgages will also possess its own maturity dates that bear on the reward to risk ratios. This is why the investment banks create these tranches into smaller pieces which each contain their own particular common set of financial characteristics that appeal to certain investor scenarios. For any investors who desire to put their capital to work in MBOs, they are able to select the specific tranche kind that will best suit their level of risk tolerance as well as their hoped- for return.

Each of the tranches gets its ultimate value from the mortgage pools which underlie them. The investors who purchase these MBOs are allowed to hold them for longer term, smaller gains that come from the interest payments. They might also decide to attempt to sell them early on for a rapid profit. It is also possible to pursue a combination of strategies, trying to obtain slower steady income for a certain amount of time before selling them off at a profit.

The monthly payments come from pieces of the total interest payments mortgage holders make each month (to their mortgage holder) within the given tranche. This is why those investors who purchase them will obtain a monthly cash flow from the specific MBO tranche in which they invest, so long as they hold on to the tranche.

Transfer of Interest

A Transfer of Interest refers to an individual, business, or other organization choosing to transfer over its ownership in an asset or object. This could be a business entity, piece of Real Estate, or asset that the owner shifts to another party. Most commonly the term becomes utilized regarding the transferring of an entity's ownership of an interest in a business. This could involve transfers between parties in a limited liability company, a partnership, a privately held sole proprietorship, or even a corporation. In the vast majority of cases, such a transfer occurs with a contract known as a transfer of interest agreement.

In theory, any time individuals or businesses engage in a purchase, they are becoming party to a contract. Such contracts are actually making a Transfer of Interest in some form of real property in the vast majority of cases. As a concrete example, when an individual buys food off of a supermarket or produce stand, this literally represents an implied contract (evidenced by a receipt as proof of purchase). The end result is that the buyer becomes the transferring new owner of the food purchase. The same is true when people buy clothing from a department store. The ownership of the clothes becomes officially transferred by the contract which the store makes with the buyer when money changes hands in exchange for a receipt and the articles of clothing.

Any type of Transfer of Interest is affected with whatever terms the two parties agree upon at the time of transfer. These could involve legal restrictions and stipulations on the kind of interest which they will transfer between them. The appropriate agreement only has to state clearly the interest which will be transferred, the parties who are involved, and the sum being delivered in consideration of the interest transfer. After the transaction intent is clearly stated by the actions and/or verbal promises of the two parties in question, the agreement will be officially concluded so that the transfer becomes finalized.

Naturally the universe of Real Estate has its own highly evolved and carefully developed procedures for such an important Transfer of Interest. They commonly call this an assessable transfer of interest. It refers to the reality of taxation which goes along with tangible interest in and de facto ownership of Real Estate. These transfers mandate that the property will be appraised and fully re-evaluated in the tax year that follows the transfer. All transfers of Real Estate done either with a contract, trust, or deed will be treated as such by the taxing authorities in the relevant jurisdiction. Leases that last for more than 20 years also come under this requirement. The reason for such an evaluation of the property value is to be certain that the taxes are fairly and fully assessed on the Real Estate involved in the contractual transfer transaction.

It is many times the same when there is a Transfer of Interest in a business accomplished through a sale. This event often produces an assessable event which will require a tax assessment to be done. When the business is at least 50 percent sold, this will commonly be required. When a business is instead forfeited or foreclosed on and the change of status does not lead to an income tax event, then this is an exception to the tax assessment rule.

When a transfer occurs among an affiliated group's members, this is also an applicable exception to the assessment case. There are often these substantial tax ramifications to such a transfer of a business that the government will usually require that the business value be reassessed following the execution of the business transfer transaction in question.

Underwriting

Underwriting refers to a means of determining if a consumer is eligible or not for a particular kind of financial product. These products vary depending on the person's or business' requirements. They might include home mortgages, insurance coverage needs, business mortgages, lines of credit, or financing for venture start up projects. The bank or other financial institution undergoing the underwriting evaluation procedure will look into the odds of the business transaction successfully providing them with a profit in exchange for their offer of financial help.

As banks and insurance firms go through the underwriting process, two different things will occur. The first of these is showing an interest in the project that the borrower is proposing for finance. They demonstrate this by offering the financial aid that the customer is requesting. Next, with a bank or institution underwriting an insurance policy, residential or commercial mortgage, or venture, they are looking to make money on their investment one day in the future. They might either gather these profits at one time in the form of a lump sum at a future date or little by little in monthly payments. In these underwriting activities, compensation is expected, which is commonly paid via finance charges or other fees.

Underwriters contemplate more than simply the amount of risk that an applicant demonstrates. They also consider the potential risk that working with the new customer might bring to other customers of their company. In order to ensure that the bank or firm does not suffer too much harm to keep up with commitments made to already existing clients, they have developed underwriting standards.

Insurance companies heavily rely on underwriting in performing their business. Health insurance is one example of this. Health insurance providers seriously look into the past and present health of a person applying. Sometimes their underwriting will show that they need to exclude various pre-existing conditions for a certain amount of time when they insure the person. Other times, underwriting will reveal a medical history that demonstrates too much risk for the company. In this case, a health insurance company will refuse to provide the requested health insurance coverage. Their goal is to not insure individuals who they believe will need significant medical treatment over time, so that they can provide a solid financial backing for their existing clientele.

In business, underwriting is commonly employed to determine if new ventures should be given financing. An example of this might be a company that has created a new technology that it wishes to sell. These underwriters will consider how marketable the product appears, the applicant's marketing plan, the expense of creating and selling the new items, and also the odds of the company realizing profits on every piece that they sell. Sometimes, underwriters of these business ventures will express an interest in having shares of stock in the start up company as a portion of their payment for services. Other times, they will only require a set interest rate for the dollar amount invested.

UniCredit Bulbank

UniCredit Bulbank proves to be the biggest bank in the Republic of Bulgaria. Until 1994, this state-controlled and -operated bank bore the name of the Bulgarian Foreign Trade Bank or BFTB. It was in 2007 that the UniCredit Bulbank became formed when Bulbank, Hebros Bank, and Biochim merged together as individual subsidiaries of UniCredit Group from Italy.

Bulgarian Foreign Trade Bank first arose in 1964 in its headquarters of Sofia, Bulgaria. The at the time completely state-owned and -founded bank held an initial paid in capital of 40 million Bulgarian leva when it opened. This proved to be a large sum of capital in this day and age. At the time under the heyday of the communists in Bulgaria it specialized in foreign finance and foreign trade payments.

The bank realized that to effectively pursue foreign trade and finance, it needed several well placed good international branches. The bank then began to open important representative offices in London, Vienna, and Frankfurt throughout the subsequent decades. In 2015, the operation boasted substantially greater assets amounting to nearly 9 billion Euros and 2015 era equity of nearly 13 billion Euros.

Once Communism collapsed in Bulgaria during the successful national coup in 1989, the country established the Bank Consolidation Company in 1991 to operate the state- controlled banking sector and to help with the eventual privatizing of the various national Bulgarian banks. BCC owned 98 percent of the share capital of Bulbank at the time. It became the first Bulgarian bank operation to change over to international SWIFT codes. This helped it to massively improve its transaction reliability and operational performance as a direct result.

The bank's eventual privatization from 1998 to 2000 saw UniCredito Italiano gain control of 93 percent of the capital shares while German based re-insurance giant Allianz obtained another five percent of the remaining shares. Bulbank then sold its majority stakes in Corporate Commercial Bank and minor stakes in United Bulgarian Bank and HypoVereinsbank Bulgaria.

Bulbank has continuously worked on the merger of operations and branches between the old Bulbank offices and Hebros Bank and HVB Bank Biochim since UniCredit made the decision to merge the HVB Group back in 2005. The group was renamed UniCredit Bulbank officially at this point.

The same Chief Executive Officer has overseen the company's massive successes since the year 2001. This towering figure in Bulgarian banking and finance is Mr. Levon Hampartzoumian. He heads UniCredit Bulbank still as of end of 2016 in its second decade of existence in the present foreign owned-form of the financial institution.

Part of the leading in Bulgaria success that UniCredit Bulbank has consistently enjoyed in recent decades stems from the wide range of clientele they effectively serve. They offer bank checking, current, and savings accounts, insurance and investment products, land and home mortgages, and financing and credit for individual clients, private banking customers, small businesses, large corporate clients, other financial institutions, and even Bulgarian government and other public institutions as well.

UniCredit Bulbank is not only by far and away the largest bank in Bulgaria by branches, deposits, and assets; it is also a heavily award-winning financial institution. In 2016, it received the honors of "Bank of the Year" from the Association Bank of the Year and "Best Bank for 2016" from Global Finance Magazine. It is known as the "Best Digital Bank in Bulgaria for 2016" per Global Finance Magazine. Focus Economics ranks it as the "Most Precise Overall Economic Forecast for Bulgaria." Forbes Magazine labeled it the "Most Innovative Bank in Bulgaria". It received the "Best Bank in Bulgaria" designations from EMEA Finance Magazine and K10's Kapital Newspaper annual ranking. Global Finance Magazine called UniCredit Bulbank the "Best Trade Finance Bank in Bulgaria" in 2016, as did Euromoney Magazine as well.

Vacancy Rate

Vacancy rates turn out to be statistics that are gathered and maintained on availability of homes for sale, rental properties, and hotels. When you see high rates of vacancy, this is evidence that a market is struggling. Lower vacancy rates are hoped for as they demonstrate that properties are in demand and vacancies do not stay open for much time. Government agencies and other companies that focus on economic analysis maintain the records on vacancy rates. If you are contemplating moving into a new community, then you will find that vacancy rates are worth contemplating.

Where housing is concerned, vacancy rates add up all housing units that can be lived in but are not presently occupied. The agencies compiling the vacancy rates then express this as the percent of available to be lived in housing that is presently vacant. Vacancy rates cover houses, townhouses, apartments, and other forms of housing. As vacancy rates prove to be lower, it becomes more difficult for individuals to obtain housing. This is because the types of housing that they want may not be available either for sale or rent on a regular basis.

The vacancy rate statistics can be found on various kinds of housing arrangements. This differentiates on vacancy rates between townhouses, apartments, and single family homes. Landlords read these vacancy rates to be appraised of the rental situation, since changes in this number impact how much rent they can charge tenants. If landlords' tenants are constantly leaving, causing high rates of turnover, then they may wrestle with high vacancy rates personally.

When you see high vacancy rates in housing, it indicates that economic recession or depression is evident. High rates of vacancy can also happen if a great number of individuals leave a particular community, causing significant quantities of homes to lie vacant. Developers incorrectly estimating how strong a market is for housing in a local community might also cause them. Another factor that leads to higher vacancy rates proves to be rents that are high. When individuals can not pay an area's rent, then they will look for other places to live. Hotel vacancy rates demonstrate the strength or weakness of an area economy more profoundly, since high hotel vacancies mean tourism in the area is down.

Businesses are concerned with commercial vacancy rates. These are commonly figured up separate from residential vacancies. In the business vacancy rates figure are commercial buildings like factories and warehouses, and also empty retail storefronts and offices. Lower rates mean that people are supporting the businesses by spending their dollars in those areas. When consumers see a large number of empty storefronts, even when the economy is doing well, it will discourage them from frequenting that plaza or area.

Any individual who wants to see the vacancy rates for a given community can get them. A good place to start looking is at a local government office and in census data. Besides this, Realtors commonly maintain statistics on area vacancy rates, as do Internet sites that keep demographic information on different communities.

Wealth

Wealth proves to be the abundant possession of material things or other resources that are considered to be valuable. People, areas, communities, or nations who control these assets are said to be wealthy. The word for wealth comes from the old English word 'Weal' and 'th', which means 'the conditions of well-being'.

The ideas of wealth have great importance for every part of the study of economics. This is particularly the case with development economics. Since the definition of wealth often depends on the situation in which you use it, no universally accepted definition for wealth exists. Different individuals have expressed a number of varying ideas of wealth in differing scenarios. Stating the concept of wealth often involves ethics and moral issues, because the accumulation of wealth is viewed by many people as the highest goal.

Wealth is not evenly distributed throughout the world. In the year 2000, world wealth estimates ranged around $125 trillion. The citizens of Europe, North America, and a few high income Asian countries have ninety percent of all of this wealth. Besides this shocking statistic, only one percent of all adults on earth possess forty percent of the planet's wealth. This number declines to thirty-two percent when wealth is calculated according to purchasing power parity, or equivalency of what it buys from one country to the next.

Wealth and richness are two separate words that are used interchangeably. They mean slightly different things. Wealth describes gathering up resources, whether they are common or abundant. Richness relates to having such resources in abundance. Wealthy countries and people possess many more resources than do poor ones. The word richness is similarly employed to describe peoples' basic needs being fulfilled through sharing the collective abundance. Wealth's opposite proves to be destitution, while richness' opposite is known as poverty.

It is a concept that requires a social contract of ownership to be set up and enforced. Ideas of wealth are actually relative. They range from not only one society and people to another, but even between varying regions or areas of the same society or nation. As an example, having ten thousand dollars throughout all of the United States does not make a person among the richest in any area of the country. But this amount in desperately poor developing nations would represent a huge quantity of wealth.

The idea of wealth changes in different times too. Thanks to the progress of science and machines that save labor, even the poorest in America today benefit from a higher standard of living than the wealthy used to enjoy not so long ago. Assuming this trend continues, then the wealthiest people's standard of living today will be considered poor in the future.

Wire Transfer

A wire transfer is the quickest, safest, most reliable means of sending money within the United States, in other countries, or around the world. They are often essential in the more critical financial activities of life such as purchasing a house. The reason larger transactions occur in this form of payment is because the recipient can receive and verify the funds transfer the same day it is done, or as near to immediately as possible (besides Western Union and Money Gram, which cost substantially more to utilize).

A wire transfer actually represents a means to electronically transfer money from one party to another via a bank as intermediary. A traditional and typical wire transfer starts at a credit union or bank and electronically processes through either Fedwire or SWIFT networks. Another common name for such a wire transfer is a bank wire, which also encompasses the standard bank to bank transfers.

Ultimately the wire transfers have become so successful and utilized throughout the United States and rest of world simply because they are capable of moving even enormous sums of money to any destination bank in the world in only a day or two. If they are affected within the same country such as the United States then same day wires can be done. For an international transfer via wire transfer, it often requires another day or even two to complete.

Since the funds move rapidly through the financial system, recipients are not required to wait a material amount of time for the funds to become cleared. This means they can access and utilize the money without significant delays. No holds are typically placed on wire transfer monies. The safety issue means that merchants prefer the wire mechanism. This is because checks can bounce because of insufficient funds, while wires never do so. In other words, these are guaranteed funds.

There are some particular requirements that wire transfers need in order to be possible to transact. At least in the United States, both parties would require a functioning bank account in order for a bank to act as intermediary. Since thieves can not open a bank account too easily, nor bank anonymously in the United States, it is difficult for them to carry out scams using bank wires. This is because it leaves a paper trail which is easy for law enforcement officials to follow.

This does not mean that wire transfer scams are unknown entirely. It is possible for a person to be tricked into wiring money to a fraudster for a purchase or service they never receive. Examples of this are fake insurance policies or false retirement or investment products. Once the wire has cleared the recipients account, they can either withdraw the funds in person or wire it to an offshore overseas account.

By the time the victims realize that they have been scammed, the funds sent by wire will be long gone. They would no longer be recoverable by traditional U.S. law enforcement or even court order methods once they have been transferred offshore. Pulling money back after it has been dispatched via bank wire is extremely difficult in any case. This is true even if the funds remain in the recipient's bank account.

Wire transfer fees can be significant. In many parts of the United States, they run as high as $40 to dispatch a bank wire. Many banks charge upwards of $10 in order for a bank wire to be received into an account. The costs to send one are higher if the wire is funded by utilizing a credit card cash advance. Cash advance fees would then apply, as well as typically large interest rates, plus the wire transfer fee. This is why it is typically most financially sound to effect a bank wire directly from the sender's bank account.

Zoning Laws

Zoning laws are statutes that mandate the ways that you are able to utilize your property holdings. Townships, counties, cities, and alternative local governments affect zoning laws so that they are able to create standards for development that benefit all residents in common.

It does not matter how big or how small a property is; it will be impacted by zoning laws. If you contemplate improving your property or purchasing another piece of property, you should be certain that you are fully aware of zoning restrictions that will affect you in advance of making any kind of commitment.

As an example, properties can be zoned according to residential or commercial restrictions. Commercial buildings will never be permitted to be constructed in a residential area, while residential dwellings can not be put up in commercial zones, unless the zoning laws of the area are changed.

Getting the zoning laws for a property altered proves to be extremely difficult. You would first have to give out public notice before getting an approved variance from the responsible government agencies in charge of zoning plans. Many times, neighbors will stalwartly resist your proposed zoning changes.

Zoning laws allow for a variety of different zoning designations and uses. Among these are commercial zoning, residential zoning, industrial zoning, recreational zoning, and agricultural zoning. These categories are generally further subdivided into other categories. Residential zoning might have sub zoning categories under it including multiple family use, for condominiums or apartments, or single family houses.

Zoning laws include a number of limitations to the property and potential improvements. The total size and height of buildings on the property is commonly restricted. The buildings can only be placed so close to each other. There will be limits to the total area percentage that is allowed to have buildings on it. Perhaps most importantly, the types of buildings that can be built on a given land's zone will be mandated.

You can learn about the zoning laws and ordinances simply by getting in touch with the area planning agency. Alternatively, you might go on the Internet to the local and state search engine to learn about your county and city zoning rules. Local planning organizations will tell you what must be done to get a variance to the area zoning.

www.ingramcontent.com/pod-product-compliance
Lightning Source LLC
Chambersburg PA
CBHW051210170526
45166CB00005B/1829